Berlitz® HANDB

EGYPT

Contents

FAMILY FRIENDLY SYMBOL 👪

This symbol is used throughout the Handbook to indicate a sight, hotel, restaurant or activity that is suitable for families with children.

Top 25 Attractions

1 **Abu Simbel by cruise ship** Ply Lake Nasser's coast to see Nubia's treasures, including this temple dedicated to Rameses II *(see p.170)*

2 **Diving in the Red Sea or Sinai** Egypt offers some of the best dive sites in the world – the variety of sealife is mesmerising *(see p.30)*

3 **Be captivated by Karnak** Explore the wonders of Egypt's largest ancient religious site *(see p.133)*

4 Shopping in the souqs Haggle for papyrus, alabaster, spices and more in the colourful markets *(see p.44)*

5 Dawn at St Catherine's Monastery Watch the sunrise from the world's oldest Christian monastery *(see p.204)*

6 Sunset at the Mena House Oberoi The best view of the Pyramids is from a classic hotel *(see p.114)*

7 Dinner at Sofra in Luxor Authentic Egyptian cuisine in a restored mansion *(see p.138)*

8 Stroll Alexandria's Corniche Enjoy sea breezes and striking architecture in this atmospheric old city *(see p.179)*

9 **Whirling dervishes** Watch this entrancing rhythmic dancing and spinning by Sufis *(see p.281)*

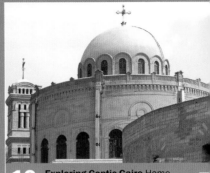

10 **Exploring Coptic Cairo** Home to ancient churches and Egypt's Christian community *(see p.71)*

12 **Tour Thebes by bicycle** Pedal along Luxor's West Bank to see the Colossi of Memnon *(see p.139)*

11 **Camel ride around Giza** An alternative vantage point from which to see the Pyramids *(see p.104)*

13 ***Koshari*** Egyptians love this dish, a spicy mix of lentils, tomatoes, fried garlic and macaroni *(see p.284)*

15 **Sound and light shows** See the ancient sites light up before you (see p.116)

14 **Experience Nubian hospitality** Take a boat to one of Aswan's islands to enjoy dinner and entertainment Nubian-style (see p.160)

16 **Calèche ride through Luxor** Clip-clop your way through town in a horse-drawn carriage (see p.150)

17 **Ultimate luxury in Sharm Al Sheikh** Egypt's glittering resort is now an international hotspot (see p.199)

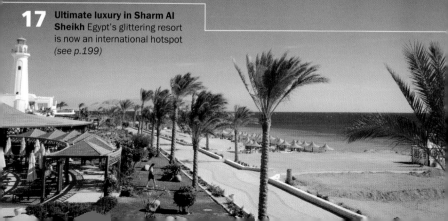

18 **Charter a *felucca* up the Nile** A cruise on the Nile is still one of the best ways to visit the temples and sample peaceful life along the river (see p.24)

19 **Visit the Egyptian Museum** See the spectacular exhibits such as the Royal Mummies and Tut-ankhamun's gold mask (see p.68)

20 **Coffee and sheesha** Pull up a chair and let the scent of apple tobacco envelop you (see p.56)

21 **Hurghadah Aquarium** Marvel at the vibrant sealife without getting wet *(see p.221)*

22 **Daraw camel market** See the professionals haggle over these 'ships of the desert' *(see p.156)*

23 **Alexandria's library** A masterpiece of modern architecture *(see p.182)*

24 **Temple at Dandarah** One of the least visited sites but one of the most impressive *(see p.123)*

25 **The homes of Siwah** This oasis is home to the world's only mud-brick bank *(see p.239)*

Egypt Fact File

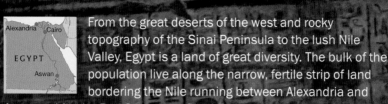

From the great deserts of the west and rocky topography of the Sinai Peninsula to the lush Nile Valley, Egypt is a land of great diversity. The bulk of the population live along the narrow, fertile strip of land bordering the Nile running between Alexandria and Aswan, while the Red Sea coast, Sinai Peninsula and Western Desert oases have smaller, yet rapidly growing communities.

i BASICS

Population: 77,420,000
(16th in world)
Area: 1,002,450km²
(30th in world)
Official language: Arabic
State religion: Islam
Capital city: Cairo
President: Hosni Mubarak
National anthem: Bilady, Bilady, Bilady (My country, my country, my country)
National symbol: The Eagle of Saladin
National sport: Football (soccer)
National airline: Egyptair

TIME ZONE
GMT +2 (late April to late
September no change)
New York: 5am
London: 10am
Cairo: noon
Sydney: 7pm
Auckland: 9pm

 CURRENCY
Egyptian Pound (LE or E£)
LE1 = 100 piastres (or *qirsh*
in Arabic)
The following figures are approximate:
£1 = E£9
€1 = E£8
$1 = E£5.8

 KEY TELEPHONE NUMBERS
Country code: +20
International calls: 00 + country
code + number
Police: 122
Ambulance: 123
Fire: 125
Tourist Police: 126

 POSTAL SERVICE
Post offices are open Sat–Thur
8.30am–2pm. Some city-centre
locations have extended hours.
Mailboxes on street corners and
outside post offices are red for
regular Egyptian mail, blue for
overseas airmail and green for within
Cairo. Allow seven days for airmail to
Europe, 14 days to America.
Cost to send a postcard: E£1.50.

 AGE RESTRICTIONS
Driving: 18 – but 25 is the minimum
age to rent a car
Drinking: 18
Age of consent: 18

Smoking is common throughout
Egypt, with the exception of inside
airports. Smoking bans are gradually
being introduced, for example
in public buildings and in some
restaurants and cafés, but they are
rarely enforced.

 OPENING HOURS
Opening hours are quite fluid in
Egypt, so the times below are a guide
only. The weekend is Friday and
Saturday. Note that during Ramadan,
offices, museums and tourist sites
keep shorter hours.
Banks: Sun–Thur 8.30am–1.30pm.
In larger cities they may open again
from 5–7 or 8pm.
Businesses: Typical hours Sat–Thur
10am–2pm and 4–8pm but they do
vary widely.
Government offices: Sun–Thur
8am–2pm; closed most holidays.
Tourist offices stay open longer.
Shops: Sat–Thur 9am–1pm and
5–10pm in summer; Sat–Thur
10am–6pm in winter.

 ELECTRICITY
220 volts. Visitors from the UK and US
will need an adaptor. American items
may also need a transformer.

Trip Planner

WHEN TO GO

Climate

Egypt is hot and dry almost year-round, with the north experiencing some cooler weather during the winter from December to February. Winter months see pleasant temperatures ranging from about 20°C (68°F) in Cairo to 26°C (79°F) in Aswan.

In the summer it is very hot, with temperatures ranging from anything between 30°C (86°F) on the Mediterranean coast to 50°C (122°F) in Aswan and Abu Simbel.

The most rain falls in Alexandria – about 18cm (7 in) a year – while in the south it hardly ever rains. The average rainfall in Aswan is 10mm (⅓in) over five years.

In the desert, the heat is intolerable during the day, while the nights are bitterly cold. Much of the country is affected by the *khamsin*, a dry, hot

The Western Desert

Public Holidays

1 January New Year's Day
7 January Coptic Christmas
25 January Egypt Police Day
25 April Sinai Liberation Day
1 May Labour Day
23 July Revolution Day
6 October Armed Forces Day

Holidays that do not fall on a set date (varies according to the Muslim calendar):
Monday following Orthodox Easter
Sham An Nessim (Spring Festival)
First day of Muharram, the first month of the Islamic calendar Islamic New Year
Third month of the Islamic calendar
Prophet Muhammad's birthday
Last day of Ramadan Eid Al Fitr
70 days after end of Ramadan
Eid Al Adha
Government offices, banks and post offices will be closed on all public holidays. Shops, historic sites and souqs will usually remain open.

wind which blows in from the Western Desert between March and April, covering everything in a fine dust.

High/Low Season

The tourist high season in Egypt is the winter (December to February), when cooler temperatures make exploring much more comfortable. Summer (June to August) is the low season in most of the country except along the coasts, and prices tend to reflect this.

The temples at Abu Simbel were moved to avoid them being flooded by Lake Nasser

The best time to visit depends on where you want to go. Summer in Cairo is very hot and sticky, Aswan and Luxor even more so, with daytime temperatures of around 40°C (104°F). However, if you want a holiday roasting on the beach, then summer is the time to head for the Red Sea or the beaches of southern Sinai. Winter is the best time to visit Luxor and Aswan, although the cooler temperatures also bring greater crowds. Probably the ideal time to explore Egypt is spring (March to May) or autumn (September to November).

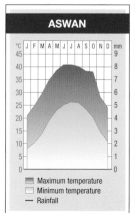

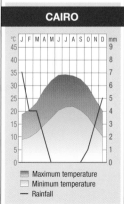

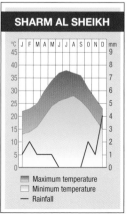

ESSENTIAL EVENTS

Seller of festival hats for Ramadan

Most Muslim festivals are determined by the Islamic calendar, based on the lunar cycle. As lunar months are shorter than our solar months, the dates vary from year to year.

Ramadan

The main event in the Islamic calendar is Ramadan, the ninth month, when all Muslims fast between sunrise and sunset. Sex, smoking and drinking liquids of any form are also prohibited.

Fasting during daylight hours is considered one of the five pillars of Islam – and the practice is thought to 'burn away the sins' of the year before. A cannon shot announces the time for breaking the fast, when *iftar,* the evening meal, takes place and the night-long party begins.

Tourists sometimes choose to avoid visiting during Ramadan, believing everything to be either closed or offering limited options – but there are advantages to visiting during this time. Office and opening hours at most sights will be reduced, but holiday package costs are often reduced to entice more holidaymakers, and it is likely to be quieter.

Restaurants and cafés outside international hotels or resort areas will not be open during the day, so you will need to stick close to your hotel. Some hotels may create an enclosed tent or patio area away from the view of Muslim patrons or staff as, although non-Muslims are not expected to fast, it is considered impolite to eat or drink in public during fasting hours.

Ramadan dates for the next few years are:

1 August–29 August 2011
20 July–18 August 2012
9 July–7 August 2013

Eid Al Fitr

Eid Al Fitr marks Ramadan's end, with celebrations, family visits and gifts. Traditionally, new clothes are worn during this period to symbolise the new year and 'cleansed state' of all who have undergone the fast. Strangers are often invited to join family feasts according to custom.

Pilgrimage to Mecca

Eid Al Adha (or **Eid Al Kabir**) marks the time of the hajj, the pilgrimage to Mecca. Those who can afford it buy a sheep to slaughter for the feast, which generally lasts three days. Immediately before and after the hajj, the port cities of Nuweiba, Suez, Port Safaja and Al Qasr are crowded with pilgrims on their way to and from Saudi Arabia.

Moulid An Nabi celebrates the Prophet Muhammad's birthday, with street parties and Sufi gatherings near the main mosques.

Coptic Easter

Coptic Easter is the most important day of the calendar for Coptic Christians – even more important than Christmas. Copts fast for 210 out of 365 days in the calendar year, with the 40-day lead-up to Easter a period of great austerity. The breaking of the fast begins on Easter Sunday, when Copts enjoy a week of feasting and celebration.

Spring Festival

Sham An Nessim Spring Festival is held on the first Monday after Coptic Easter. For this important festival – the name means 'sniffing the breeze' – Egyptians, Muslims and Christians all take part in festivities directly descended from Ancient Egypt to celebrate the resurrection of Osiris and the return of spring. Families traditionally have a picnic of *fasikh*, dried fish with eggs and onions.

Secular holidays

Sinai Liberation Day on 25 April (a public holiday only on the Sinai Peninsula) commemorates the day the peninsula was returned to Egypt by Israel following the signing of the Camp David agreement.

Armed Forces Day on 6 October is a great holiday for fans of military displays, with parades and precision marching taking place in Cairo to commemorate the first day of the October War against Israel in 1973.

Priest celebrating Coptic Easter

ITINERARIES

Egypt is a vast country, but sights of interest are concentrated over a relatively small area. For those interested in Ancient Egypt, the strip along the Nile will be the focus, specifically the cities of Aswan, Luxor and Cairo. Divers will want to head for the Red Sea coast and Sinai Peninsula, while those looking to top up their tan will stick to the beach resorts of the Red Sea and Sinai.

A week will give visitors enough time to enjoy a whistle-stop tour of historical sights or a more relaxed stay on the sandy beaches of a resort. A two-week stay allows you to slow down and explore more out-of-the-way spots, perhaps take a brief cruise or do some diving. With a whole month at your disposal, intrepid types can follow up sightseeing with a stay on a dive boat and a desert safari.

You can take a camel or horse ride round the pyramids at Saqqarah

One Week for Egyptologists

Days 1–2: **Cairo.** Visit the Pyramids, Memphis and Saqqarah, and enjoy sunset drinks at the Mena House Oberoi. The following day, explore the treasures of the Egyptian National Museum, followed by a spot of shopping at Cairo's souq, Khan Al Khalili, and coffee and sheesha at Al Fishawy.

Days 3–5: **Luxor.** Travel down to Luxor and visit the west bank, Karnak Temple and the temples at Dandarah and Abydos. If it's not too hot, explore the west bank by bicycle and, for an alternative perspective, see Karnak by night at a sound and light show.

Days 6–7: **Aswan.** Cross by ferry to Elephantine Island before going south of the city to Philae and the Nubia Museum, then head to Abu Simbel as part of a day trip by either plane or coach.

Two Weeks for Cruise-Lovers

Days 1–5: Arrive in Luxor and begin your cruise upriver, visiting Esna, Edfu and Kom Ombo on the way to Aswan. Going in this direction will take a day longer than if you travel from Aswan due to the current.

Cruise ships at Kom Ombo

Days 6–8: Relax in Aswan to enjoy a *felucca* trip to Seheyl Island and a jaunt to Philae for the sound and light show before continuing your journey.

Days 9–14: Cruise Lake Nasser, stopping off at the numerous Nubian temples, including Kalabasha, ending at Abu Simbel.

Three Weeks for Bedouin Delights

Week one: Explore the Western desert with Bedouin guides, including stops in Siwah and Bahareyyah. Be sure to take a dip in the geothermally heated pools.

Week two: Base yourself in Hurghadah for desert adventures in the Eastern Desert. Spend a night in a Bedouin camp or take a horse ride to ancient Roman mines.

Week three: Take the ferry to Sharm Al Sheikh and transfer to Dahab for more desert fun, including a trek to St Catherine's Monastery and a climb up Mount Sinai.

One Month for Sporting Enthusiasts

Week one: In Alexandria dive for treasures offshore, then head back to Cairo to play golf under the Pyramids at the Mena House Oberoi.

Week two: Transfer to Sharm Al Sheikh by ferry and trek up Mount Sinai or enjoy hiking through the interior, then dive or snorkel the world-class reefs offshore.

Week three: Take the ferry to Hurghadah and continue diving in the extraordinarily rich waters of the Red Sea, or book a Nubian adventure in the Eastern Desert.

Week four: Transfer to Luxor and take a *felucca* south to Aswan then fish for Nile perch on Lake Nasser.

BEFORE YOU LEAVE

Visas and Entry Requirements

Visas can be obtained on arrival in Egypt if you are arriving by air. Those arriving by ferry are advised to apply in advance from their closest Egyptian embassy or consulate. The cost of the visa depends on nationality, ranging in price from US$15 and US$20. Your passport must be valid for at least six months after entry and have a blank page available.

Nationality	Visa Required
UK	✓
US	✓
Canada	✓
Australia	✓
New Zealand	✓
Ireland	✓
South Africa	✓

Embassies and Consulates

Australia: 1 Darwin Avenue, Canberra; tel: 612-6234 437; www.egypt.org.au
Canada: 454 Laurier Avenue East, Ottawa; tel: 613-234 4931; http://www.mfa.gov.eg/missions/canada/ottawa/embassy/en-gb/
Ireland: 12 Clyde Road, Dublin; tel: 1-660-6566; www.embegyptireland.ie
South Africa: 270 Bourke Street, Pretoria; tel: 12-343 1590
UK: 2 Lowndes St, London SW1; tel: 020-7235 9777; www.egyptian

consulate.co.uk; www.egyptianembassyuk.org
US: 3521 International Court NW, Washington DC; tel: 202-895 5400; 1990 Post Oak Boulevard, Suite 2180, Houston; tel: 713-961 4915; 500 N Michigan Avenue, Suite 1900, Chicago; tel: 312-828 9162/64; www.egyptianembassy.net

Vaccinations

No vaccinations are required to enter Egypt unless you are arriving from a region with reported cases of yellow fever.

Booking in Advance

If you are planning on visiting in high season (December–February), you should book your accommodation in advance. There are no requirements to book attractions or tours prior to arrival in Egypt. In fact, many deals can be negotiated by booking once you are in the country.

Tourist Information

Egyptian Tourist Authority; www.egypt.travel
Canada: 2020 Rue University, #2260 Montreal, H3A 2A5; tel: 514-861-8071.

Sharm Al Sheikh tourist information centre

Calèche in Edfu

UK: 3rd floor, Egyptian House, 170 Piccadilly, London W1J 9EJ; tel: 020-7493 5283
US: New York: Suite 2305, 630 Fifth Avenue, NY; tel: 212-332 2570
Los Angeles: Suite 215, 8383 Wilshire Boulevard, Beverly Hills, CA; tel: 213-653 8815

Maps and Books
Maps produced by the tourist authority are not very helpful. The most common (and handy) maps are those produced by Kümmerly & Frey or Macmillan, both available online.

Books to read to give you a flavour of the country include:
Alexandria Quartet by Lawrence Durrell. Lives and loves of expats before the revolution.
Flaubert in Egypt by Gustave Flaubert. Evocative descriptions of the sights of Egypt.
Midaq Alley by Naguib Mahfouz. Character-filled masterpiece from Egypt's Nobel Prize-winning author.
The Mistress of Nothing by Kate Pullinger. Compelling historical fiction telling the story of a Victorian writer travelling down the Nile.
A Thousand Miles up the Nile by Amelia Edwards. Classic piece of 19th-century travel literature chronicling a Nile cruise.
The Yacoubian Building by Alaa Al Aswany. Multi-viewpoint epic set in downtown Cairo.

Websites
www.egypttoday.com – lifestyle
www.touregypt.net – guide to sites
www.drhawass.com – website of the Secretary-General of the Supreme Council of Antiquities
www.horus.ics.org.eg – for children
www.sis.gov.eg – information
http://weekly.ahram.org.eg – Egypt's English-language newspaper online
www.red-sea.com – diving
www.yallabina.com – for Cairenes
www.thebanmappingproject.com – chronicling excavations in the Valley of the Kings

Trip Planner

Packing List

- Long-sleeved cotton or linen shirts and long trousers or dresses (if visiting religious centres)
- Sturdy walking shoes
- Insect repellent
- Sunscreen and sunglasses
- Cotton or linen shopping bags (so you don't need to take any plastic ones)
- A scarf to cover your hair if you are a woman travelling through conservative parts of the country
- Photocopy of your passport
- ISIC card (if you're a student)
- Upset stomach and headache medication

UNIQUE EXPERIENCES

Nile Cruising

The Nile cruise has been an indelible part of the Egyptian experience since the days of the pharaohs. Today, a jaunt on the river is part of almost every package tour to the country – but it's still one of the best ways to enjoy the sights.

Thomas Cook, a printer from Leicester, England, and a member of the Temperance Society, decided to promote tourism in the 1840s as a means of diverting people from drunken idleness. At that time the only viable way to see the sites of Egypt was by boat, so he organised Nile cruises. It was only along the river that the country had ever been habitable; Egypt was, in fact, the Nile. Everything was built along the river – ordinary houses depended on bricks made out of Nile mud, and the huge blocks of limestone and granite used to build the temples and pyramids were transported by water.

Ancient Cruising

In Egypt's early days, navigation on the Nile was efficient but not foolproof. The River Nile was the main highway with an immense amount of river traffic. Massive barges sailed south from Aswan to Giza with granite blocks for the pyramids and also to Luxor, transporting massive monolithic granite obelisks. Sails, originally square but later 'lateen', or triangular, under Arab influence, had to be disproportionately large or at least set high to catch wind passing above the shelter of high banks.

The royal boats were in a class of their own, symbolic of the boat that took the sun-god Ra across the heavens, and hence acquiring the title 'solar boats'. An example can be found at the Solar Boat Museum on the Giza Plateau (see p.104) near the foot of the Great Pyramid.

Onboard Developments

By the Middle Ages there were reputed to be around 36,000 ships working the Nile. The Arab historian Abd Al Latif

River life seen from a cruise boat

One of the larger cruise ships which ply the Nile

remarked on ships known as *dahabiyyas* with 'a wooden chamber over which is elevated a dome with windows, and in the daytime furnished with shutters, and which give a view over the river in each direction. There is in this chamber a private cabinet and latrines, and they decorate it in various colours, with gilding, and the most beautiful varnish'.

In the end, of course, these beautifully crafted sailboats yielded to changing circumstances, and, in the 19th century, Thomas Cook introduced the paddle-steamer, a far more practical vessel for the tourists he was taking to Egypt. This in turn was replaced by the modern, diesel-powered cruise ship. Today *dahabiyyas* are enjoying a revival in popularity, providing a quieter and more exclusive alternative to the larger Nile cruise vessels.

Practical Information

The idea of enjoying a golden sunset over the West Bank of the Nile with a gin and tonic in hand is usually enough of an incentive to book a cruise. The pharaohs regularly floated down the Nile to survey their lands, and today's boats try to emulate the regal experience (not all succeed).

The traditional cruise takes passengers between Aswan and Luxor, stopping at Kom Umbu, Esna and Edfu along the way. Trips are sometimes extended as far as Abydos. A recent addition to Egypt's cruising options is on Lake Nasser, which takes in the relocated temples of Nubia. One of the perks of a Lake Nasser cruise is the chance to see Abu Simbel at daybreak when few tourists are around. Additionally, many of the temples on Lake Nasser are virtually unreachable overland, meaning that you and your fellow cruisers will have the temples to yourselves.

Currently, cruises along the entire length of the Nile are not running due to security fears. The removal of the convoy system in large sections of Middle Egypt is giving hope to a reinstatement of itineraries from Aswan to Cairo, but nothing has been finalised to date.

Trips between Aswan and Luxor generally last from three to six nights. Trips going south are usually longer than those going north because they go against the tide. On most cruises, meals are included in the cost in addition to stops at the best temples and sites along the route. Cruise ships vary in quality from little more than glorified ferries with simple rooms right up to five-star facilities boasting lavish interiors. For ultimate splendour, consider chartering a *dahabiyya* – private sailing boats inspired by the luxurious sailing vessels of the past.

Booking a *Felucca*

If budgets are tight, a *felucca* trip offers an affordable alternative. These triangular-sailed, flat-bottomed boats have changed little over the last few hundred years, and can be rented for both day trips and extended tours. Because they do not need special mooring sites, they can stop at small islands and get nearer to the ancient temples.

With *feluccas*, the boat layout is the same no matter which one you choose. The deck will be covered in mattresses and a canopy will be erected over the top during the day.

Feluccas sailing from Aswan

At night, the canopy will come down and be turned into 'walls' to shield you from the cold.

Feluccas carry a minimum of six passengers and a maximum of eight. If you have fewer people in your group and don't want to join with others, you'll have to pay a supplement for the missing people. The Aswan or Luxor tourist offices can give you a basic guide as to what you should be paying.

Meals are usually included in the price; don't try to haggle the price down too low, as the captain will then scrimp on food during the journey. It's a good idea to have a look at the boat before departing, so you can examine the quality of life-preservers, cooking facilities, decks and cushions. You'll need to take with you plenty of water to drink, a sleeping bag and toilet paper. Toilet facilities are basic.

Fans of *feluccas* argue that the experience is authentic, putting you in touch with everyday river life. The environmental cost is also far less than cruise ships, as wind power pushes you along for most of the way. While tour operators do book *feluccas*, it is just as easy to negotiate direct with the captain. Simply stroll along the Corniche in either Aswan or Luxor and wait for someone to approach.

Nile Cruise Ships

When selecting your ship, remember you get what you pay for. More expensive boats tend to have fewer and larger cabins and will make the effort to prepare good food. All boats provide guides to accompany passengers to the sites, and some have

Cruise ship on the Nile

Day Trips

If you can't afford a full week on board or can't spare the time, consider instead a day cruise in order to experience the magic of the Nile.

In Aswan, the two most popular day trips take visitors to Seheyl Island, with its Nubian village south of the city, or around Elephantine and Kitchener's Island for leisurely visits to the botanic gardens and ancient ruins.

Luxor's popular day trip is to Banana Island for a spot of sunbathing and swimming. From Cairo, boats ply the waters, offering sunset cruises. Some larger vessels also offer buffet dinners, belly-dancing shows and dancing under the stars. Prices will always be cheaper if you book direct; however, quality will be guaranteed if you arrange your day trip through a tour operator or travel agent.

Cruise ships offer exuberant on-board entertainment

ship's manager and not the captain. The manager will speak better English and is the one in charge of guest relations. Competition amongst cruise ships is high, so if you can wait until a ship is just about to depart, you will get the best deal. Check your room in advance before parting with any money and have a walk around to determine onboard facilities. Be sure to confirm that the price includes all extras and that you won't get hit for additions after leaving port.

With over 300 cruise boats now plying the waters, travellers are spoilt for choice and are sure to find a ship that suits their style and budget. Cost-cutting options include choosing a boat moored further along the riverbank, or wedged between other boats and therefore lacking Nile views. Check with your travel agent if booking before arrival to see what features your ship will have.

small libraries on Egyptian history and culture.

It's usually easy to book a cruise after you have arrived in Egypt. Your best bet is to ask to speak with the

Summary of Cruising Options

- *Feluccas*
  Feluccas are simple, triangular-sailed boats. Sleeping arrangements are communal and the captain and his crew take care of meals.
  Who do they appeal to? Eco-travellers, those with a sense of adventure, people who like 'authentic' experiences and the chance to meet locals.

- *Dahabiyyas*
  Dahabiyyas are private floating vessels made popular in the 19th century. Furnishings are traditional yet luxurious, and there are usually a maximum of ten cabins on board.

  Who do they appeal to? Those with deep pockets who want to travel in style; people who want privacy and the ability to go wherever they want in their own time.

- **Cruise ships**
  Cruise ships range in size from a few cabins to 100 or more. Guests have their own cabins, and entertaining activities are arranged daily.
  Who do they appeal to? Tourists who like the security of package tours and set itineraries; those who want to experience Egypt, yet don't want to give up home comforts.

As there are so many boats to choose from we have just listed a few that have more character, atmosphere or history than most.

M/S Philae

Mena House Oberoi Hotel
Shari' Al Ahram, Cairo; tel: 3377-3222
www.oberoiphilae.com

The award-winning *Philae* is designed as an old-fashioned paddle-steamer. There are 54 comfortable wood-panelled rooms, all with their own bathroom and balcony, four deluxe suites and a great library.

M/S Senator

Travco 19 Shari' Yehia Ibrahim, Zamalik, Cairo; tel: 735-4890
www.mssenator.com

The *Senator* is the ultimate in Nile cruise luxury, with just 17 large and luxurious suites, all with panoramic windows, international phone, satellite TV and en suite bathrooms.

M/S Star Goddess

Sonesta Cruise Collection
3 Shari' Al Tayaran, Nasr City, Cairo; tel: 2262-8111

www.sonesta.com

Palatial all-suite cruise ship with just 33 cabins – all named after famous composers. All of the suites feature private terraces, in case you don't want to mix and mingle with the *hoi polloi*.

M/S Sudan

Seti First Travel
16 Shari' Ismail Muhammad, Zamalik, Cairo; tel: 736-9820
www.setifirst.com

The only old-fashioned steamer on the Nile, a gift from Queen Victoria to King Fuad, and used in the movie *Death on the Nile*.

M/S Sunboat IV

Only available through Abercrombie and Kent; tel: 574-8334
www.abercrombiekent.com

Small cruise boat offering large, luxurious cabins, spacious sun decks with plunge pools, excellent food and very good mooring facilities at Luxor and Aswan in central locations. The boat has onboard internet access, satellite TV, and daily deliveries of international newspapers.

The old-fashioned steamer *Sudan* was used in the film *Death on the Nile*

M/S Triton

www.roadtoegypt.com
The most luxurious boat on the Nile, with only 20 suites, an indoor and an outdoor pool and a great restaurant. Book through upmarket travel agencies outside Egypt.

Dahabiyyas

To get a real feel of what cruising used to be like before the traffic jams on the Nile, take a *dahabiyya* (Arabic for a golden boat). Nineteenth-century travellers such as Flaubert, Amelia Edwards, Pierre Loti and Florence Nightingale sailed the Nile on these wooden boats with cabins, propelled by two lateen sails. Some have been restored, others are being built in the same style, but all are much smaller than the cruise boats. They make the journey from Luxor to Aswan slowly, typically taking six or seven days, and stopping at sites such as Jabal As Silsilah and Al Qab, where the bigger boats cannot moor.

Assouan

Tel: 010-657 8322
www.nourelnil.com
Built in the style of the magnificent 19th-century vessels, with eight double cabins, each with a fully equipped en suite bathroom.

Dongola

Tel: 010-699 3889
www.nile-dongola.com
One of the larger *dahabiyyas* on the Nile. The boat, once the private yacht of Sultan Hussein (who ruled from 1914 until 1917), has been carefully restored, with one suite and four cabins.

Royal Cleopatra

5 Shari' Muhammad Ibrahim, Dokki

Tel: 012-717- 8225
www.nilecruiseegypt.net
The *Royal Cleopatra* is a luxurious lateen-rigged Nile sailing vessel, with sleeping accommodation for one to seven people.

Sonesta Amirat

Sonesta Cruise Collection
3 Shari' Al Tayaran, Nasr City, Cairo; tel: 02-2262-8111
www.sonesta.com
The newest *dahabiyya* to launch on the Nile, this exquisite boat has just six cabins and two suites, plus an open-air Jacuzzi on deck.

Vivant Denon

Tel: (00 33) 06 10 15 37 89/(00 33) 01 48 46 40 98 (France)
http://membres.lycos.fr/Dahabeya
This boat is only available for some weeks a year between October and April; the summer is possible too, but it gets very hot without air conditioning.

A cruise round Lake Nasser is a popular alternative to a Nile cruise

Cruises on Lake Nasser

Another way of experiencing the peace and quiet of the Nile is a cruise on Lake Nasser. Several boats now offer 3–4-day cruises, visiting the ancient temples and Nubian monuments on the shores of the lake. Watch Abu Simbel at dawn before the crowds descend, and take your sunset aperitif by one of the rarely visited rescued temples on the shore *(see also p. 170)*.

Eugenie and Qasr Ibrim
Belle Epoque Travel
17 Shari' Tunis, New Madi, Cairo
Tel: 02-516 9649
www.kasribrim.com.eg
www.eugenie.com.eg

Two beautifully decorated and very elegant boats, built in the style of an old steamship, offering five-star luxury on Lake Nasser. In 1993 the *Eugenie* was the first boat to offer luxurious cruises on the lake; since then several other boats have joined her, including the following: *Prince Abbas* (Mövenpick Hotels; tel: 02-690 1797; www.moevenpick-hotels.com),

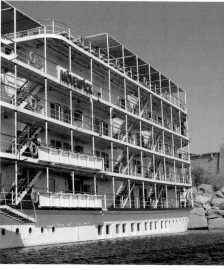

The *Prince Abbas*, one of the largest cruise boats on Lake Nasser

Nile Cruising

Nubian Sea (High Dam Cruises; tel: 02-240 5274; email: nubiansea@mistnet.net), *Queen Abu Simbel* (Naggar Travel; tel: 10-140 7753; www.naggartravel.com) and *Tania* (Travcotels; tel: 02-3854 3222; www.travcotels.com).

Top 5 Nile Mystery Novels

Need a good page-turner to read as you sail? Mystery writers have been inspired by Egypt for decades, attracted by the potent combination of sun, sand and a rich and colourful history. Here are a few:

- *Death on the Nile* by Agatha Christie. Classic whodunit set on a cruise ship taking in the sights of the great river.
- The *Amelia Peabody* series by Elizabeth Peters. Mystery series set in Luxor featuring excavations and murders in the sand.

- The *Vengeance of the Gods* series by Christian Jacq. Young scribe Kel is unjustly accused of murder. Can he prove his innocence in time?
- *The Amerotke Mysteries* by Paul Doherty. Respected Theban judge Amerotke oversees cases of murder and intrigue during the reign of Thutmose II.
- *The Mamur Zapt Mysteries* by Michael Pearce. The head of the Khedives secret police solves mysteries in the souqs and alleys of turn-of-the-20th-century Egypt.

Diving and Snorkelling

The sealife and corals of the Red Sea are among the world's finest, attracting thousands of divers and snorkellers each year. Even the inexperienced can enjoy this underwater world of vibrant colours and astonishing variety.

The main reason visitors come to the Red Sea every year is to see the closest coral reefs to Europe. The clear waters and amazing marine life here have been attracting divers ever since Hans Haas and Jacques Cousteau made their first Red Sea underwater films in the 1950s.

World-class dive sites are all along the coast, with the main interests split between the numerous wrecks, large pelagic fish, and a wide range of corals attracting smaller reef fishes. Each dive site is very specific in what it offers, with visibility, currents and types of large fish changing through-out the seasons.

The only way to see a sunken ship close up is to get a qualification and join the many divers exploring the famous wrecks – such as the World War II *Thistlegorm* from Sharm Al Sheikh or Hurghadah, and the *Salem Express* off Safaja. There is also the option of joining a 'liveaboard' for a few days, to reach the more remote reefs and wrecks that tend to be in better condition.

Learning to dive in Egypt is easy thanks to the numerous dive centres that offer training at all levels. All centres are affiliated with a certify-ing body such as PADI (Professional Association of Diving Instructors).

Avoid touching the coral when diving as you could kill it

The basic qualification takes five days to complete, and with it you can dive with an instructor to a depth of 18m (60ft). Most training centres also offer an introductory diving session to see if you like it before you start.

Marine Life

The key to a reef site is the quality of its coral, for this is what brings fish in abundance. Coral is a living organism which comes in two different types: soft and hard. The Red Sea has both versions in abundance. By day – when most divers visit the reefs – corals are quiet creatures. But by night, the colourful show truly kicks off as the polyps (small cylinders surrounded by tentacles) that make up the coral emerge to feed. Reds, oranges, greens, blues and purples are all common colours that can be seen – often in vibrant shades.

Fish are drawn to the coral as a food source and refuge from bigger prey. The coral reefs and surrounding vegetation make for excellent places to breed and feed. Common species include snapper, grouper and parrotfish. Sharks are another regular visitor, including tiger sharks, black- and white-tipped reef sharks and the occasional hammerhead or whale shark (but usually in open water only).

Leatherback turtles, hawksbill turtles and green turtles are all native to the Red Sea, but their numbers are rapidly dwindling. While they aren't hunted, they are often caught in fishing nets and accidentally killed.

Turtles are becoming increasingly rare

How to Pick Your Dive Centre

Here are a few key questions you should ask before signing up to a diving course:

- Are they certified members of the Egyptian Underwater Sports Association and Red Sea Diving and Watersport Association?
- Are you insured? Are they? Ask to see proof. Check their safety record.
- Are they PADI-registered?
- Can you understand the instructor's English?

Diving the Sinai Peninsula

The Sinai is one of Egypt's biggest tourist hotspots, especially the southern tip of the peninsula which makes up the Ras Muhammad National Park; this is one of the best dive sites in the world. A national park since 1983, Ras Muhammad is an unspoilt site of remarkable beauty and exceptional natural interest.

Both the land and surrounding water are considered part of the park. Offshore the marine life is wonderfully varied; divers can see a huge range of corals and fish, including turtles, sharks and eels.

Further to the northeast, at the gateway to the Straits of Tiran, is Tiran Island – off limits to visitors due to its proximity to Saudi Arabia. While you can't step foot on Tiran, the area around the island is a wonderful location to visit as part of a day trip; four coral reefs occupy the centre of the strait, all of which are extremely

Diving and Snorkelling

colourful yet lacking the crowds of other sites. The coral reefs off the southeastern coast of Tiran and to the northwest are considered to be the best preserved near the Sinai coast.

The difficulty in navigating the waters means there are plenty of wrecks to explore. The western side of the peninsula has the largest con-centration of wrecks in the Red Sea, including the *Thistlegorm (see p.37)*.

Dive Centres
in the Sinai

There are dozens – if not hundreds – of dive centres in the Sinai, especially in Na'ama Bay and Dahab. While technically part of Sharm Al Sheikh, Na'ama Bay lies to the north of the old town along the Sinai coast. Dahab is further east, approximately halfway between Sharm and the Israeli border.

Backpackers and laid-back travellers tend to choose the centres of Dahab, while luxury-lovers stick to Na'ama Bay. Prices reflect the division, with deals available the further away you go from the five-star resorts. Prices and operat-ing styles do vary, so it is worth shop-ping around for the best deals.

Operators based in Sharm Al Sheikh include: **Red Sea College** (Na'ama Bay; tel: 069-360 0145; www.redseacollege.com), which was recently voted 'Best dive centre in the world' for the fourth year in a row by British-based *Diver* magazine; **Shark's Bay Diving** (Umbi Diving Village, Shark's Bay; tel: 069-360 0942; www. sharksbay.com), offering a wide range of Sinai and day-trip offerings includ-ing dives to the *Thistlegorm* wreck; and **Sinai Divers** (Ghazala Hotel, Na'ama Bay; tel: 069-360 0150; www. sinaidivers.com), an outfit known for its range of liveaboards and advanced packages. At Dahab, **Fantasea Red Sea** (Coral Coast Hotel, tel: 069-364 1195, www.fantasearedsea.com) pro-vides sampler courses and packages – some even including a combined tour with adventure options into the Sinai interior, giving you the best of land and sea. Other recommended oper-ators include the Mövenpick Hotel's Swiss-operated outfit, **Subex** (Na'ama Bay, tel: 069-360 0122; www.subex. org) and **Emperor Divers** (Na'ama Bay, on Sharm Na'ama Bay Road; tel: 069-360 1734; www.emperordivers.

Snorkelling is the easy way to see underwater life

One way of entering the water

At Hurghadah, **Diving World** (beside Old Sheraton Hotel, Sakala; tel: 065-344 3582; www.divingworld redsea.com) and **Emperor Divers** (tourist harbour, Al Mina; tel: 065-345 0537; www.emperordivers.com) are your best bets for safety and sustainability while out on the reefs.

If you prefer quality over cost, then head to Safaja, 20km (12 miles) south of Hurghadah along the coastal highway, where operators have a better reputation for environmental maintenance.

At Safaja, **Nemo Dive** (Maglis Madina, Corniche Street; tel: 065-325 6555; www.nemodive.com) is often mentioned as a good option with lots of package selections to choose from and a strong adherence to sustainable diving practices.

com), a dive company that charges a little more than most, but offers packages suitable for all ages.

For a full list of qualified diving operators in the Sharm area, contact the Sharm Diving Union on 069-366 0418.

Dive Centres along the Red Sea Coast

While the reefs near Hurghadah have been pretty much decimated due to crowds and pollution, the sheer volume of travellers who come to Hurghadah means the resorts are the best in the region. The further south travellers go, the more 'authentic' the diving experience. Experienced divers tend to travel south to Marsa 'Alam towards the Sudanese border to avoid the crowds, although quality in terms of fish and reef colours is diminished. The benefits are in the lack of day-trippers who tend to clog the reefs and cause damage.

Conservation of the Reefs

Unfortunately, the water around Hurgadah has been overexploited and the

> **Internet Research**
>
> There are a number of good internet sites available to help you research your diving itinerary prior to arrival:
> - GoRedSea.com (www.goredsea.com) – index of regional dive centres and liveaboards
> - Red Sea Virtual Dive Centre (www.redseavdc.com) – detailed descriptions of over 70 dive locations
> - Reef Check (www.reefcheck.org) – environmental charity with a mandate to save the coral reefs of the planet – good resource to check for updates on reef damage in Red Sea hotspots.

reefs have been damaged as a result. Measures have been taken to stop the decline, but there are still operators around Hurghadah with a reputation for lax environmental measures. If you notice any unsavoury practices (such as anchoring on a reef, not providing divers with enough information on care of the reefs before they dive, allowing divers to chip off coral for souvenirs), then report the operator to the Red Sea Association for Diving and Watersports (tel: 065-344 4802) when you are back on dry land.

Costs and Packages

Courses, day dives and liveaboards are usually cheaper from Hurghadah and Safaja than from any of the resorts on the Sinai. A typical four- or five-day PADI open-water course from a reputable diving centre should cost from US$280, including the certificate. A two-day advanced course will be around US$175. Add about 10–15 percent to the cost for Sinai prices.

Those new to diving should book themselves in for an introductory dive before they commit to full lessons. This will help determine if diving is really for you. Expect to pay between US$50–75 including equipment.

Diving is better away from the coast

For those looking to expand on their skills, a five-day open-water diving course is the next step. Any good course must include classroom theory. This will then lead to dives in a hotel swimming pool or just offshore followed by a couple of boat-dives at the end.

Liveaboards

If you are already PADI-certified and want to do a lot of boat diving, dive

Unique Experiences

The Golden Rules of Reef Conservation

- Do not collect, remove or damage any material, living or dead (including coral, fish and plants).
- Do not stir up sand, as it is difficult for coral to remove sand particles and may result in stunted growth.
- Do not drop litter – especially cigarette butts and crisp bags.

- Do not walk or anchor on any reef area. You should time snorkelling with the high tide so you can swim – and not walk – over the living reef.
- Do not feed the fish, as this disturbs the reef's ecological balance.
- Do not touch or tread on coral as this will cause permanent damage.

packages or liveaboards are recommended. A liveaboard sees you going out to sea and sleeping on board for the duration of the package booked. You'll probably want to arrange this with a group or meet up with your potential boat-mates in advance of the trip to ensure you enjoy your stay.

A five-day dive package, including two dives per day, will cost approximately US$300, but deals can be had – especially if a small group of divers is looking for an extra body to lower the cost of their trip. Once again, add a 10–15 percent mark-up for Sinai operators.

All liveaboards should include full board, transfers, tanks and weights in the package. Diving equipment and alcohol will be extra.

Which Site to Choose?

The following guide outlines a selection of the best sites, depending on what you are looking for from your experience:

Best sites for beginners
Sha'ab Al Arg
Easily accessed from Al Gunah, this dive location is in a shallow lagoon that is sheltered from the tides and heavy winds, making it a gentle site for beginners to wet their fins. Brain corals and the occasional visiting manta ray or dolphin family provide the visual excitement.

Al Qaf
An easy dive through a canyon of corals that sometimes sees shark visits. Access is from the shore 10km (6 miles) north of Al Qasr.

Hamada
The wreck of a cargo ship lies atop this inshore reef 60km (37 miles) north of Berenice. Fish and coral are lacking, but the chance to explore a wreck site as a beginner diver is what makes this location so tempting.

Best for fish and dolphins
Gota Abu Ramada
Filled with fish, this diving spot 5km (3 miles) south of the Giftun Islands is popular with night divers and photographers due to the colours on display.

Ras 'Om Sid
Opposite Hotel Royal Paradise, Sharm Al Sheikh, this dive site is one of the most popular in the region due to its wealth of reef fish. If you're lucky, you may spot a passing manta ray or whale shark.

Sha'ab Samadai
Also known as Dolphin Reef, this lagoon is home to a school of spinner dolphins. An ideal dive site for beginner and intermediate divers 18km (11 miles) southeast of Marsa 'Alam.

Best wreck sites
Salex Express
Hundreds of travellers returning from the hajj lost their lives when the passenger ferry *Salem Express* sank in South Safaja Bay in 1991. While the wreck is considered one of the best by divers, respect should be paid to the many who died here.

Sha'ab Abu Nuhas
More ships have succumbed to this reef, in the southeastern straits of

Gubal, than anywhere else in the Red Sea. You'll need to be on a liveaboard to reach the numerous wrecks that can be found here, including the 1879 wreck of the *Carnatic*.

Thistlegorm

The most famous wreck in the Red Sea, the *Thistlegorm* was sunk by German bombers in 1941 *(see box, opposite)*.

Best challenges
Blue Hole

This massive sinkhole claims lives every year and is considered the holy grail of sites amongst advanced divers. Located 8km (5 miles) north of Dahab, access is via a narrow cut in the reef called the Bells.

Elphinstone

Strong currents draw seven species of shark to this remote reef wall covered in soft corals about 125km (78 miles) north of Marsa 'Alam. Not for the faint-hearted.

Shark Reef

Often ranked as one of the top 10 dive sites on the planet; divers must battle strong current to reach the remains of the *Jolande*, a Cypriot freighter that met its watery fate in 1980. The site is located at the southern tip of Ras Muhammad Park and can only be reached by liveaboard.

Best sites for coloured corals
Islands

Located just offshore to the south of Dahab, this dive site is renowned for the quality of its coloured corals. It's a good site for beginners, however. The table corals are extremely delicate, so if you have trouble with buoyancy and make it a habit of stepping down onto the ground while diving, you might want to avoid. The colours are so intense that it has been described as a near-hallucinogenic experience.

'Om Qamar

You'll need a day trip or liveaboard itinerary to reach this dive pot, 9km (5½ miles) north of the Gistun Islands near Hurghadah. Suitable for intermediate divers, the site features three towers of purple soft coral.

Snorkelling

While snorkellers don't see the same variety of underwater life as divers, there is still plenty to astonish. Many activity centres sell or rent snorkel, mask and fins, and there are numerous safe bays in which to practise using the

The variety of coral is extraordinary

equipment. Your best bet is to book through your hotel's activity centre, as dive centres tend to focus their attention on divers, giving snorkellers less attention when they go out on the reefs. If your selected property doesn't have an activity centre, then go to the nearest international standard hotel chain (eg Hilton, Hyatt, etc) and book through them. Hotels have greater experience catering to the casual snorkeller and will spend more time answering your questions. Snorkellers should be aware of the designated areas in which they are free to swim, away from the dangers of boats and other watersport activities. Daily boat trips take snorkellers to secluded reefs and marine parks such as Ras Muhammad to see the pristine coral formations and reef fish.

Windsurfing

Safaja is popular with windsurfers as it is notoriously windy. The best-known place is the **Shama Safaja Village**, north of town, where kitesurfing is also available. Two other recommended operators specialising in wind- and kitesurfing are **Club Nathalie Simon** (Menaville Hotel, Safaja; tel: 012-117 0793; www.fun-kite.com), named after the two owners who founded the centre after moving to Egypt in 1999, and **Club Mistral** at the Shams Hotel (information from their German head office; tel: +49-881-909 6010).

Glass-Bottomed Boats and Submarines

Many operators also offer rides in a glass-bottomed boat or submarine. In Sharm Al Sheikh, **Discovery** provides

Snorkelling from a boat

glass-bottomed boat trips which depart from the Hilton Fayrouz Pier, Na'ama Bay. Tickets are booked through your hotel concierge or via tour operators. The **Sindbad Group** (www.sindbad-group.com) operates a Hurghadah-based submarine – the perfect experience if you want to go underwater without getting your hair wet.

Thistlegorm Wreck

The wreck of the English freighter *Thistlegorm* is famous within the diving world and can be dived in a long day from Sharm Al Sheikh. It lies almost in the middle of the Gulf of Suez, west of Ras Muhammad National Park, in Sha'ab Ali, and was sunk by German bombers in 1941. The explosion ripped the ship in half, but much of the cargo remains intact, including Norton and BSA motorbikes, tanks, army supplies and even railway engines.

Desert Safaris

A quintessential image of Egypt is that of the great desert explorer, crossing the vast expanse of dunes on camel. Plenty of tour operators now offer the chance to relive the 'Lawrence of Arabia' experience – plus a few more adventurous options – in the great sands of the Sinai, and the Eastern and Western Deserts.

Over 90 percent of Egypt's land is desert, and desert trips are becoming increasingly popular as a perfect antidote to stressed urban life. You can take safaris lasting from one to three days on camel, or by four-wheel-drive (where all supplies are included), or simply head off on quad bikes for an afternoon of fun and frolics.

But the deserts of Egypt are more than just an opportunity for a change of scene and pace; they are also home to some of the most fascinating and intrepid tribespeople of North Africa

– the Bedouin. Constant travellers, the Bedouin can lay claim to having an older culture and way of life than the relatively recent arrivals to the region, the Copts and Muslims.

Sitting in a Bedouin tent after a long day trekking through the desert is a seductive experience. The Bedouin are famous for their hospitality, and happy to welcome strangers into their home.

Guides and Logistics

The two regions most popular for safaris are the Western Desert, where

Getting kitted out for a desert safari

oases flourish amid endless dunes, hot springs and weirdly eroded rock formations, and the Sinai, which is more rocky and rugged. The Eastern Desert is another option, where you can combine a diving holiday with a desert safari.

Nights are spent in goatskin or camelskin tents large enough to accommodate the entire group. At campsites toilets are usually a pit dug in the ground, but luxury facilities are not the priority when enjoying the intense peace and solitude of the desert.

Guides will charge approximately E£60–100 per day, with camel journeys priced at the high end of the scale for day trips near the major Sinai and Red Sea resorts. In the Western Desert, prices can be slightly more due to the isolation of the region. This price should include meals and the cost of registering the trip with the police. Drinking water may or may not be included; check before you go, as this will clearly add to your costs.

Day Trips

If you are short on time, day trips can be arranged to suit any itinerary. A

On the road in the desert

camel ride including a stop for Bedouin tea costs US$20, or US$35 with dinner. Horse-riding trips through the desert can be arranged for both beginners and more advanced riders at the **Sofitel Hotel Equestrian Centre** (tel: 069-360 0081) in Sharm Al Sheikh. Excursions cost US$30 per hour, with overnight journeys starting from US$100.

Quad runners are immensely popular, but you should think twice if you are environmentally conscious, as the wheels destroy the fragile desert eco-

Wedded Bliss

All-night Bedouin weddings are worth attending if you manage to find a guide who knows one that you can be invited to. These colourful functions provide a rare opportunity for young Bedouin men and women to mix and mingle. The women wear incredibly sequined and embroidered wedding shawls that catch the light of the full moon (and hopefully the eye of a future prospect). The men, in turn, dance intricate dances in the hopes of impressing a potential bride. Tour operators may sometimes boast that a wedding feast is part of the package, but these will invariably be synthetic affairs put on just for the tourist. Your best bet is to head for Dahab or Nuweiba, where the independent Bedouin guides who offer their services on the street will have better connections to try to get you an invitation to the real thing.

system. Canyon Safari at the Pigeon House (tel: 069-360 0997) in Sharm offers packages starting from US$20 per hour.

The Tribes of the Sinai

Fifty thousand Bedouin call the Sinai Peninsula home. It's a harsh and unforgiving environment to live in, especially in the north where most choose to congregate. There are 14 distinct tribes, all with ties across the Middle East to families in the Negev, Jordan and Saudi Arabia.

The largest Bedouin tribe in the Sinai are the Sukwarka. The centre of their community is Al 'rish on the Mediterranean coast – so while they make up a large proportion of the Bedouin population, you will probably have the least contact with them if you are sticking to the resort communities in the south. Other important tribes scattered throughout the

Camel safari

north and centre of the peninsula include the Tarabin, the Tyaha and the Haweitat.

The Arabs of Al Tor

The seven tribes in the south of the Sinai are collectively known as the Towara or 'Arabs of Al Tor'. Members of these tribes work as guides for tourists wishing to travel into the Sinai interior, and are known to have almost encyclopaedic knowledge of every trail, rock and plant in the peninsula. The benefit of travelling with the Bedouin is their years of learning, passed from father to son.

Trekking up Mount Sinai

By far the most popular experience in the Sinai is a trek up Mount Sinai at dawn. Known in the Old Testament as the place where Moses was given the Ten Commendments, Mount Sinai is the dramatic setting for the 6th-century St Catherine's Monastery *(see p.204)*.

The best time to set off is around 2am so that you reach the summit at sunrise (the climb usually takes around 3½ hours, including frequent rest stops). It can be cold, especially in winter, but the views and the quality of the early morning light more than make up for it. Enthusiastic types can try going up a set of stone steps, which take an hour to climb, or you can go up on a camel in about two hours.

Camels and Bedouin line the path if you decide to go up independently and want to arrange transport upon arrival. Alternatively, Sheik Sina Bedouin Treks (El Milga, St Catherine; tel:

Campfire in the desert

069-347 0880; www.sheikhsina.com) is recommended for trekking itineraries or climbs.

Booking a Sinai Desert Tour

The Bedouin experience is now a firm fixture on the tourism trail, and hiring a Bedouin tour guide is actually quite easy. St Catherine's, Dahab and Nuweiba are the best locations from which to arrange a desert adventure in the Sinai, as they have large Bedouin guide communities. Operators offer a wide range of camel or jeep safaris into the Sinai interior from the resort towns or monastery. Their length depends on your chosen itinerary and mode of transport. Camels may feel more 'authentic', but they will also take two to three times longer to get to their destination.

Two organisations that can put you in touch with experienced Bedouin guides in the Sinai are the **Centre for Sinai** (Dahab; 069-364 0702; www. centre4sinai.com) and **Man & the Environment Dahab** (069-364 1091; www.mate-info.com).

The Western Desert

Despite being home to a tiny fraction of the Egyptian population, the Western Desert makes up over 80 per cent of the nation's landmass. The region is harsh – inhospitable, stark, yet fascinating. Some of the highest temperatures recorded on the planet have been measured here.

Travelling through the region requires experience, knowledge and a strict adherence to safety measures. As such, it is recommended only to travel with a tour operator.

Longer safaris in the Western Desert are available from **Khalifa Expedition** (tel: 012-321 5445; www. khalifaexp.com), **Peter Gaballa** at Egypt Off Road (tel: 010-147 5462; www.egyptoffroad.com) and **Hisham Nessim** (tel: 012-780 7999; www.raid-4x4egypt.com).

Desert Safaris

Top Five Desert Experiences

- A dip in the geothermal hot springs located near the town of Mut or close to Siwah Oases.
- Trekking up Mount Sinai before dawn to enjoy the sunrise.
- A night under the stars at a Bedouin campsite in the Eastern Desert.
- Witnessing the wonder of Mother Nature as you drive through surreal rock formations in your jeep.
- Enjoying complete silence in the desert, with only the whisper of the wind creating the occasional sound.

Excursions in the Western Desert

The very isolation of the Western Desert's oases has bred a culture distinct from the rest of Egypt. Primarily Berber-speaking, the residents of this remote outpost are fiercely proud of their independence and value tradition above all else. Desert experiences in the oases often focus on the region's isolation and hidden natural wonders.

Tours come in two categories: day trips from the various oases or extended treks that travel between the oases. Popular day trips take in hot springs or oases that are close to your home base. For instance, if you are staying in Siwah, guides will take you to Bir Wahed, El Maraqi, Abu Shrouf or 'in Schiffar. All tours are accompanied by Bedouin or Egyptian guides – when in doubt, try to choose a company with local guides, as they will be more familiar with specific sites of interest in the region.

The Eastern Desert

In the Eastern Desert, native tourist guides are much less experienced when it comes to dealing with tourist needs. The best guides will be employed by a larger-scale operator. It is better to arrange your Bedouin desert treks through a recognised tour operator such as **Al Badawiya** (Al Badawiya Hotel; tel: 02-575 8076; www.badawiya.com) or the Bedouin-guided **Red Sea Desert Adventures** firm based in Marsa 'Alam (tel: 012-399 3860; www.redseadsertadventures.com). Red Sea Desert Adventures is a safari company run by a Dutch geologist and her Austrian partner. They have lived in Marsa 'Alam for over a decade and are authorities on the art and culture of local Ababda tribespeople. Tours are tailor-made and can include walking, camel rides or jeep

Jeep safaris are a popular way to explore

Camel ride at Giza

explorations throughout the area. A typical camel safari will cost approximately €80 per day.

In the oases, most hotels double up as tour operators, but standards can vary, especially on longer treks. Good reports have come out of the **Siwah Safari Paradise** (Siwah Town; tel: 046-460 1590; www.siwaparadise.com) and the **Palm Trees Hotel** (Shari' Torrar, Siwah Town; tel: 046-460 1703).

Voluntourism

Visit the Sinai Wildlife Clinic non-profit organisation to see how locals are attempting to conserve the native wildlife. In autumn the most important work is done, and volunteers are taken on to help work on the clinic's various projects. Those with veterinary or nursing skills are especially welcome. Ring in advance for details (tel: 069-360 1610 ext. 241).

Day Trips in the Eastern Desert

Geological jeep safaris and Bedouin barbecues are popular day trips for those who want a bit of time away from the beach. Marsa 'Alam offers a number of highly regarded operators who provide bespoke and large group options. Recommended operators include **Mazenar Tours** (Marsa Shagra, Shari' Port Sa 'id; tel: 065-333 5247; www.rockyvalleydiverscamp. com) and eco-champions and bird-watching specialists Fustat Wadi Al Jemal (Wadi Jemal; tel: 012-240 5132; www.wadielgemal.com). At Al Gunah, arrange camel and horse rides at the Mövenpick Resort or through the Swiss-managed Yalla Horse Stables near Abu Tig marina (tel: 065-354 9702/010-136 6703; www.elgouna. com). Horses and camels are also available along all the main beaches for shorter beach or desert rides.

Shopping in Souqs

To experience Egypt fully, you must enter its markets – for it is here that travellers can see what has seduced countless invaders, explorers and merchants for centuries. Souqs are the heart and soul of the country; prepare your five senses for a delightful onslaught.

In Egypt, the market, or souq, is where you go if you want to buy something. Not for this nation the orderly shopping experiences of London, Paris and New York. Instead, the souq is a chaotic mass of colours filled with beckoning and yelling, people coming and going, and goods piled up high wherever you turn. Look past the stuffed camels and cheap souvenirs to see the finest the country has to offer – spices, colourful fabrics, heaps of fruit and vegetables, crafts, silver and gold, backgammon sets, metalwork, sheesha pipes, papyrus scrolls, alabaster items and bellydance outfits... You name it, you'll find it in the souq.

Crossroads of the World

Egypt has been known as a trading centre for centuries – ever since the early Egyptians of the Old Kingdom began travelling beyond their borders to bring in treasures from afar. The empire was situated at the crossroads of the known world and was the gateway for trade between Africa, Asia and Europe. Traders from Saharan and sub-Saharan Africa would wind their way to Egypt, either on foot, by boat along the Nile, Mediterranean and Red Sea coasts or on camel or horseback, their beasts stacked high with gold, ivory and spices to trade. In

Fine silk for sale at Luxor souq

return they would take home papyrus, alabaster, grain and precious stones mined from the Eastern Desert.

The ancient trade routes remain today, but the methods of travel have changed, with sailboats replaced by freighters and horses overtaken by long-distance trucks. Camel travel remains important from the Sudan, but the volume of traders reduces each year as nomadic communities become more sedentary.

The Souq Experience

An Egyptian souq is a place of frenetic activity, filled with noise, rich colours and pungent smells. Goods will be transported by wheelbarrow, donkey and on porters' backs all around you, so watch your back and hold on tight to your money.

Expect vibrant colours to dazzle you at every turn, sparkly products thrust into your line of vision and soft silks placed in your hand for you to admire. It's common for sellers to try to get your intention with hisses and verbal patter. Every few steps you will hear 'best spice here', 'free gift', 'just one Egyptian pound' or questions about where you are from. Some aggressive touts may even grab your arm and steer you into their shop. Stay calm and be firm but polite when saying no. A simple 'no shoqran' should do the trick to end the sales pitch – at least until the next stall.

Haggling at a spice store

Food markets may feel particularly alien, as entire animals are hung on display complete with heads and tails. Despite the smell, standards of hygiene are high, with animals slaughtered on the same day their meat is

How to Haggle

Haggling is an integral part of the Egyptian shopping experience and should be considered a game, rather than a battle. Here are a few tips:

- Ask the seller what the price is – never quote an offer first.
- Most dealers start their offers at an exorbitant price; suggest half of what the seller quotes you and go from there. The vendor will ridicule the amount you quote but keep smiling and stay firm.
- Don't show too much interest in the item you want to buy.
- Only engage in the bargaining process if you are serious about buying, but be prepared to walk away empty-handed if the price is too high. You may be followed and offered a lower price once out in the street.
- Take a relaxed approach; talk to the dealer at length, enjoy the tea you may be offered and do not feel under any obligation to buy if you can't get the right price.
- Get an idea of prices by trying several shops and checking out the 'fixed-price shops' where haggling is not necessary.
- Don't feel guilty about managing to get a low price; a vendor will not sell without making a profit.

Aswan souq is best for spices and CDs of Nubian music

sold. Meat is a luxury in Egypt, so butchers ensure they sell the very best to make customers want to come back for more. If you're squeamish, explore the market early in the day, as the smell gets worse as the day goes on and the sun gets hotter.

Choosing your Souq

If you are travelling widely throughout Egypt, you may want to restrict your shopping to the items each souq is known for. For instance, Luxor is known for its alabaster products, while Aswan offers great spices and Nubian items. Bedouin crafts can be found in the Sinai, and Cairo is essentially a one-stop-shop for all things Egyptian. Additionally, some souqs are much more relaxed than others to shop in – so if you are a bad bargainer

or just hate all the hassle, you may want to avoid the high-pressure atmosphere found in some of the more aggressive markets. Of all the souqs in Egypt, the one in Luxor tends to generate the most complaints in terms of persistent salesmen and scams – so this may be the souq to avoid. Try to bring a reusable bag with you to limit the number of plastic bags being thrown out after a single use.

The Confident Haggler

If you've never haggled before, a great way to start out is to watch how local experts do it. Egyptian women never express much delight at finding an item for fear of giving the seller a bargaining advantage, and they will walk away before agreeing to any price they think is too high.

Traditionally, stallholders in the souqs were men. This remains the case, and it is very uncommon to see a woman working in the markets. If travelling as a couple, merchants will try to persuade women with their wares but negotiate the final price with men. The assumption is that women are the ones who like to shop while men have the wallets.

The more expensive the item, the more elaborate the bartering may become. You may be invited into the store to look at a wider selection, offered a soft drink or cup of tea; stallholders may even invite you to visit their homes to dine with their families. Relax and stay a while, as rushing a negotiation is seen as rude and sellers are genuinely interested in finding out more about you. *For more tips on the art of haggling, see the box on page 45.*

Navigating the Souq

With the exception of the souq of Aswan (which lies along one long strip of road) and the modern souqs of the Sinai and Red Sea resort towns, Egypt's markets are maze-like and difficult to get your bearings in. Don't even think about trying to navigate your way around with a map, as the winding and claustrophobic alleyways are sure to confuse you within minutes, and maps can't cover the

Handy Market Vocabulary	
How much is it?	Bikam da?
I'm just looking.	Bat farrag bas.
I'll take it.	'Akhudha.
Do you accept credit cards?	Bi to khud kredit kard? (m) Bi ta khudee kredit kard?(f)
Can you give me a discount?	Mumkin tidee ni takh feed?
I don't like it.	Mish 'a gibni.
0	Sifr
1	Waahid
2	Itnayn
3	Talaata
4	Arba'a
5	Khamsa
6	Sit'ta
7	Saba'a
8	Tamanya
9	Tis'a
10	'Ashara
20	Ishreen
100	Miy'ya

Scented oils for sale at Aswan souq

small alleys and backways that make up most of the souq. The key is to wander and explore. The greatest finds usually hit when least expected – so don't just stick to the main avenues.

Pretty much anything can be purchased in the souqs, from Arabian perfumes and spices to sheesha pipes and jewellery. There once was an un—official rule of thumb that merchants who sold an item tended to stick closely together. So, if you wanted perfume, you went to the perfume part of the market; copper could be bought in the copper market, etc. As the tourist trade has taken over the souq, this division has relaxed in most cases. You will still find gold, copper and spice merchants clustered together, but it's no longer the hard and fast rule it once was.

Sensory Delights

One of the highlights of the souq is to see how wares are displayed. The Egyptian version of the shop window can be quite visually stunning, as most stall owners put a lot of effort into showing off their stock. Once your eye has been attracted, the rest of your senses will be disarmed as you are encouraged to touch, taste and smell items for sale.

Don't be afraid to handle stock – an Egyptian buyer wouldn't think twice about testing every aspect of an item's quality before buying it. This holds especially true in Aswan, as this souq specialises in spices. Sellers will gladly take you through their wares and hold, crush, pound and sift spices to demonstrate quality. You may even be offered a glass of *karkadeh* (hibiscus

Luxor souq

Papyrus-making demonstration, Luxor

flower) tea to help you as you make your decision.

People-Watching

As a tourist, you are bound to stand out and receive attention as you shop, making people-watching a challenge. Instead, do as the locals do and pull up a chair at an *qahwa* (coffee house or café) and order a drink. You'll find them pretty much everywhere in the souqs, designed to serve merchants and tourists alike. From a street-side table, it's easy to absorb the atmosphere and enjoy the show, as children approach you to sell you trinkets and smaller items like gum or cigarette lighters.

Scams to Avoid

The vast majority of Egyptians are honest and hard-working, but for a minority, the temptation of lots of tourists and easy money is too great. Here are a few shopping scams to watch out for:

- **The bait and switch**
  You pick an item out and get home to find that the wrapping contains another item of inferior quality. Avoid getting caught out by ensuring the item is wrapped in your presence.

- **The antique boutique**
  The seller says the item is an antique treasure. There are numerous ways to age items artificially, and scam artists know every trick. All antiques that leave Egypt must have documents provided by the government for export – and these are rarely given.

- **The not-so-genuine article**
  Alabaster is not always of the highest quality. To see if you are being sold the genuine article, look for cracks and wax deposits – wax is commonly used to fix flaws in the stone. A top-quality item should have no cracks and little or no wax. Hold it up to the light; true alabaster is translucent.

Nubian Culture

The creation of the Aswan High Dam nearly decimated the Nubian people – a community of traders whose traditional homeland lay between the First and Sixth Cataracts of the Nile. But despite the loss of their homeland, the Nubian people endure, keeping their traditions alive in villages throughout the region.

As the gateway to Africa, Nubia has been prized since the dawn of ancient Egyptian civilisation. This arid stretch of land of about 22,000 sq km (8,500 sq miles) situated between the Sudanese border and the Egyptian town of Aswan may have lacked the fertility of areas to the north, but its value as Egypt's key continental trading route made it a prized possession.

Today, Nubia is no longer. In 1972, this once great area disappeared under the largest artificial lake in the world, Lake Nasser. The Nile was tamed once and for all by the building of the High Dam outside Aswan, which created the vast lake, but the Nubians paid a high price.

Scattered to the four winds, they dwell in cities and towns up and down the Nile, no longer able to visit the homes where their ancestors were born and raised.

Nubian woman, c.1900

A Short History

To understand the drama of the Nubian diaspora, it is necessary to understand the importance of ancient Nubia. Known as Kush, the region protected Egypt's southern frontier and was an essential gateway for Egyptian trade with Africa. Around 1550BC, the Theban pharaohs turned their attention to conquering Kush. However, it took them over a century to subdue Lower and Upper Nubia.

As Nubia was a largely barren land, the Nile played a crucial role in the life of the Nubian people. Their small riverside villages, each usually comprising one extended family, were supported by growing crops, fishing and cultivating date palms, which provided a nutritious source of food, fibre for ropes and wood for construction and furniture.

Nubian Versus Egyptian

From the middle of the 18th Dynasty, Upper and Lower Nubia were ruled by a viceroy appointed by the Egyptian pharaoh, and a process of Egyptianisation ensued.

During the New Kingdom the Nubians worshipped a deity in ram form, which the Egyptians accepted as another form of their god Amun. From that point on, the Nubians played a more important role in Egypt. Most of the 25th Dynasty Kushite pharaohs were of Nubian descent, and some authors even believe that

A view of Aswan

Cleopatra was a Nubian woman from Wadi Halfa on the Sudanese border – *kilu baba tarati*, the possible derivation of Cleopatra, is Nubian for 'Beautiful Woman'.

Bridging Cultures

Aswan has been the link between the Egyptian and Nubian cultures for thousands of years. In antiquity, Elephantine, the largest of the islands, situated immediately opposite Aswan, was known as Yebu or Elephant Land, because it was the trading post for ivory (although another theory for the island's name points to the shapes and textures of the rock formations).

The island commanded the First Cataract that formed a natural boundary to the south, and gave Egypt a loose sovereignty over Nubia. The Nubians, moving with their herds of sheep and goats, relied on Egypt for grain and vegetable oil.

Nubian Weddings

The Egyptianisation of the Nubian people has meant that there are no distinct festivals unique to the Nubian people. The one exception to this is when Nubians get married. Weddings can last as long as two weeks (though three days is more common now) and are vibrant affairs, with Nubian musicians playing an important role.

According to tradition, several gifts are passed from the groom to the bride and her family including lavish garments, silks and jewellery. The presents are loaded on a camel, which may also be considered a wedding gift.

The sheer cost of the event means that Nubian men tend to marry relatively late in life in order to save up enough money to cover the ceremony costs.

Nubian Culture

Preserving Nubian Culture

Although Nubia was strategically important as a buffer zone to the ancients, historically the Egyptians have always looked down on the region as a vast barren area, and its loss was considered inconsequential. However, a growing realisation of the cultural value of what had been destroyed gathered momentum in the 1980s, and in the late 1990s a new Nubia Museum, backed by international interest and funds, opened its doors in Aswan *(see opposite)*.

Nubians Today

Despite their plight in the modern world, the Nubians have managed to retain their distinct identity and are immensely proud of their inheritance and culture. They rarely marry

Nubian boatman

Egyptians, even when they live in Cairo or Alexandria, and, as is discernible from the many Nubian boatmen in Aswan, they speak their own language, which is totally different from Egyptian Arabic. Other elements of traditional Nubian culture survive in the villages on Elephantine Island and neighbouring islands – many women, for instance, still wear the Nubian-style dress of a black transparent gown over a brightly coloured dress. Wedding celebrations last at least three days, and include performances by Nubian musicians *(see box on p.51)*. Nubian music is well known in the west *(see opposite)*.

Nubians are making their mark in Egyptian society, particularly in the arts. Probably the most famous person of Nubian descent was Anwar Al Sadat, the late president of Egypt and Nobel Prize-winner, whose mother was Nubian.

Nubian Architecture

The internationally renowned Egyptian architect Hassan Fathy (1900–1989) found his inspiration in vernacular Nubian architecture. Writing about his first visit to Elephantine Island in 1941 in his *Architecture for the Poor*, he said: 'It was a new world for me, a whole village of spacious, lovely, clean and harmonious houses each more beautiful than the next. There was nothing else like it in Egypt; house after house, tall, easy, roofed cleanly with a brick vault, each house was decorated exquisitely around the doorway with claustra-work-mouldings and tracery in mud'.

Fathy believed in adapting

View of the Nile from Aswan

traditional materials, designs and techniques to create modern, attractive and economical solutions to housing the poor.

Speaking Nubian

The Nubian language differs from Arabic and is spoken widely amongst the Nubian people. As many Nubians work in the souq of Aswan, you will find they also speak Arabic and English, making it unlikely that you will ever get a chance to learn any words for yourself.

The Nubian dialect spoken in Aswan and southern Egypt is Kenzi-Dongolawi – one of six dialects recorded by linguistic researchers. Debate continues over how to write the language down properly, as there is argument over the way letters should be written and words transliterated. As such, there are no Nubian–English dictionaries or phrasebooks currently on the market.

The **Nubia Museum** is a good one-stop-shop for information on Nubian architecture. The museum was built using Nubian construction and design principles, but is currently undergoing restoration, meaning that sections may be closed. Alternatively, ask Muhammad Sobhy to guide you around the village of Siou on Elephantine Island. Mohamed can be reached at the Animalia Café; tel: 231 4152.

The Nubian Beat

Nubian music is the means by which Nubians are starting to stamp their influence on Egyptian culture. Songs produced by stars of the Nubian music scene are incredibly popular in Egyptian society, and Aswan is a great place to sample the sound. Many Nile-side restaurants feature nightly performances given by talented locals, and there are souq sellers who specialise

constantly. Performances usually fall into one of two categories: traditional or contemporary. Traditional performances will feature village songs using drums and handclapping to set the beat. Contemporary performers will take the traditional songs and mix them with influences from jazz, trance, funk and classical styles.

Hamza Ad Din is widely considered to be the father of the contemporary Nubian sound. An accomplished oud (lute) musician, his playing has been included in recordings and concerts made by some of the leading lights of 60s music, including the Grateful Dead, Bob Dylan and Joan Baez.

in selling Nubian music CDs. When making a purchase, ask them if they know of any performances coming to town, as venue locations change

Aswan

When the flooding of their homelands resulted in dispersal of the

Top Five Nubian Items to Buy

Nubians are renowned for their craftsmanship and culture. The following, which are all sold in Aswan's souq, make good souvenirs:

- **Basketry**
  Nubian women are well-known basketweavers. A common style is a round, flat-based cone used to serve food.
- **Nubian music**
  Nubian music is distinctive; more accessible than Arabic music, it has a rhythmic quality, mixing simple melodies with soulful vocals. At Aswan souq there are several music shops selling CDs where you can listen to the music before you buy.

- **Henna tattoo**
  Henna, a natural dye, has been used in Nubia for centuries (traces of it have even been found on mummified pharaohs). Traditionallly, women decorate their hands and feet prior to getting married. You can get a tattoo in the Nubian villages on Elephantine Island.
- **Jewellery**
  Women supplement their income by making simple beaded jewellery.
- **Spices**
  Almost all the spice merchants in Aswan are Nubian. They know their quality and will happily let you try before you buy.

Nubian population, many Nubians settled in Aswan (or within an easy drive of the city). Aswan souq is a good source for genuine Nubian arts and crafts, including daggers, hand-woven rugs, jewellery and baskets *(see box opposite)*.

Aswan can sometimes seem overwhelmed by tourists and their interests, but in general it manages to shoulder the burden of tourism while preserving much of its unique character. The market streets are often filled with visitors from Sudan or tribes from the Eastern Desert as well as with Western holidaymakers.

Dinner under the Stars

There are a number of islands scattered along the Nile near Aswan, many of which house Nubian restaurants. Hop aboard one of the free ferries from the pier located opposite the Egyptair office on the Corniche in order to experience delightful Nubian dishes. In most cases, island restaurants aren't completely authentic, offering a mix of Western, Nubian and Egyptian food. Ask your waiter for help to ensure you get a taste of real Nubian treats and not the tourist version.

Kenzi House (Seheyl Island; 012-415 4902; opening times vary, ask for Gelal Muhammad Hassan to arrange transfers, music and meals) is located within a much larger Nubian community, giving visitors the chance to experience a bit of Nubian village life, while **Nubian Duka** (Essa Island; 097-230 0307; opening times vary, call ahead to arrange a table and transfers from the pier opposite the Egyptair office) puts its focus on a folklore show in order to give patrons a 'taste' of Nubia.

Nubian Culture

Nubian selling jewellery

Coffee Houses

For Egyptians, a coffee house is far more than a Middle Eastern version of Starbucks. It is and has been for centuries a place of reprieve, a place of social exchange and an integral part of the local neighbourhood.

Ever-popular Al Fishawy coffee house in Khan Al Khalili bazaar, Cairo

The coffee house is an essential part of urban Egyptian life, but coffee has had a chequered history in Egypt. Although now integral to the lives of thousands, it once invoked the wrath of the clergy, who saw it as a dangerous drug.

To the average Egyptian man, going for coffee represents more than just a means of having a hot drink. Ever since coffee beans arrived in Egypt from Ethiopia and Yemen in the late 15th century, men have gathered in coffee houses to exchange news, gossip, make plans, play games and – in some cases – plot.

In a land where homes are crowded and small, the coffee house is a place of refuge and respite. But they are a far cry from a Westerner's idea of a café. No discerning Egyptian would be seen with a foamy cappuccino or blended drink in his hand. Instead, this is a largely masculine world of dense Egyptian coffee, sweet tea and sheesha smoke, often with football on the TV screen, games of chess and backgammon on the tables and loud music to add to the din. Women may feel uncomfortable in some establishments, especially those located off the beaten track or in rural locations. Coffee houses in tourist areas, souqs and cities will be less intimidating.

The *qahwa* (in formal Arabic; *ahwa* in informal Arabic) – meaning both 'coffee' and 'café' – is defined loosely. It can be anything from a bench, a patch of charcoal, a tin pot and three glasses to a cavernous saloon reverberating with the clack of dominoes, the slap of cards and the crackling of dice.

The ideal café adjoins a small square in the backstreets of a popular quarter. The few outdoor tables will be shaded by a tree or vine, while the ground will have been sprinkled with water to keep down the dust. A pungent sweetness emanates from the interior, where sawdust covers the floor.

An elaborate brass sarabantina, which resembles a cross between a steam locomotive and a samovar, occupies pride of place on the counter at the back of the room, behind which striped glass jugs for smokers' water pipes line the walls.

Cheap and Cheerful

One of the reasons behind the popularity of the *qahwa* is the affordability

Women will feel more at home in modern coffee houses

of going to one. A couple of coffees and a sheesha can run to less than E£2, making a night out within the realm of possibility for even the poorest of men. Gambling professionals will even set up shop in the coffee house to make their salaries, challenging locals to games of backgammon, dominoes or chess for money. Don't worry if you're just looking for a casual game, as there are plenty of

57

Coffee Houses

Ordering Your Drink

When selecting your drink, use one of the following terms to help place your order:

- *Scitto:* Arabic coffee without sugar.
- *Mazboot:* Arabic coffee with medium sugar (the most common order).
- *Ziyada:* Arabic coffee with lots of sugar.
- *Karkade:* a refreshing tea made from the flowers of the hibiscus plant, served hot or cold.

- *Chai soqar bosta:* tea with sugar on the side – in most cases, tea is always brewed with sugar already added.
- *Chai qamseena:* tea in a small glass.
- *Chai menno feeh:* special tea with milk added – the milk is heated, followed by the tea leaves.
- *Vanillia:* hot chocolate.
- *Nescafé:* Western-style coffee.

free tables and individuals looking to have a bit of fun.

Making the Perfect Cup

Arabic coffee is still prepared and served in centuries-old style, without the fancy gadgetry of European invention. Sugar, then powdered coffee are added to hot water and brought to the boil in a brass kanaka. The *qahwagi* (waiter) brings the kanaka and cup on a tin tray and pours the liquid with care, preserving the wish – the 'face' or thick mud that sits on the surface before settling. In the better cafés, a dark blend spiced with cardamon is used. In all establishments, customers should specify how they want their drink *(see box on p.57)*. In some 'European cafés', *qahwa Faransawi* or French coffee is served, and newer, modern cafés have Italian espresso machines.

A Smoker's Paradise

The Egyptian café is a paradise for smokers, where there are ample opportunities to enjoy the ultimate tool for smoking toboacco; the sheesha, or water pipe. Increasingly popular in the West, the sheesha is a colourful bulbous glass pipe filled with water; charcoal is used to heat the tobacco, and the smoke passes through the water, which cools and lightens the taste of the burning leaves, and makes a pleasing gurgling sound as it does. The sheesha is a traditional feature of coffee houses from Alexandria to Aswan. If smoking is your thing, then the sheesha is an instrument of meditation to be savoured serenely.

If you decide to indulge, you'll need to choose your type of tobacco. Most popular is *ma'assil*, a sticky blend of chopped leaf fermented with

Coffee shop, Aswan

Unique Experiences

molasses. It is pressed in small clay bowls that are fitted into the sheesha and lit with charcoal. This tobacco is also sold with a smoother apple flavour *(tuffah)*, or sticky cherry, strawberry and even cappuccino flavours. *Tumbaq*, another variety, is loose dry tobacco wrapped into a cone with a whole leaf. While *ma'assil* is easy to smoke, a cone of dry *tumbaq* may take up to an hour to exhaust.

The govenment has started to take action to limit smoking in Egypt, but it's an uphill struggle. Egyptians smoke the most cigarettes in the Arab world. In 2010 Alexandria became the first no smoking city, with a ban on lighting up in government buildings.

Sheeshas (water pipes) are very popular

Where to Find a Café

Alexandria

Walk along the Corniche to find a comfortable *qawah*. While many are tourist-oriented with inflated prices, the views and breezes make up for it.

Aswan

There are numerous *qawahs* located in the Aswan souq. Hours vary – just find one that looks comfortable and pull up a chair.

Cairo

Cairo is filled with coffee houses of all kinds; old-fashioned intimidating cafés and more modern brasserie types. The most famous of all is Al Fishawy (Khan Al Khalili, just off Meadan Al Husayn; no phone). Apparently open since 1773, this exotic café in the heart of the souq is a great place to hang out, have a cup of mint tea or smoke a sheesha.

Luxor

Like Aswan, Luxor's coffee houses are located within the souq. Wander the lanes of the market and then take a break when the haggling and hassle get too much.

Coffee House Reading

Drinks, television and games may draw the crowds, but for many the coffee house is also the place to read and listen. Tables are filled for hours with newspaper readers, storytellers and people reciting poetry, historic passages and political tracts.

This was captured perfectly by Egypt's greatest storyteller, Nobel Prize-winner Naguib Mahfouz. Novels such as *Midaq Alley* and *The Cairo Trilogy* chronicle the lives, loves and passions of Cairo's coffee-house aficionados. Pull up a chair with a copy of one of his books and compare the words to the colour around you. You'll be surprised by how similar they are.

PLACES

Getting Your Bearings

From space, Egypt looks like a mass of yellow cut through by a thin strip of green, running from the southern border with Sudan until it reaches the Mediterranean via the Nile Delta. The yellow is of course desert, and the strip of green is the Nile Valley, home to over 90percent of Egypt's population of almost 80 million.

It was along this valley that a mighty kingdom flourished for over 3,000 years. Preserved by the country's hot, dry climate and often buried by the sands, many of Ancient Egypt's tombs, temples and pyramids have survived, and are a major draw to the country.

To the west is the largest region of the country – yet also the least populated – the Western Desert, dotted with oases. East lie the Sinai and Eastern Desert, where you find the popular tourist resorts of Hurghadah and Sharm Al Sheikh. The climate, beaches and extraordinary marine life along the coast attract thousands of visitors.

For easy reference when using this guide, the main tourist regions of the country have a whole chapter dedicated to them and are colour-coded for quick navigation. Detailed regional maps are found at the beginning of each chapter.

A listings section can be found at the end of each chapter which features the best hotels, restaurants, cafés and activities the town or region has to offer. The listings cater to all budgets, from those on a shoestring through to those who like to travel with no expense spared.

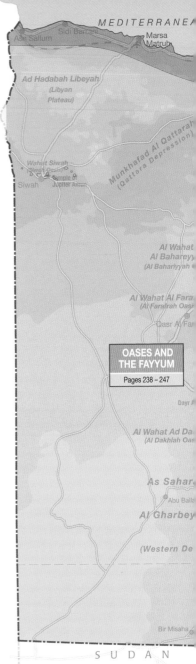

MEDITERRANEA

Ask Sallum   Sidi Barrani   Marsa Matruh

Ad Hadabah Libeyah
(Libyan Plateau)

Munkhafad Al Qattarah
(Qattara Depression)

Wahat Siwah
(Siwah Oasis)
Temple of
Siwah   Jupiter Amun

Al Wahat
Al Baharey
(Al Bahariyyah

Al Wahat Al Fara
(Al Farafrah Oasi

Qasr Al Far

OASES AND THE FAYYUM
Pages 238 – 247

Dayr

Al Wahat Ad Da
(Al Dakhlah Oas

As Sahar

Abu Balla

Al Gharbey

(Western De

Bir Misaha

S U D A N

ALEXANDRIA AND THE NORTH
Pages 178 – 197

GIZA, MEMPHIS AND SAQQARAH
Pages 98 – 117

CAIRO
Pages 64 – 97

SINAI
Pages 198 – 219

MIDDLE EGYPT
Pages 118 – 127

LUXOR
Pages 128 – 151

RED SEA COAST
Pages 220 – 237

UPPER EGYPT
Pages 152 – 177

Cairo

The largest city in Africa and the hub of the Arab world, Cairo is a diverse and fascinating metropolis. Nearly 18 million residents live in this booming, bustling capital city, with more arriving each year from the countryside. Dive into the swirling mass and you'll uncover amid the noise and chaos an absorbing city of extraordinary treasures, including the jewel in the crown, the Egyptian Museum.

Population: 17,800,000

Local dialling code: 02

Local tourist office: 5 Shari' Adly; tel: 02-2391 3454; www.egypt.travel. Other branches at Cairo International Airport and Rameses Train Station.

Main police station: Next to main tourist office (see address above) on 1st floor; tel: 02-2390 6028.

Main post office: Meadan Al 'Atabah.

Banks: Banks with ATMs are dotted throughout the city.

Hospitals: Anglo-American Hospital, Shari' Hadayaq Al Zohoreya, Gazirah; tel: 02-2735 6162.
As Salam International Hospital, Shari' An Nil, Ma'adi; tel: 02-2524 0250.

Local newspapers/listings magazines: Egyptian Gazette; www.egyptiangazette.net.
Al Ahram Weekly; http://weekly.ahram.org.eg.
Egypt Today; www.egypttoday.com.

Cairo (Al Qahirah) is a beguiling city. This metropolitan melting pot battles daily to meet the needs of its vast population. With almost 18 million people now calling Cairo home, the city faces severe overcrowding, infrastructure challenges, traffic congestion and some of the worst air pollution on the continent.

And yet despite the chaos, noise and traffic, it's hard not to feel Cairo's charm – this is, after all, Africa's greatest city. You'll be struck by golden sunsets over the Nile as the traffic beeps around you and the call to prayer rings out; dark passages swirling with spiced, sweet smoke in the medieval alleyways of the market; a quiet room in the Egyptian Museum filled with dusty artefacts in an unvisited corner of the galleries.

While the city itself seems to be one vast urban sprawl, if you break it down into its neighbourhoods it is in fact quite manageable. Downtown is the centre for business, the Egyptian Museum and five-star tourist hotels along the Nile. To the east lie the labyrinthine roads of Islamic Cairo, with beautiful mosques and many architectural gems. To the south is where you will find the Coptic community and

Cairo's oldest synagogue, while to the west is cosmopolitan Zamalik, home to the fashion-conscious with trendy cafés, restaurants, boutiques and clubs.

Cairo's Beginnings

Despite the presence of the Pyramids nearby, Cairo is not a Pharaonic city. The Pyramids were built at a time when Memphis, 20km (12 miles) south of the Giza Plateau, was the capital of Ancient Egypt.

The Romans built a fortress at On (modern-day Heliopolis), but the foundations of the city were laid in the 10th century when the Fatimids marched in from what is now Tunisia. The Fatimid caliph decided to call the city Al Qahira ('Victorious'), which Europeans corrupted to Cairo. Many great buildings from this era, such as Al Azhar mosque and

View of Cairo's minarets

university and the three great gates, remain today. It wasn't until the mid-19th century that the city's appearance was radically altered. Under the reign of Ismail, grandson of Muhammad Ali, modern central Cairo was built, and what had been a marshy swamp was transformed into a city of European standing.

Following the July Revolution of 1952, Cairo expanded dramatically and continues to do so as city planners try to keep pace with the rapidly growing population.

Downtown

Downtown Cairo (Misr to residents) is a noisy, busy commercial district where you'll find budget accommodation and cheap restaurants, upmarket hotels along the Nile, and several key sights.

Meadan At Tahrir

If Cairo has a heart, then it is **Meadan At Tahrir ❶** (Liberation Square). Created in the 19th century, the square is surrounded by an ocean of traffic, with the famous pink building of the Egyptian Museum to the north and

Apartment block, Downtown Cairo

the Nile Hilton (currently under renovation) on the western perimeter. Other significant buildings here include the Mosque of Umar Makram, used for funerals of important Cairenes, a Soviet-style building devoted to Egypt's notorious bureaucracy, and the American University in Cairo.

Much construction is now going on around the square, as plans are in motion to transform the block into a pedestrian-friendly showpiece. It should be a couple more years until redevelopment is complete; until then, visitors will find the square particularly difficult both to reach and to navigate around.

The American University

Serving the square is Sadat Station, one of Cairo's busiest metro stops.

Cairo Transport

 Airports: Cairo International Airport, 20km (12 miles) northeast of the city centre in Heliopolis; tel: 02-2265 5000; www.cairo-airport.com. To and from the airport: buses depart from the car park outside the arrivals level of Terminal One. Route 356 runs every 20 minutes from 7am to midnight between the airport and the Egyptian Museum. Cost is E£2 per passenger plus E£1 per bag, and the journey takes an hour. Cheaper still is Route 27, which makes the same journey, and Route 400, which runs 24 hours a day. The fare is 50pt per person, but there's no air conditioning. There are plenty of taxis outside the airport; the going rate is anything between E£50 and E£100 depending on your bargaining skills and when you arrive.

 Cairo metro: There are currently two lines, both running in an approximate north–south direction from 6am–11.30pm. The metro is convenient for trips to Coptic Cairo, Downtown, Gezirah and Giza, but is not as useful for Islamic Cairo as few stations serve the area. The cost is E£1 for all rides, regardless of distance. Tickets can be purchased through machines at each metro stop turnstile or from a ticket seller in the station. Hold on to your ticket until you leave the metro.

 Buses: Buses are slow, crowded and get caught up in traffic. The metro and taxis are far more efficient ways of getting around. The Downtown hub at Meadan Abdel Moniem Riad, behind the Egyptian Museum (under the underpass), is the central location for bus journeys to depart. Tickets, which you buy on boarding the bus, cost between 50pt and E£2, depending on the length of your trip.

 Taxis: Most taxi drivers in Cairo work independently, and the quality of your experience will vary greatly with each car. New yellow taxis have arrived which promise better standards, including adherence to Cairo's meter charges and air conditioning, but there are far fewer of them in the city and they are always in demand. To book a yellow taxi in advance, call 19730. If using any other kind of taxi, negotiate the price before you get in.

 Car hire: Driving a car in Cairo is not recommended as it's very dangerous. The narrow and traffic-clogged streets also mean that parking is incredibly difficult. Hiring a car and driver is a better option. Budget, Terminal 1, Cairo Airport; tel: 02-2265 2935; www.budget.com. Hertz, Ramses Hilton, Corniche An Nil; tel: 02-2575 8914; www.hertz.com.

A small palace dating from 1878 lies just behind the entrance. This is the former headquarters of the **American University in Cairo**, where children of the country's elite were educated. Space constraints in the city forced the university to move to the suburbs a few years ago, but arts performances and openings still take place on the old campus grounds, and the school's English-language bookstore remains in the iconic building – this is the best bookshop in Cairo. There's also a small café (daily 10am–5pm) and changing exhibitions.

For most visitors, however, the main appeal of the square is the world's finest collection of Egyptian artefacts held at the Egyptian Museum.

The Egyptian Museum

The **Egyptian Museum ❷** (Meadan At Tahrir; tel: 02-2579 6748; daily 9am–6.30pm, entry not permitted after 4.45pm; Ramadan 9am–4pm; charge **ⓜ**) contains a vast collection of Ancient Egyptian artefacts, including Tutankhamun's exhibits. Packed to the rafters with priceless treasures, the museum is both inspiring and frustrating, as the poor labelling and number of visitors can get in the way of your enjoyment (*see p.70 for tips on how to avoid the crowds*).

What is currently on display is a mere fraction of the finds actually held by the Egyptian Museum's vaults. These are currently being cleared and catalogued, and a new museum, south of the Giza Pyramids, called the Grand Egyptian Museum, is being built which will ease the strain on the overstuffed Cairo building.

To do the museum justice, you should budget at least half a day looking round, and ideally make two visits. After going through security, you'll notice a staircase rising to your right. This leads to the upper floors

Highlights of the Egyptian Museum

The following is a list of the Egyptian Museum's top 20 highlights, chosen by Professor Dr Zahi Hawass, Secretary General of Egypt's Supreme Council of Antiquities, and head of the museum. GF = Ground Floor; UF = Upper Floor. The number tells you which room it's in.

- Statue of Akhenaten (GF 3)
- Statue of Rameses II as a child with the sun-god, Horus (GF 10)
- Bust of Thutmose III (GF 12)
- Statue of Meritamun II (GF 15)
- Copper statue of Pepy I or his son, Merenra (GF 31)
- Statuette of dwarf, Seneb, and his family (GF 32)
- Four statues of Intyshedu (GF 32)
- Ka-Aper (Skeikh Al Beled) (GF 42)
- Statue of Khafra (GFl 42)
- Statue of the dwarf Perniankhu (GF 42)
- Narmer Palette (GF 43)
- Statue of Kai (GF 46)
- Three triads of Menkaura (GF 47)
- Statue of Djoser (GF 48)
- Golden mask of Psusennes I (UF 2)
- Golden mask of Tutankhamun (UF 3)
- Portrait of two brothers from the Fayyum (UF 14)
- Golden throne of Tutankhamun (UF 35)
- Innermost coffin of Yuya (UF 43)
- Mummy of Hatshepsut (UF 56)

and the Tutankhamun treasures, the Royal Mummy Rooms and some toilets, which are almost always very busy. Many go straight to the upper floor, avoiding the ground floor artefacts if they are pressed for time.

Climbing the steps to the first floor, and the Tutankhamun exhibit, look out for the wonderful display of ancient papyri on the walls of the staircase, still with remarkably fresh colours. Objects found in the boy king's tomb take up two of the four sides of the upper floor and include the stunning gold death mask, the two innermost golden anthropoid coffins, jewellery, wooden shrines, chariots, beds and footwear. The thousands of items in the corridor include his magnificent golden

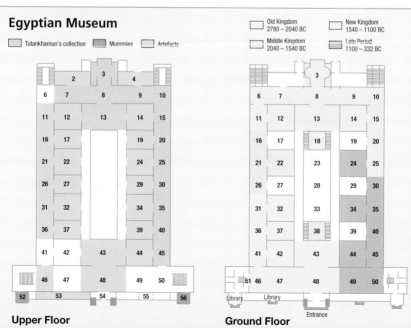

Egyptian Museum

☐ Tutankhamun's collection ☐ Mummies ☐ Artefacts

☐ Old Kingdom 2780 – 2040 BC   ☐ New Kingdom 1540 – 1100 BC
☐ Middle Kingdom 2040 – 1540 BC   ☐ Late Period 1100 – 332 BC

Upper Floor

Ground Floor

Decoration on Coptic church in Old Cairo

throne and footrest, plus two life-size guardian statues.

On the first floor are the Royal Mummy Rooms (additional fee), displaying the skills of the mummification process on the bodies of some royal rulers, including Sety I and Rameses II. Nearby is Room 53, which displays mummified animals considered sacred to the ancient Egyptians; it is fascinating to recognise animals such as gazelles, snakes and baboons wrapped up for eternity.

Other rooms not to be missed include the Royal Tombs of Tanis, Ancient Egyptian Jewellery, and the beautiful paintings and statues in Room 32 (downstairs).

The basement now offers a great museum for children, with an activity centre and playroom, sponsored by Lego. Models of the Pyramids and temples at Karnak are displayed in Lego – much more appealing to little ones than the cabinet displays.

Old Cairo

Known to the Greeks, Romans and early Christians as Babylon (not to be confused with the Mesopotamian city-state of the same name), the old fortified town around which Cairo grew is known to Egyptians as Misr Al Qadimah and to Westerners as Old Cairo. The area is now home to the city's Coptic community. Copts ('Egyptian Christians') were one of the earliest groups to embrace Christianity. Today, the Copts comprise around 15 percent of Egypt's population.

It was here that the Romans decided to build their fortification, creating a 'steeping stone' between Memphis and Heliopolis. In the Late Period, construction of a canal began during the reign of the Persian occupier Darius I (521–488BC), linking the Nile to the Red Sea at this point, cementing the strategic importance of the growing population.

Numerous churches were built here through the centuries due to the area's association with the Holy Family, who, it is believed, visited on their way south to Asyut. Today the neighbourhood thrives with activity, especially on Sundays, when it seems Cairo's entire Coptic population descends on the area to attend services and catch up with friends and family.

Visiting Coptic Cairo

Getting to Coptic Cairo is very easy. From Downtown, take the metro and get off at Mari Girgiss Station on Line One. Go down the steps and turn left as soon as you leave the station. The entrance to the Coptic Museum is across the street, and the ticket office is in a small room at the base of a tower, one of two which remain from the riverfront fortification and dating from AD98.

The grounds of the **Coptic Museum** Ⓐ (Shari' Mari Girgiss; tel: 02-2363 9742; www.copticmuseum.gov.eg; daily 9am–5pm; Ramadan 9am–3pm; charge) begin south of the tower and are entirely within the fortress walls. Founded by private benefactors on land belonging to the Coptic Church, the museum was taken over by the government in 1931. Though there are many ancient Christian sites in Egypt, there are none in which the churches themselves have not been abandoned, destroyed or rebuilt inside and out. It is therefore only the Coptic Museum that gives an idea of what the interior of a 5th-, 6th- or 7th-century church was like. Objects that were excavated in Upper Egypt and in the monastery

Inside the Coptic Museum

Coptic cemetery tomb

of St Jeremiah at Saqqarah are of particular interest.

The museum's most prized relics are the Coptic textiles and the 'Nag Hammadi Codices', a collection of nearly 1,200 papyrus pages bound together as books – the earliest so far known with leather covers – sometime soon after the middle of the 4th century. Written in Coptic, the codices draw syncretically upon Jewish, Christian, Hermetic, Zoroastrian and neo-Platonic sources and have thrown extraordinary light on the background of the New Testament, particularly the Epistles, by revealing that Gnosticism, hitherto supposed to be only a Christian heresy, was in fact a separate religion.

The Coptic churches

The **Church of the Blessed Virgin Mary ❸** is popularly known as the Hanging Church (Al Kanissah Al Mu'allaqah; Shari' Mari Girgiss; daily 7am–5pm; Mass on Fri 8–11am, Sun 7–10am; free but donations welcome) as it is perched on the two bastions that were originally the southern gates of the Roman fortress. It dates from after the Arab conquest and has certainly been rebuilt many times. Try to visit during a service, when the incense can be smelled as soon as you alight from the metro station. A large plasma screen shows the priest's rituals behind the iconostasis, decorated with gold images of the saints, as streams of silver light from the high windows pierce the incense smoke. Despite its modern appearance, it has a very rustic and ancient feel.

Backtrack to the museum ticket office, from which a stairway leads down to the stone-paved main street of the Coptic enclave. The **Church**

of St Sergius **⊙** (Abu Sarga; daily
8am–4pm) lies down the street to
the right. Traditionally regarded as
the oldest in Misr Al Qadimah, it is
said to have been built in the 5th or
6th century over a cave where Joseph,
Mary and the infant Jesus stayed after
fleeing to Egypt to escape persecution
from King Herod of Judaea.

The **Church of St Barbara ⊙** (Sitt
Barbara; daily 8am–4pm) is further
down the main alleyway, then to the
left. Though continuously rebuilt, it
has a fine inlaid medieval iconostasis,
one of the few surviving medieval
icons of St Barbara, and an extraordinarily beautiful 13th-century icon of
the *Virgin with Child Enthroned*.

A few steps away is the **Ben 'Ezra
Synagogue ⊙** (daily 9am–4pm), used
as a church in the 8th and 9th centuries,
closed under the fanatic Caliph Al

Hakim (996–1021), then sold to the
Sephardic community. From the 11th
century onwards, it served as a *geni-
zah*, a repository for discarded documents, which were discovered when
it was rebuilt in the 19th century and
have since provided a wealth of information about the life of the Jewish
community around here in the 11th–
13th century. The spring next to the
synagogue is supposedly where Mary
collected water to wash Jesus, and also
where the Pharaoh's daughter found
the baby Moses in the bulrushes.

The shortest route back to the
main road outside the fortress
returns past the Church of St Sergius,
then curves round to the **Convent
of St George ⊙** (Dayr Al Banat;
daily during services), where modern
believers wrap themselves in chains
in remembrance of the persecution of

73

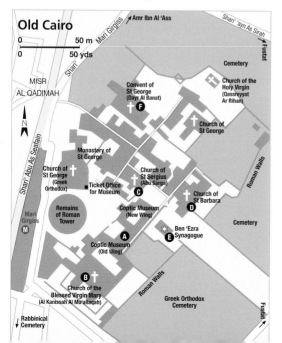

Old Cairo map

Interior of the
Hanging Church

☃ TOUR OF ISLAMIC CAIRO

Cairo contains among the oldest and most revered Islamic buildings in the world. Densely packed into a relatively small area, Islamic Cairo and the nearby Citadel make a great half-day's exploration.

This quarter is home to magnificent mosques and medieval madrasahs (religious schools) and khanqahs (residences), as well as the Citadel, which served for centuries as the seat of Egypt's rulers.

Cairo's oldest-surviving intact mosque is the **Mosque of Ibn Tuloan** (Shari' As Salibah; daily 8am–6pm; free), built between 876–9 by the Abbasid ruler Ahmed Ibn Tuloan. Constructed of red brick and stucco,

the gigantic structure covers an area of over 3 hectares (7½ acres). From the minaret, there are stunning views over the Citadel and Old City.

A gateway near the mosque exit leads to the **Gayer-Anderson Museum** (Bayt Al Kiretleyyah; Shari' Ibn Tuloan; tel: 02-2364 7822; daily 9am–4pm; charge). Gayer-Anderson, an English army doctor, served as physician to the royal household from 1935–42 and also avidly collected oriental antiques, which he housed in the two adjoining 16th-century buildings.

Shari' As Salibah, the main street of the quarter, follows the **Qasabah**, the principal thoroughfare in medieval times, and is still lined with old palaces, mosques, madrasahs and khanqahs.

Exterior of Sultan Hassan Mosque

Tips

- Distance: 3.5km (2 miles)
- Time: half a day
- Women and men should dress respectfully: long trousers and sleeves are best; women will also require a headscarf for some mosques (though this can often be provided). Shoes should be left outside the mosque or with the shoe guardian; sometimes shoe covers are provided.
- Avoid visiting on Friday afternoons, when the mosques are closed for prayers.
- Bring a few small bills to tip custodians.
- Inside the mosque, eating, drinking and talking loudly are frowned upon, though photos are usually permitted.

At the southern end of Shari' As Salibah lies Meaden Salah Addin, a square used for horse racing in Mamluk times.

The **Mosque-Madrasah of Sultan Hassan** (Meadan Salah Addin; daily 8am–5pm; summer to 6pm; charge) was built between 1356 and 1363. Covering over 10,000 sq m (12,000 sq yds), it's the largest medieval religious monument in the Islamic world, and Cairo's finest example of Mamluk architecture.

Opposite lies the **Mosque of Ar Rifa'i** (daily 9am–5pm; free, but small charge for royal tombs). Built between 1869–1912, this neo-Mamluk confection houses the remains of various VIPs. Across from the mosque lies the **Bab Al 'Azab** (Meadan Salah Addin; free), the Citadel's main gate in Ottoman times.

Cairo's imposing **Citadel** (Al Qal'ah; Shari' Salah Salim; tel: 02-2512 1735; daily 8am–5pm; summer until 6pm; free) was built in 1176 by Salah Addin

Courtyard of the Mosque of Muhammad Ali

to fend off the Crusaders, and is the largest fortification in the Middle East. Egypt's ruler resided here for over 700 years, until Ismail, Ali's grandson, relocated to the Abdeen Palace.

Sadly, few original buildings remain; instead, there's a fairly motley collection of mosques, palaces and museums, but the views from the terraces are worthwhile.

Conspicuous for its size and gleaming alabaster facing is the **Mosque of Muhammad Ali**. Completed in 1848, it is classic Ottoman in style with its repeating domes and pencil minarets. Nearby, the 14th-century **Mosque of Nassir Muhammad** is the quarter's only remaining Mamluk monument. It boasts a cedarwood ceiling.

Walking Tour of Islamic Cairo

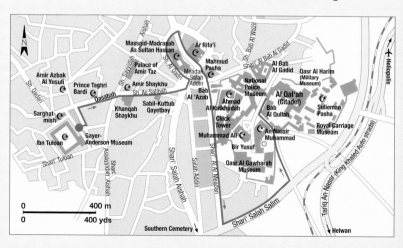

0 — 400 m
0 — 400 yds

Southern Cemetery ↓   Shari' Salah Salim   ↓ Helwan

St George. The convent incorporates a remarkable room with wooden doors 7m (23ft) high, thought to have originally formed part of a Fatimid (12th-century) house.

The island of Roadah

Across a narrow branch of the Nile from Old Cairo onto the island of Roadah is the earliest Muslim structure still extant in the city: the Roadah **Nilometer** ❸ (Manisterli Palace, Shari' Al Malik Assalah; daily 9am–5pm; charge), built in 861 by the governor of Egypt on the order of the Abbasid caliph. The building's conical dome is not part of the original Nilometer, but a replica of the Ottoman-style dome that covered it in the 17th and 18th centuries. Nilometers measured the height of the annual flood and thus the richness of the harvest, which would determine the level of taxes for that year.

The **Manisterli Palace** (Qasr Al Manisterli), next to the Nilometer, is the *salamlek* or reception kiosk of a palace complex built in the 1830s by the founder of a distinguished Cairene Turkish family. The palace was restored in the 1990s, and part of it is now an elegant venue for concerts, while another part houses the **Umm Kulthum Museum** *(see box opposite)*.

Islamic Cairo

To the east of Meadan Attaba is Islamic Cairo. This is a fascinating area of the city, filled with narrow streets, twisting alleyways, suberb mosques and great medieval facades.

Islamic Cairo is no more Islamic than other parts of the city, but the name reflects the fact that it is home to the city's most important mosque and sacred shrine and also a profusion of minarets.

Interior of Mosque of Muhammad Ali

Mosque of Ibn Tuloan

is a massive courtyard of nearly 2 hectares (4 acres) with an ablution fountain in the middle. You can climb the spiral minaret for great views of the Citadel and the city.

Built against one end of the mosque are the two old houses that compose the **Gayer-Anderson Museum** (Shari' Ibn Tuloan; tel: 02-2364 7822; daily 8.30am–4.30pm; closed Fri noon–1pm; charge), also known as Bayt Al

The best way to explore is to spend a couple of days wandering through the neighbourhood. Etiquette should be followed in order to respect local customs – for example, women should cover their legs and arms, men should wear long trousers, and shoes must be removed before entering prayer halls. (The guardian who looks after the shoes should be given some baksheesh.)

The Mosque of Ibn Tuloan

At the centre of the Abassid quarter is the congregational **Mosque (Mass-gid) of Ibn Tuloan ❹** (Shari' As Salibah; daily 8am–6pm; free). Built between 876 and 879 by Ibn Tuloan, who had been sent to rule Egypt by the caliph of Baghdad, it is one of the great masterpieces of Muslim architecture and all that remains to testify to the magnificence of the period. Echoing the architecture of Baghdad, it consists of a square enclosed by a huge flat-roofed arcade of baked brick, which is covered with fine plaster and surmounted by anthropomorphic cresting. In the centre of the mosque

> **Who was Umm Kulthum?**
>
> Egypt's answer to Edith Piaf, Umm Kulthum was the nation's favourite female singer throughout much of the 20th century. Umm Kulthum was born in the Delta region in 1904 and soon became a regular performer in the region. Familiar to audiences on the blossoming club circuit, her star didn't really shine bright until 1935, when she recorded her first song in a feature film. Her Thursday evening radio show was so popular that the streets would empty and businesses would shut in order to allow everyone the chance to hear their favourite daughter perform.
>
> If you want to find out more about the woman whose voice could stop a nation, head to the **Umm Kulthum Museum** (Manisterli Palace, Shari' Al Malik Assalah; tel: 02-2363 1467; daily 10am–4pm; charge), housed in a wing of the Manisterli Palace. This interesting small museum displays photographs, the signature sunglasses and good-luck scarves of Umm Kulthum, and shows a short film that chronicles important episodes in her life.

Kiretleyyah. The British major John Gayer-Anderson restored two beautiful 16th- and 17th-century houses, and filled them with his collection of Islamic objets d'art and paintings. James Bond fans may recognise it from one of the scenes in *The Spy Who Loved Me*.

To the Citadel

Shari' As Salibah, running east of the Mosque of Ibn Tuloan, is lined with monuments, most of them restored after earthquake damage in the 1990s. The street leads to Meadan Salah Addin, above which towers the **Citadel ❺** (Al Qal'ah; Shari' Salah Salim; tel: 02-2512 1735; daily, winter 8am–4pm, summer 8am–5pm; charge). The entrance to the citadel is from Bab Algabal off the Shari' Salah Salim.

Built in 1176 by Salah Addin, the fortress was home to Egypt's rulers for 700 years. Both a fortress and a royal city, the Citadel continued the tradition among Cairo's rulers of building enclosures for themselves and their retainers. Various dynasties have contributed structures to the complex, making it a hotchpotch of ideas and architectural styles.

For example, the inner court of one mosque is a virtual museum of reused pharaonic and Roman-period columns, while its two minarets show Persian influence in their upper pavilions, which are covered in green tiles.

Under the rule of Muhammad Ali Basha (1805–48), the outer walls of the Citadel were rebuilt to suit the needs of a modern army and the decaying medieval buildings in the interior were replaced by new palaces,

barracks, military schools, armament factories, and his own colossal **Mosque of Muhammad Ali**. The Ottoman-style mosque (also known as the Alabaster Mosque), completed nearly 1,000 years after the Ibn Tuloan, dominates the fortress, and indeed the Cairo skyline. The mosque and Citadel are popular with tourists, probably because of their size and imposing setting, but they are relatively unimpressive (and expensive) compared to other sights in the city.

Mosque of Sultan Hassan

On Meadan Salah Addin immediately below the Citadel, opposite the Bab Al 'Azab, soar the walls of the **Mosque and Madrasah of Sultan Hassan ❻** (daily 8am–5pm except during Friday prayers; free), who was the seventh son of Nassir Muhammad.

The noblest and most outstanding example of Bahri Mamluk architecture, this mosque was begun in 1356 and finished seven years later. In contrast with the congregational Mosque of Ibn Tuloan, built to be a gathering place, this is primarily a theological school, combining four residential colleges (madrasahs) with a mausoleum. From the towering main entrance, with its canopy of stalactites, a bent passageway leads to the cruciform central court. Here four great arched recesses, or *iwans*, create sheltered spaces for instruction in each of the four schools of Islamic jurisprudence.

Across the street is the **Ar Rifa'i Mosque** (Meadan Salah Addin; daily 9am–4pm except during prayers; free), begun in 1869, six centuries

Minaret of the restored mosque,
Darb Al Ahmar

15th-century Cairo. At the southern end of Al Azhar Park is the **Mosque of the Amir Aqasunqur** (1347), also known as the Blue Mosque due to the blue-grey marble on the exterior and the tiles inside. It contains the tomb of Kuchuk, the brother of Sultan Hassan, murdered in 1341 at the age of six. Over 300 years later (1652) it was half-heartedly renovated by an Ottoman officer, who had the walls partially covered with Damascene tiles.

Until the 19th century, the enclosed city of medieval Cairo (Al Qahirah) later than the mosque of Sultan Hassan, and completed in 1912. Because it was planned as a complement to its Mamluk neighbour in scale, fabric and architectural style, tourists frequently mistake it for an ancient monument. In it are interred the Khedive Ismail and other members of Egypt's royal family, including King Farouk, whose body was moved here from the Southern Cemetery, and the last Shah of Iran.

Darb Al Ahmar

The Darb Al Ahmar (Red Alley) runs from the Citadel to Bab Zowaylah, and is lined with medieval buildings, some of them undergoing restoration. This was the heart of 14th- and

Surviving the Traffic

For the uninitiated, traffic in Cairo can be daunting. Pedestrian crossings and lights do exist, but they are few and far between and never seem to be in existence anywhere you might want one. As such, trying to cross the street (especially major roadways with multiple lanes, like those surrounding Meadan At Tahrir) can put fear into the hearts of even the bravest tourists. Despite this, there are (unofficial) rules to crossing the street. When you're ready to go, step off the sidewalk and cross in a regular pace until you reach the other side. Drivers will adjust to you and swerve around as long as you don't zigzag or make unexpected changes to your speed. If all this sounds too risky, then wait until a local is crossing and follow directly behind them, keeping your pace and course exactly the same, as they'll have a better idea of how to do it properly.

was encircled by 60 gates, of which only three remain. The imposing gate of **Bab Zowaylah** ❼ (daily 8.30am–5pm; charge), dating from 1092, marks the southern boundary of Al Qahirah.

Just outside Bab Zowaylah is the 14th-century Souq Al Khayyameyyah (Tentmakers' Bazaar), where you will see tentmakers sitting cross-legged on raised platforms in tiny shops on either side of the street, stitching away at the bright appliqué from which temporary pavilions are made.

A continuation of the Darb Al Ahmar, which here changes its name to Shari' Ahmad Mahir, heads past Bab Zowaylah west towards the **Museum of Islamic Art** (Shari' Boar Sa'id; recently restored; times of opening not available as this book was going to press), containing one of the world's finest collections of Islamic arts.

Along Al Azhar Road

Where the Qasabah meets the Shari' Al Azhar are the giant buildings associated with Qansuh Al Ghuri, one of the last Mamluk sultans, who displayed his wealth by building on Cairo's most prestigious street. On the left is the **Al Ghuri Mosque/ Madrasah**, part of the complex that was supposed to contain his tomb, but his body was never returned after he died fighting the Ottomans near Aleppo in Syria.

The open courtyard of the mosque has several circular-shaped flooring slabs of green-and-red marble, and four large *iwans* (vaulted, open-ended halls), illuminated by lamps suspended from the ceiling. Near here is Al Ghuri's *wikala*, the best-preserved example of a merchants' hostel in Cairo, and the venue for performances of whirling dervishes (see p.281).

Cairo

Khan Al Khalili market

Al Azhar Mosque

Further down this same street, on the left, is the **Al Azhar Mosque** ❽ (daily 8am–6pm, except prayer times; free), the first mosque built by the Fatimids, in AD972. The mosque has been enlarged and rebuilt over the years, but the overall impression is harmonious and the atmosphere venerable. The main gateway to the mosque is known as the Barber's Gate, where students had their heads shaved before entering the attached Al Azhar University, one of the world's oldest universities, dating from AD988. It is now the world's foremost centre of Islamic theological teaching.

At the rear of the Al Azhar Mosque is the **Bayt Zainab Khatun** (daily 9am–5pm; charge), a 15th-century Mamluk-style house complete with courtyard and grand reception hall. It is unfurnished, and the best reason to visit is for the magnificent views across Al Azhar from the roof of the property. To the east is the 30-hectare (75-acre) **Al Azhar Park**

Finding Your Way in the Souqs

While the alleys of the Khan Al Khalili can feel downright confusing, there was once a method to the madness. Years ago, before the advent of souvenir shopping, merchants clustered together geographically to help customers find their way around the shops. If you wanted spices, you'd go to the spice street, while jewellery shoppers would head for gold alley. Now that souvenirs have taken over the bulk of stores, this strict formation has relaxed, but you can still see some of the older shops adhering to the ancient rules. Examples include the spice and perfume merchants, who are generally found near the southern entrance to the market, and the gold and silver merchants found to the northwest.

(daily 10am–midnight; admission fee), opened in 2005, a welcome and refreshing escape from the hurly-burly of the city. Accessed from the Salah Salim expressway, it was developed by the Aga Khan Foundation to improve the quality of life of Cairo's inhabitants. The graceful water channels and pools, meandering walkways and cafés are a peaceful and rubbish-free retreat, offering great views over the city. There's also a small open-air theatre and playground.

Khan Al Khalili bazaar to Bab Al Futuh

Returning to the Qasabah, use the footbridge to cross the busy Al Azhar Road and enter the bustling centre of **Khan Al Khalili** bazaar ❾ (Mon–Sat early morning to sundown), Cairo's buzzing souq district. Merchants have been selling to Cairo's residents here since as far back as the 12th century. Despite the tour groups and the tat, it still has an exotic atmosphere, especially amid the perfume, gold and spice stalls. You can buy just about anything here, from everyday items to precious stones. Watch the locals bargaining for goods before you start to haggle *(see p.45)*. The streets and alleyways were memorably brought to life by Nobel Prize-winning author Naguib Mahfouz in his novel *Midaq Alley*.

One of the most popular spots in the bazaar is **Al Fishawy Coffee house**, in an alley one block west of Meadan Al Hussain. Claiming to have

Bayt As Sehaimi and shops in the bazaar

been open continuously for 200 years (except during Ramadan), Al Fishawy is a great place to sit and soak up the atmosphere.

At the eastern edge of the Khan Al Khalili is the **Mosque of Sayyedna Al Hussain**, which has a silver-grilled shrine containing the head of the Prophet's grandson, who was murdered in AD680. This, Cairo's official mosque, is a place of pilgrimage for Shia Muslims, and non-Muslims are not allowed to enter.

North of Khan Al Khalili is the former grand thoroughfare of medieval Cairo, with many superb Islamic buildings. Dominating Bayn Al Qasrayn is a splendid monumental ensemble built by a succession of Mamluk sultans. The largest is the **Madrasah and Mausoleum of Qalawoan** (9am–5pm), built in 1284 for the Bahri Mamluk Sultan Qalawoan, who founded a dynasty that lasted almost a century. The mausoleum is particularly beautiful, decorated with inlaid stone and stucco. Next door is the **Madrasah of An Nasir Muhammad**, built in 1304, and the third important building is the **Madrasah and Khanqah of Barquq**.

Further up the road, where the street splits, is the wonderful recently restored **Sabil Kuttub Adb Arrahman Katkhudah**, with interior blue-and-white tiling. A *sabil kuttub* combines a public drinking fountain at street level and Quranic school above. Taking the left fork, the small **Al Aqmar Mosque** on the right, dating from 1125, is reached down a few steps (the original street level over 1,000 years ago).

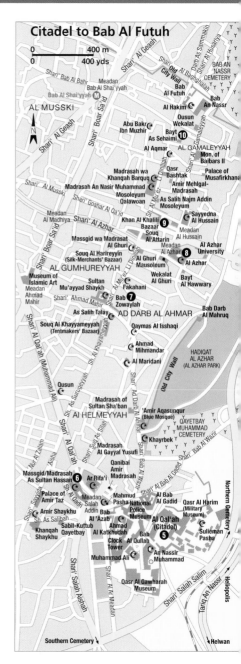

Investment is being made in this area in order to restore the large Ottoman-period merchants' houses along Haret Al Darb Al Asfar. Pride of place goes to the 17th-century **Bayt As Sehaimi**  (daily 9am–5pm; charge), a fine townhouse which shows how the Cairo heat could be tempered with a central courtyard, trees, fountains and cooling *mashra-biya* wooden window screens. Music and theatre programmes are performed here regularly.

Just before the Bab Al Futuh gateway is the **Al Hakim Mosque** (daily 9am–5pm; charge), completed in 1013 for the sixth Fatimid ruler of Egypt. The mosque stands against a section of the North Wall that connects the Bab Al Futuh with the Bab An Nassr. The walls and towers are well worth exploring, and the views southwards take in countless domes and minarets.

City of the Dead

To the north and south of the Citadel are two vast cemeteries known as the City of the Dead. Opposite the Al Azhar Park entrance, across the other side of the Salah Salim expressway, is the **Northern Cemetery** . Many 15th-century Mamluk sultans are buried in large ornate tombs, protected by guardians who organise the funerary processions, anniversaries and festivals. Guardian families have always lived here, but as Cairo has expanded, many others have taken up residence in other mausoleums. The City of the Dead is now a huge community with its own shops, schools and bus services. In the southern

Tombs in the City of the Dead

Flower shop in Zamalik

section is the **Mosque of Qayetbay** (1472), depicted on the Egyptian one-pound note. Widely regarded as the pinnacle of Islamic building in Cairo, the mosque's dome is exquisitely carved with floral and star designs. Climb the minaret for amazing views of Islamic Cairo below.

Sections of the **Southern Cemetery** ⑫ are much older, some dating to the 12th century. Surrounded by walled areas of thousands of graves and tombs are two main mausoleums, both about 2.5km (1½ miles) south of the Citadel. Imam As shafi'i is a popular local saint, credited with founding one of the four main schools of Sunni Islam. He died in 820 and his tomb is the oldest part of the complex, dating from 1211. Money and written wishes are piling up inside the tomb, which has a

carved marble column marking the position of his head. About 100m/yds away is the multi-domed **Hoash Al Basha**, containing the extravagant and colourful tombs of Muhammad Ali's family.

Zamalik and Gazirah

Designed for the upper classes, the streets of Zamalik on the island of Gazirah feel decidedly leafier than other points in the city. Here is where the bulk of international embassies call home, drawn by the relative calm and wider avenues. The area has less character than it used to but remains a prized address for good shops, bars and restaurants. Fashionable Cairenes have injected new life into Zamalik, transforming many an old cruise boat or mansion into a sumptuous restaurant, bar, coffee house or nightclub.

★ BELLY DANCING

The art of belly dancing has been around in Egypt for a long time – so long that no one quite knows how to trace its origins. Some say it is an extension of traditional folk dances, others point to images of dancers carved onto the walls of Pharaonic temples that exhibit similar movements. The Victorian era's fondness for all things exotic brought the dance to the eyes of Westerners, and new generations have been seduced ever since.

Despite the fact that belly dancing has been around for centuries, the dance only came to the attention of Europeans in the late 18th century, when Napoleon's troops saw it for the first time. During this period, most dancers were prostitutes offering their services to Europeans seduced by the exotic, with belly dancing as an added bonus.

The writer Gustave Flaubert, who chronicled his experiences touring the Egyptian countryside, wrote of his encounters with a belly-dancing prostitute by the name of Kuchuk Hanem. As European influence began to trickle into Egyptian society in the early 20th century, belly dancers shed their image as women of the street and emerged as highly proficient performers, admired for their technical prowess and beauty. Cabarets and performance halls popped up all over Cairo, and some dancers starred in Egypt's early films, including Fifi Abdou, Nagma

Up close and personal with a belly dancer

Belly dancer, 1862

Fouad, Saima Gamal and Naima Akef.

Following independence, the authorities considered the dance to be too sexual and immoral. Stars who had once been celebrated for their prowess were prevented from performing.

Now belly dancing can be seen in Cairo, though it's likely to be for the benefit of tourists; many of the dancers come from Russia, Romania and other Eastern European countries, where there is no social intolerance for the so-called provocative moves. Belly dancing lessons are also given as a way to keep fit; in fact, belly dancing tours are becoming increasingly popular, including visits to shows, opportunities to buy costumes and lessons with the experts.

If you want to learn belly dancing, try:

• Samir Hesein, former dancer and choreographer of the famous Mahmoud Reda Troupe; tel: 010-688 6343; email: redatroup@hotmail.com.

• Amora Dance; tel: 010-440 1231; email: amoradance@hotmail.com.

To watch belly dancing:

• Haroun Al Rashid at the Semiramis Intercontinental, Corniche An Nil, Garden City; tel: 02-3795 7171; performances every day except Wednesdays, from 11pm until 3.30am. Reservations are recommended, especially on Thursdays, when Dina performs.

• Nile Maxim, ship docks opposite Cairo Marriott Hotel in Zamalik; tel: 20-2728 3000. Dinner cruise and belly-dance entertainment. Book in advance.

To purchase belly-dancing costumes:

• Mahmoud Abd Al Ghaffar; 73 Shari' Ghawar Al Qaid; tel: 02-2589 7443. A wide selection of costumes.

You can take belly dancing lessons in Cairo

The Opera House

Further south lies the **Opera House** ❸ (Gazirah Exhibition Grounds; tel: 02-2739 8144; www.cairoopera. org), which shares a complex with the **Museum of Modern Egyptian Art** (Tue–Sun 10am–2pm, 5.30–10pm), collectively known as the **Gazirah Arts Centre**. There are over 10,000 works on display chronicling Egypt's art scene from the early 20th century to the present day.

The **Cairo Tower** (Shari' Al Borg; tel: 02-2735 7187; daily 8am–midnight; charge) provides panoramic views over the city. Designed like a tall lotus, it stands 182m (600ft) high, with an occasionally revolving bar-restaurant at the top. Even if you aren't staying in Gazirah, a visit to Gazirah Palace (now the Marriott Hotel) is recommended. Built in 1869 as a guesthouse for noble visitors attending the opening of the Suez Canal, the palace grounds now feature an elegant shopping arcade and a number of cafés. The hotel, along the river at 16 Shari' Al Gazirah, is about to undergo a two-year renovation which may see some wings closed to visitors and guests.

Cairo's Opera House

The original Opera House was commissioned in 1869 to celebrate the opening of the Suez Canal. The Khedive then commissioned an opera to celebrate Egypt's history and pair it with European culture, resulting in Verdi's masterpiece *Aida*. Contrary to popular belief, *Aida* did not open the Opera House. In fact, its first performance in Cairo wasn't until 1871. Unfortunately, the great Opera House burnt down in 1971. A new Opera House built with Japanese funds was opened in 1988.

ACCOMMODATION

Cairo is well stocked with five-star and budget properties, but tends to lack anything to accommodate the middle ground. Standards for hotels that call themselves five-star can vary wildly, as the tourism industry evaluates accommodation according to amenities and not by the actual standards of rooms and services.

Many hotels in the city are in dire need of renovation. The Nile Hilton recently closed for a much-needed refurbishment, and other properties will follow suit in the next few years.

Cairo Marriott
16 Shari' Saray Al Gazirah, Zamalik
Tel: 02-2728 3000
www.marriott.com
This opulent hotel is built around the former palace of the Khedive Ismail, constructed to commemorate the opening of the Suez Canal in 1869. Antique furniture graces the halls and public rooms. There are several good restaurants and the popular Harry's Pub on site. **$$$$$**

Carlton Hotel
21 Shari' 26th of July, Downtown
Tel: 02-2575 5181
www.carltonhotelcairo.com
Near the Cinema Rivoli, the Carlton seems to be stuck in a time warp. The rooms have some 1950s detail, but vary in size and comfort, so check them out beforehand. Very good value and central location. **$$**

Golden Tulip Flamenco Hotel
2 Shari' Al Gazirah Al Wusta, Zamalik
Tel: 02-2735 0815
www.flamencohotels.com
Modern hotel in a quiet, tree-lined street in the residential part of Zamalik, with some rooms overlooking the Nile and even the Pyramids on a clear day. **$$$$**

Horus House
21 Shari' Ismail Muhammad, Zamalik
Tel: 02-2735 3634
A home away from home, the Horus is often booked up by returning guests. The restaurant offers a good-value lunch, popular with older residents. Book well in advance. **$$$**

Lialy Hostel
3rd floor, 8 Meadan Tala'at Harb, Downtown
Tel: 02-2575 2802
Very clean and welcoming budget option on one of Downtown's most picturesque squares. The rooms are large and very clean, albeit a bit noisy. Staff are very friendly, and there is a good internet café. **$**

The Marriott in Zamalik

Longchamps Hotel
21 Shari' Ismail Muhammad, Zamalik
Tel: 02-2735 2311
www.hotellongchamps.com
Longchamps is an old-time favourite for
those who visit Cairo often. The rooms
are spotless, and many have great shady
balconies overlooking the leafy streets of
Zamalik. **$$**

Radwan Hotel
83 Shari' Gawhar Al Qaid, Meadan Al Azhar
Tel: 02-2590 1311
A popular option for budget travellers, with
clean and comfortable rooms as well as a
communal satellite TV lounge and internet
access. Good base for exploring Islamic
Cairo. **$**

Ramses Hilton
1115 Shari' An Nil, Downtown
Tel: 02-2577 7444
www.hilton.com
Until the Nile Hilton reopens, the Ramses
is the next best option. Located across the
street from the Nile Hilton, the Ramses is
currently the closest hotel to the Egyptian
Museum. Rooms are a good size, and all
feature balconies. **$$$$**

Sheraton Cairo Hotel, Towers and Casino
Shari' Madis Qaset Al Fhoarg, Gazirah
Tel: 02-3336 9800

The Ramses Hilton

www.starwood.com
Located a short walk away from the Opera
House and Egyptian Museum, the Sheraton
is a city within a city. At night, a choice of
restaurants and a popular casino provide
diversions. **$$$$$**

Talisman
39 Shari' Tala'at Harb, Downtown
Tel: 02-2393 9431
www.talisman-hotel.com
Cairo's first boutique hotel, in a lovely Down-
town apartment building. It has spacious
and stylish rooms decorated in oriental style
and an atmospheric breakfast room, as well
as salons to relax in following an exhausting
day's sightseeing. **$$$**

RESTAURANTS

With a large expat, business and
tourist population, Cairo offers a wide
range of food from all over the world.
You can try Egyptian staples from
stallholders serving up the best *koshari*
and *ta'amiya* you've ever tasted, or
eat at one of the five-star hotels for a

Restaurant Price Categories
Prices are for a two-course meal for one, not including a drink or tip.
$ = below E£15
$$ = E£15–E£40
$$$ = E£40–E£75
$$$$ = over E£75

more refined experience. Reservations are best made for fine dining and trendy
locations, especially if you intend to try them out on a weekend evening. Café-
going is a way of life in Cairo, and there are many famous tea and coffee houses
in the city. *For more on Egypt's coffee culture, see p.56.*

Abou Shakra
69 Shari' Qasr Al Aini, Downtown
Tel: 02-2531 6111
Known as 'the King of the Kebab', this is one
of the best places to eat kebabs, and prices
are very reasonable. **$**

Abou Al Sid
157 Shari' 26th of July, Zamalik
Tel: 02-2735 9640
Very atmospheric Egyptian restaurant set
in an old building, furnished with traditional
Louis Farouk-style furniture and work by
local artists on the wall. Very busy at week-
ends, and trendy, so book ahead. **$$**

Al Fishawy
Khan Al Khalili, just off Meadan Al Hussain,
Islamic Cairo
Apparently open since 1773, this exotic café
in the heart of the souq is a great place to
hang out, have a cup of mint tea or smoke a
sheesha (water pipe), at any time of the day
or night. It's a great place to watch the world
go by. No alcohol. **$**

L'Asiatique
Le Pacha 1901 Boat, Shari' Al Gazirah,
Zamalik
Tel: 02-2735 6730
Superb dishes impeccably served in a
relaxed and youthful atmosphere. Definitely
the best (and most expensive) Asian cuisine
in town. **$$$**

Aubergine
Shari' Sayed Al Bakry, Zamalik
Tel: 02-2738 0080
Intimate and chic, this is a popular vegetar-
ian restaurant. **$$**

Café Riche
17 Shari' Tala'at Harb, Downtown
Tel: 02-2392 9793
Founded in 1908, the legendary Café Riche
is steeped in history. This is where the
singer Umm Kulthoum started her career,
and where her contemporary Gamal Abd
An Nasser planned his revolution, later
becoming president. Nowadays it is still a
good place to meet for a drink or a simple
Egyptian lunch. **$**

Cilantro
31 Shari' Muhammad Mahmoud, opposite
AUC, Downtown (other branch on 157 Shari'
26th of July, Zamalik)
Tel: 02-2792 4571
Popular café that serves good coffee with
fresh croissants for breakfast, healthy sand-
wiches and delicious fresh juices. **$**

Felfella
15 Shari' Hoda Sharawi, Downtown
Tel: 02-2239 2833
The original Felfella restaurant, which now
has several branches in Cairo and other
Egyptian cities. Started as a cheap vegetar-
ian restaurant, it still serves plenty of cheap
vegetable dishes and meze. **▓ $**

Groppi
Meadan Tala'at Harb, Downtown
Tel: 02-2574 3244
Only vaguely reminiscent of its former
grandeur, this is a popular place to meet for

The once grand coffee house of J Groppi

Fine dining in Cairo

Citadel, this is a perfect choice for a lunch, sunset tea or dinner. **$$**

Justine
Four Corners, 4 Shari' Hassan Sabri, Zamalik
Tel: 02-2736 2961
Creative French cuisine and a cosy, luxurious atmosphere in the most upmarket of the Four Corners restaurants. **$$$**

Rossini
66 Shari' Omar Ibn Al Khattab, Heliopolis
Tel: 02-2291 8282
In a renovated villa in one of Cairo's nicest neighbourhoods, Rossini offers delicious seafood cooked with Mediterranean flair. **$$$**

coffee and pastries. Even if it's not at all like the old days, the waiters are still smiling. **$**

Hilltop Restaurant
At the Al Azhar Park, Shari' Salah Salim
Tel: 02-2510 9151
In an impressive, Fatimid-style building, overlooking the formal gardens and with a magnificent view over historic Cairo and the

Sabaya
Semiramis InterContinental, Shari' An Nil, Garden City
Tel: 02-2795 7171
Excellent Lebanese restaurant serving meze, the best *kibbeh nayyeh* (raw pounded lamb) in town and a wide selection of Lebanese specialities. Very friendly waiters and an elegant contemporary Middle Eastern decor in subdued tones. **$$$**

NIGHTLIFE

Clubs are opening up, but Cairo still doesn't have the party-on reputation of the Red Sea coast, Sinai or other Middle Eastern capitals like Beirut. Instead, the growing middle and upper classes prefer fruit juice and cocktail bars in hip joints – usually in the elegant neighbourhood of Zamalik. Tastes change as rapidly as a Cairo taxi driver switches lanes, so it's best to check listings magazines or with your hotel concierge prior to going out for the evening.

Bars
After Eight
6 Shari' Qasr An Nil, Downtown
Tel: 010-339 8000
Tucked away down a small alley, this café is hard to find but worth seeking out, particularly at night when there are live jazz/salsa and Arabic music performances by local and foreign bands.

Cairo Jazz Club
197 Shari' 26th of July, Aguza, opposite the Balloon Theatre
Tel: 02-3345 9939
The best jazz club in Cairo, with regular live performances and good food.

Estoril
12 Shari' Tala'at Harb, Downtown
Tel: 02-2574 3102

This bar serves cold beer and good food to a young and trendy crowd.

La Bodega
157 Shari' 26th of July, Zamalik
Tel: 02-2735 0543
Cool bistro with Mediterranean dishes, from tagines and couscous to pastas and tapas. The über-trendy (for Cairo at least) lounge bar serves good fusion food in a minimal Asian decor, to a Buddha Bar beat.

Live Music Venues
Al Sawy Cultural Centre
Shari' 26th of July, Zamalik, under the bridge to Aguza
Tel: 02-2736 8881
www.culturewheel.com
Excellent Arabic jazz venue, often showing documentaries and hosting seminars.

Arab Music Institute
22 Shari' Rameses
Tel: 02-2574 3373
Twice-weekly centre for classical Arabic music performances.

Bayt Al Suhaymi
Darb Al Asfra, Al Hussan, Islamic Cairo

Cairo Jazz Festival

Tel: 02-2591 3391
Folk music performances every Sunday at 8pm. Special shows during Ramadan to break the fast.

Cairo Opera House
(The Egyptian Education and Culture Centre)
Gazirah
Tel: 02-2739 0114
www.cairoopera.org
Cairo's Opera House stands at the Gazirah Exhibition Grounds, with three theatres, an art gallery and library.

ENTERTAINMENT

When it comes to being entertained, there's a wealth of options to explore in Cairo. Like Aladdin's Cave, there's something inside this city for everyone to enjoy. Fans of belly dancing will be pleased to know that Cairo is considered the birthplace and mecca for practitioners of this seductive dance form. But that's not all – Sufi dancing, contemporary dance, opera, traditional and modern theatre can all be found on most nights of the week. Consult *Al Ahram* or the *Egyptian Gazette* for weekly listings.

Art Galleries
Al Sawy Cultural Centre
Shari' 26th of July, Zamalik, under the bridge to Aguza
Tel: 02-2736 8881
www.culturewheel.com
Excellent gallery for local artists.

Hanager Arts Centre
Opera House Grounds,
Gazirah
Tel: 02-2735 6861
This lively space specialises in established, contemporary Egyptian artists, and always has something of interest on show.

Townhouse Gallery for Contemporary Art
10 Shari' Nabrawi, Downtown
Tel: 02-2576 8086
www.thetownhousegallery.com
The best (and most active) contemporary art gallery in town, with an annexe for video installations and movies, and a wonderful art bookshop.

Ballet
Egyptian ballet dancers are trained at the National Ballet Institute in the City of Art complex on the Pyramids Road. The Institute was founded with Russian help in 1960 and staffed with Russian experts. In 1966 the Institute's first graduating class premiered with *The Fountain of Bakhchiserai* in the old Cairo Opera House. The Cairo Ballet currently includes Russian and Italian dancers and performs in the new Opera House.

Belly Dancing

Belly dancing is commonly offered as part of the floorshow of the floating restaurants that glide along the Nile or at some of the five-star establishments in the Downtown area. Venues open and close regularly due to growing anti-belly-dancing sentiment amongst conservative religious groups. *Al Ahram* lists belly-dancing performances in the city along with the *Egyptian Gazette*. *For more information, see the Unique Experiences feature on p.86.*

Traditional Dance Troupes
Folk dance is popular in Egypt, and there are over 150 troupes. The most prominent are the National Troupe and Reda Troupe, which perform at venues across the city.
At Tannoura Egyptian Heritage Dance Troupe gives whirling performances at the Citadel's Sarayat al Gabal Theatre on **Shari'** Salah Salim every Sat, Mon and Wed at 8.30pm (tickets are free). They perform a whirling ceremony, a form of ecstatic mystical dance, though here it is a cultural performance.

Theatre
Live Performance Venues
Al Qawmi (National) Theatre

Whirling dervish dancer

Meadan Ataba, Downtown
Tel: 02-2591 7783
Popular venue for contemporary Arabic plays.

The American University in Cairo Theatre
113 Shari' Qasr Al Ayni,
Garden City
Tel: 02-2794 2964
Performs in Wallace Theatre and Howard Theatre on the AUC campus.

Cairo Puppet Theatre
Azbakeyyah Gardens
Tel: 02-2591 0954
Dialogue is in Arabic, but the gestures and meanings aren't too difficult to follow.

Cinemas
Cairo has many cinemas, often super screens in five-star hotels and shopping malls. Most cinemas change their programmes every Monday. Films are listed in the daily *Egyptian Gazette* and *Al Ahram Weekly*.

French Cultural Centre
1 Shari' Madrasset Al Huquq Al Faransiyah, Mounira
Tel: 02-2794 7679
Weekly selection of French film, sometimes with subtitles.

Ramses Hilton Annex Cinema
Shari' An Nil, Downtown
Tel: 02-2574 7435

Renaissance Nile City
Nile City Building, Shari' An Nil, Bulaq
Tel: 02-2461 9101

Stars/Golden Stars
City Stars Mall, Shari' Omar Ibn Al Qhatab,
Heliopolis
Tel: 02-2480-2012

Townhouse Gallery
10 Shari' Nabrawi, Downtown
Tel: 02-2576 8086
Good selection of foreign and arty films.

Cultural Centres
Cultural centres tend to be very active in
Cairo, putting on concerts, lectures, film,
theatre and exhibitions. For programmes,
check with the *Egyptian Gazette*, or the *Al
Ahram Weekly*.

American Research Center in Egypt
2 Meadan Simon Bolivar, Garden City
Tel: 02-2794 8239
Excellent library for lectures and films.

British Council
192 Shari' An Nil, Aguza
Tel: 02-3300 1666

French Cultural Centre
1 Shari' Madrasset Al Huquq Al Faransiyah,
Mounira
Tel: 02-2794 7679

Goethe Institut
5 Shari' Al Bustan, Downtown
Tel: 02-2575 98577

SPORTS AND ACTIVITIES
People tend not to have sport in mind when they come to Cairo, but there are
opportunities to keep fit if you want to. Four- and five-star hotels often have a pool
and a gym, and non-guests may be able to access facilities by paying a charge.
Call in advance to check daily rates.

Cycling
The Cairo Cyclists (tel: 02-352 6310) have
regular Friday and Saturday morning cycle
rides in and outside the city, starting from
outside the Cairo American College, Meadan
Digla in Madi, at 8am.

Fitness Centres
There is a good gym and excellent pool
at the Nile Hilton, Meadan At Tahrir (currently closed for renovation). Splash at the
Cairo Marriott (Shari' Saray Al Gazirah; tel:
02-2728 3000) has rowing and cycling
machines alongside pool, sauna and floodlit
tennis facilities, and Gold's Gym, on the
8th/9th floors of the Madi Palace Mall (tel:
02-2380 3601), has a mixed gym, women-
only gym, Jacuzzi and sauna.

Football
Football is the Egyptian national sport, and
a national obsession. There is a strong
national side, mostly made up of players
from the two rival Cairo teams, Al Ahly

Football is huge in Egypt

(tel: 02-2735-2114; www.ahly.com) and Zamalik (tel: 02-2735 5690; www.zamalik.com). Both teams share the Cairo Stadium in Heliopolis (tel: 02-2260 7863), playing on Friday, Saturday or Sunday from September to May, at 3pm.

Golf

There is a nine-hole golf course at the Gazirah Club (tel: 02-2736 0434) in Zamalik, but better options can be found in the suburbs around Giza. *See p.116 for listings.*

Horse Racing

Horse racing takes place from October/November to May at the Heliopolis Hippodrome (tel: 02-2241 7086) and the Gazirah Sporting Club (tel: 02-2736 0434) on Saturday and Sunday from 1.30pm. The *Egyptian Gazette* lists details of events.

Running

The Cairo Hash House Harriers meet every

There are two riding stables near the Pyramids

Friday afternoon to run, jog or walk, and then drink beer. For information log on to www.cairohash.com.

TOURS

Almost all tour operators have a base or office in Cairo. Booking with an operator has its advantages in terms of convenience, but will require extra money to cover commissions. Offered tours tend to be quite standard across the board. Typical itineraries include trips through Islamic Cairo, Coptic Cairo or to the Pyramids at Giza and Saqqarah.

Soliman Travel
In the UK:
113 Earls Court Road, London
SW5 9RL
Tel: 020-7244 6855
www.solimantravel.com
British travellers can book their trip prior to departure with Soliman Travel, a tour operator with offices in both London and Cairo. Soliman Travel, the largest tour operator specialising in Egypt in the UK, can also book specialist tours for you.
In Cairo:
24 Khalil Elaroussy Street, Higaz Square, Heliopolis
Tel: 02-2635 0350

Eastmar
13 Shari' Qasr An Nil
Tel: 02-2574 5024
www.eastmar-travel.com
Full-service Nile tours and excursions agent. Their particular strength is in Nile cruises, as many ships are owned by the operator and can be booked at short notice.

Egypt Panorama Tours
Opposite Madi metro station
Tel: 02-2359 0200
www.eptours.com
Good choice for budget travellers, with cruises and excursions priced at the lower end of the scale.

FESTIVALS AND EVENTS

Cairo is not just the capital of the country, it's also the cultural capital of the nation. Events are held throughout the city, showcasing visual arts, the written word, music, film and performance arts. During religious festivals the streets are alive with activity and crowds, especially around Old Cairo at Coptic Christmas and Easter and in Islamic Cairo after dark during Ramadan and Eid.

January

Cairo International Book Fair
www.cairobookfair.org

Over 3,000 exhibitors draw over 3 million readers from across the Middle East to this month-long celebration of the Arabic written word. Held in the Cairo Fair Grounds.

February

Al Nitaq Festival

Growing in popularity, this annual festival attempts to champion Cairo's emerging arts scene. Cafés and cultural centres across the city join in to celebrate visual arts, music, film, theatre, dance and poetry. Live performances and exhibits are scheduled throughout the month.

May

Spring Festival

Held at venues throughout the city, this multi-disciplinary event celebrates the arts of the Middle East, and runs simultaneously in Cairo and Beirut. Through music, dance, writing and photography, the festival challenges artists to cross boundaries on a political, social and cultural level.

August

Arab Music Festival
www.cairoopera.org
Cairo Opera House
Tel: 02-2739 0114

Held at the Cairo Opera House, this festival attracts top instrumentalists, singers and established ensembles, allowing visitors to hear the best music the Arab world has to offer. Tickets often sell out well in advance for the big names.

November

Cairo International Film Festival
www.cairofilmfest.com

Cairo is often referred to as the Hollywood of the Middle East. This annual film festival, the oldest festival in the Middle East, celebrates the industry and showcases films from across the Arab-speaking world.

The Arab Music Festival, held in August

Giza, Memphis and Saqqarah

Egypt's pyramids are the oldest of the major pharaonic sites and, along with the enigmatic Sphinx, also their most iconic. This area close to modern Cairo was the power base of the Old Kingdom, and its rulers were buried in the tombs and Pyramids of Saqqarah and Giza, home to the only remaining Ancient Wonder of the World.

Giza

Population: 2,700,000

Local dialling code: 18

Tourist office: Pyramids Road. Across the street from the Mena House Oberoi and next to the main tourist police station.

Tourist police station: Pyramids Road. Across the street from the Mena House Oberoi. Tourist police officers on the Giza Plateau usually speak some English. Other police officers have very limited English, so you are advised to contact the police either through your hotel or by speaking with an on-site police officer rather than visiting the police station in person.

Banks: Banks are not hard to find in Giza. If going to Memphis and Saqqarah, make sure you have enough money with you. The closest banks to the Pyramids can be found in the lobbies of either the Mena House Oberoi or Le Meridien Pyramids, both of which are on the Pyramids Road.

Hospitals: The closest hospital of international standard is the Anglo-American Hospital, near the Cairo Tower in Gazirah. Anglo-American Hospital, Shari' Hadayaq Al Zuhreyyah, Gazirah; tel: 02-2735 6162.

Local newspapers/listings magazines: None specific to the area; however, the listings magazines of Cairo do cover Giza in their information.
Egyptian Gazette; www.egyptiangazette.net.
Al Ahram Weekly; http://weekly.ahram.org.eg.
Egypt Today; www.egypttoday.com.

The Mediterranean Sea once reached at least to the foot of the Muqattam Hills that shelter modern Cairo to the east, and probably even as far south as ancient Memphis. In other words, the vast triangle of the Nile Delta that exists today was once a wide bay. Memphis, situated at the base of the ancient Delta, was the first capital of Upper and Lower Egypt, and held the title of capital for just under 1,000 years between 2920 and 2160BC.

Even with the growth of other cities, it retained its importance as a religious and commercial centre right through to Graeco-Roman times. The necropolis of the ancient city was situated at nearby Saqqarah, location of the first ever pyramid tomb (the Step Pyramid). Subsequent Memphite kings then followed suit by erecting pyramid tombs along the desert edge over a distance of about 30km (18 miles), from Abu Rawash in the north to Dahshur in the south. However, the most spectacular was the Great Pyramid at Giza (Aggizzah).

Many hotels and travel agents offer tours of Memphis, Saqqarah and Giza, but it is easy to arrange things independently. Though it would be difficult to complete a tour of the three sites on public transport, you can hire a taxi for the day fairly inexpensively.

Tourists at the Pyramids

Camel rides around the Giza Plateau

If you prefer, you could take a taxi to Memphis and Saqqarah in the morning, then get the driver to drop you off at the Pyramids around lunchtime; from there you can hire another taxi or catch a bus back to town.

Giza

The **Pyramids of Giza** ❶ (Plateau: daily 8am–4pm in summer, 8am–6pm in winter; inside the Pyramids: 8am–4pm, 100 tickets distributed for entry into the Pyramid of Khufu twice a day at 8am and 1pm; separate charges for the Great Pyramid, the Solar Boat Museum, Khafra's Pyramid and Menkaura's Pyramid; 🅜) stand on a rocky plateau on the west bank of the Nile, 25km (15 miles) north of Saqqarah.

The outlines of the Pyramids were once smooth and covered with a limestone facing that was fitted and polished, nowhere betraying an entrance. Apart from some extractions during the First Intermediate Period (2181–2055BC), the limestone facing encased the pyramid until a 13th-century earthquake loosened some of the stones. The Arabs then removed the limestone for use in the construction

♦ TOUR OF THE PYRAMIDS

Egypt's Pyramids are the oldest of the major Pharaonic sites and, along with the enigmatic Sphinx, also their most iconic. For 46 centuries, they have impressed travellers. A visit here is a must.

The sole surviving Wonder of the Ancient World, Giza's Pyramids must rank as the oldest and most visited tourist attraction in history.

Drive to the Pyramids' ticket office (daily 7.30am–4pm; charge – cash only, separate charges for the Solar Boat Museum, and two of the three tombs of the Pyramids: Khufu, Khafra and Menkaura, which open by rotation). The oldest and largest of the three Pyramids is the **Great Pyramid of Khufu** (Cheops; 2589–2566BC). With its original limestone casing (sadly requisitioned for other buildings over the centuries), the pyramid towered 146.6m (480ft) high. Its height

has now been reduced by 9m (30ft). Three chambers were found inside, but all were empty except for Khufu's sarcophagus.

Inside, the very cramped corridor leads via the Queen's Chamber into the spectacular 47m (154ft) long Great Gallery, which ends at the King's Chamber with its pillaged and now empty sarcophagus.

Lying behind the pyramid is the **Solar Boat Museum** (charge), which showcases an extraordinary 43m (141ft) long boat. An interesting exhibition documents the excavation. Here also lie three smaller Queens' Pyramids and the ruins of the king's funerary temple.

Better preserved is the complex around the **Pyramid of Khafra** (Chephren; 2558–2532BC), Khufu's son, which lies southwest of his father's.

The Pyramids of Khufu and Khafra

Tips

- Distance: 3km (1¾ miles)
- Time: half a day
- Many visitors prefer to take an organised tour of the Pyramids, which includes transport to/from them (they lie in the city suburbs of Giza), a guide and all entry tickets.
- If coming independently, note that the sale of tickets for the Great Pyramid are limited to 300 a day, of which 150 go on sale at 1pm. Arrive early and be prepared to queue.
- Bring light clothes, a hat, good shoes, and plenty of water and sunscreen.
- Photos inside the tombs are no longer permitted.

Khafra's pyramid appears taller, but is actually built on higher ground and is slightly smaller, at 136m (447ft). Unusually, the apex is still covered by the original limestone casing. The pyramid has two chambers, one of which contains the king's sarcophagus.

Walk eastwards down the road to the remains of Khafra's Funerary Temple. The Causeway leading to his Valley Temple is guarded by the famous and ever-enigmatic **Sphinx.** Carved from bedrock, it is well preserved thanks largely to it being covered over the centuries by the sands. Sadly the Sphinx has suffered over the ages: its nose was chiselled off sometime between the 10th and 15th centuries and part of the fallen beard now resides in the British Museum in London.

Named by the Greeks after the mythical half-woman, half-lion monster of

The Sphinx, carved from an outcrop of rock, and the Pyramid of Khafra

ancient times, the origin, purpose and date of the Sphinx remain a mystery.

Back on the plateau the smaller, third **Pyramid of Menkaura** (Mycerinus; 2532–2504BC), built by Khafra's son, has a large ruined temple also dedicated to Menkaura in front of it.

From here, the road leads to a plateau from where you can enjoy the iconic view of the three Pyramids together. Later, pop into the iconic and historical Mena House Oberoi (see p.114), for a drink or cup of tea before heading back to town.

Walking Tour of the Pyramids

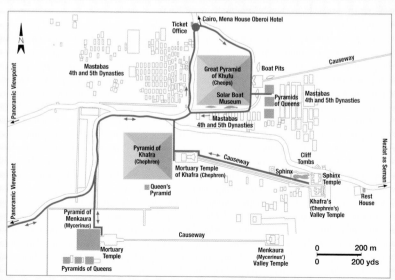

of some of the celebrated buildings of Islamic Cairo, including the Mosque of Sultan Hassan. It has been said that when the sun shone, the Pyramids could be seen glinting as far away as in the lands that make up modern-day Israel.

The Great Pyramid

The **Great Pyramid** 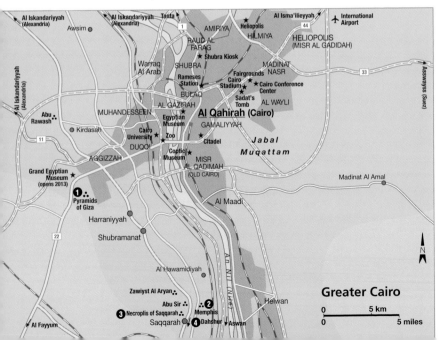, which was built in honour of the 4th Dynasty Pharaoh Khufu (Cheops) c.2600BC, is the sole survivor of the Seven Wonders of the Ancient World. Originally 147m (480ft) high and covering an area of 5 hectares (13 acres), the pyramid was constructed of some 2.3 million blocks of stone of an average weight of 2.5 tonnes (some weighed as much as 16 tonnes). The sides of the pyramid themselves were oriented almost exactly true north,

south, east and west, with the four corners again at perfect right angles. The maximum error in alignment has been calculated as being a little over one-twelfth of a degree.

Entering the pyramid is not for the claustrophobic or the very unfit, as the corridor is low and narrow, and usually crammed with tourists. The shaft leads left into the Queen's Chamber and right into the 47m (154ft) long Great Gallery, which in turn leads up to the King's Chamber with its empty sarcophagus. The main burial chamber is a small room built of red Aswan granite, as is the large open sarcophagus that still remains in the centre.

Pyramid of Khafra

The next pyramid belongs to Khufu's son, **Khafra** Ⓑ (Chephren, c.2576–2551BC), which is built at a steeper

Greater Cairo

Detail showing the entrance to the Great Pyramid

angle than the Great Pyramid. The internal structure of passages is much simpler, although no less claustrophobic, than that of the Great Pyramid, leading to a single chamber containing Khafra's large granite sarcophagus.

Pyramid of Menkaura

The third of the royal pyramids at Giza was begun by **Menkaura** (Mycerinus, *c.* 2532–2504BC), the successor of Khafra. By far the smallest, it was apparently left unfinished at Menkaura's death and hurriedly completed by his son, Shepseskaf, whose own tomb is at Saqqarah. There are signs of haste throughout the complex, even in the pyramid itself. Brick was used to finish off the mortuary

103

Giza Transport

Metro station: Giza, located on line 2. Giza metro offers convenient access to the Giza train station for travellers arriving from Cairo. However, it is a fair distance from the Giza Plateau, and visitors will need to take a taxi to or from the stop.

Train station: Located at Meadan Mahattit Al Jizah, approximately 10km (15 miles) east of the Giza Plateau. You will need to take a taxi to reach the Pyramids from here.

Main transport operators: Airport and coach services can be found in Cairo. An operator departing specifically from Giza is:
Abela Egypt; tel: 02-2574 9474; www.sleepingtrains.com.
Abela offers twice-daily departures to Luxor and Aswan on comfortable

overnight wagon-lits from Giza. Tickets can be purchased at Giza Train Station or reserved online.

Taxi companies: Almost all taxi drivers work as independent operators, and there are usually plenty around. Many people choose to visit the sights of Giza, Memphis and Saqqarah by taxi, especially if they are not taking a tour. Hail one off the street and negotiate a price with the driver (the tourist office can give you a rough idea of cost). Be clear about your agreed price or you may be overcharged on your arrival. The recent introduction of metered and air-conditioned yellow taxis that can be pre-booked is a novelty in Cairo, but they are a rare sight in Cairo and even rarer in Giza. The trip by metered taxi is also more expensive.

temple, causeway and valley temple, though they were begun in limestone and some of the blocks weigh 200 tonnes, showing that the failure to complete it in limestone was not due to a decline in technical mastery.

The Sphinx

At the end of a causeway to the east of the Pyramid of Khafra stands the **Sphinx D**, a recumbent lion with a human face – that of Khafra. Fashioned out of the bedrock of the Giza plateau, it is 255m (840ft) long and some 20m (65ft) high at its head. Repeatedly covered in sand, the Sphinx has been the victim of rescue and conservation efforts since ancient times. Between its outstretched paws

---

Visiting the Pyramids

- Included on every 'must-see' checklist, the Pyramids are at their busiest in the mid-morning when tour buses arrive and on Thursdays and Fridays when visitors from cruise ships and day-trippers from the Sinai resorts descend. Try and visit either first thing in the morning as soon as the site opens or in the last hour to avoid the masses.

- You can hire a horse or camel to explore the area around the Giza Plateau. It's best to avoid the owners near the Pyramids, who are very pushy indeed, and go to the stables near the coach park. Officially, a one-hour tour should cost E£35 and a short tour E£20, but you will need to bargain hard to get these prices.

---

a red granite slab tells the story of the first attempt at conservation under the Pharaoh Thutmose IV of the 18th Dynasty. The text relates how the Pharaoh (just a young prince at the time) was sleeping in its shadow one day, when the Sphinx appeared to him and instructed him to clear away the sand that was choking it, promising him the crown if he did so.

The Solar Boat

Behind the Great Pyramid is the **Solar Boat Museum E** (extra charge; ). The museum houses a cedar-wood boat that was discovered in a pit covered in limestone blocks and mortar near the Great Pyramid in 1954. The boat, which was painstakingly reassembled from 1,200 pieces of wood, is regarded as one of the most important finds of the 20th century and, at 4,600 years old, is one of the oldest boats in existence. Visitors must wear protective footwear to keep sand and other particles that might damage the vessel out of the museum.

The exact purpose of the solar boat is a matter of debate. It was either the funerary boat of Khufu, which carried the Pharaoh's body to Giza prior to embalming, or it was intended to carry the dead Pharaoh across the sky from east to west to be united with the sun-god Ra.

Four other boat pits have been discovered. Three of these are empty, but an unexcavated boat is known to lie under the ground beside the boat museum. In time, it, too, will be revealed, as there is evidence that the

The Grand Egyptian Museum

Construction is under way of a Grand Egyptian Museum 3km (2 miles) from the Giza Pyramids, which will mark the new entrance to the whole plateau. The museum will house the greatest treasures currently in the Egyptian Museum in central Cairo. It should be finished around 2013.

When the museum opens, it is anticipated that the downtown core will lose a lot of its package traffic, especially as Giza has more space to offer developers looking to create resort-style properties. Unfortunately, more people equals more pollution and more rubbish strewn about the site.

In addition, the massive growth of the surrounding suburb has increased road traffic greatly, meaning more air pollution affecting the Pyramid exteriors.

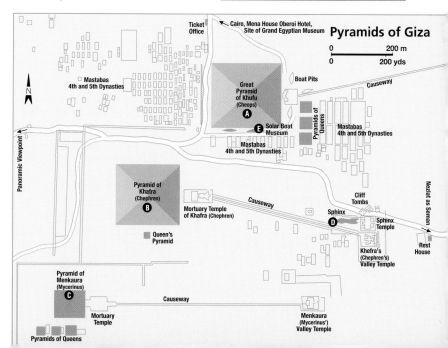

Pyramids of Giza

Statue of Rameses II at Memphis

bedrock in which it lies is not hermetically sealed, and that the boat is deteriorating.

Memphis

Memphis ❷ is situated on the west bank of the Nile some 25km (15 miles) south of Giza and almost opposite modern Cairo's suburb of Al Ma'adi. For most of the Pharaonic period Memphis was the capital of Egypt. It was honoured by Egypt's most famous kings, some of whom built palaces there. The city was lauded by classical writers in glowing terms, and was regarded as a pilgrimage destination and a place of refuge. It was so great that any who sought control of Egypt knew that they first had to take Memphis.

Essential monuments

Little remains of the ancient city today. Even the Temple of Ptah, one of the great gods of ancient Egypt, is in ruin. It is hard to imagine this derelict place as the former heart of one of the most important and heavily populated cities in Ancient Egypt.

Because of the scanty remains, most visits to Memphis focus on the monuments in the **museum compound** (daily, winter 8am–4pm, summer 7.30am–5pm; charge), where the tourist buses park and where there is a cafeteria as well as shops selling imitation antiquities.

The main feature of the compound is a statue of Rameses II in a covered enclosure. Regarded as the finest statue of this Pharaoh ever carved, it lies in a horizontal position and can only be viewed properly from the gallery. Part of the crown and the lower legs are missing, but the fine craftsmanship is apparent in the details of the king's mouth, with indentations at the corners, the muscular shoulders and the sturdy torso. The royal name, in an oblong cartouche, can be seen on the right shoulder, on the breast and on the Pharaoh's girdle.

Another object of particular note in the museum compound is the **alabaster sphinx**, the largest statue ever found made of this stone. The pair of this statue used to stand outside Cairo's railway station but has been moved to the new Grand Egyptian Museum site at Giza.

Saqqarah

To the southwest of Memphis on a very arid plateau is **Saqqarah** ❸ (daily 8am–4pm; charge), the ancient city's necropolis and one of the most important sites in Egypt. Over a period of 3,500 years this was an active burial ground, where Pharaohs and their families, officials, generals and sacred animals were buried. Its name is derived from Sokar, an agricultural god believed to dwell in the earth. Because Sokar lived underground, he also came to be regarded as one of the gods of the dead; hence the adoption of his name for the whole necropolis.

Imhotep Museum

A new complex, completed in 2008, now greets all visitors to the site. If you are taking a taxi, ask your driver to stop here so you can buy entry tickets before driving up the hill, as there is no ticket office beyond. Just behind the ticket office is the **Imhotep Museum** (daily 9am–4pm; charge), a new museum honouring the contributions made by the great architect Imhotep and filled with artefacts found at the site – many chronicling the ancient construction methods used to build the pyramid at Saqqarah.

The Step Pyramid of Djoser

Dominating the horizon of Saqqarah is the **Step Pyramid of Djoser** ❹ (entry only with special permission), the central feature of a funerary complex built by Imhotep for Pharaoh Djoser, the first king of the 3rd Dynasty, in 2686BC. Djoser's reign marks the beginning of the Old Kingdom or 'pyramid age', an era of great vision and invention.

This is the world's earliest stone monument, the precursor to all Egypt's architectural achievements. A cross-section would reveal its complexity, arising from the fact that it began as a mastaba (from an Arabic word meaning 'bench' that refers to

Part of the Step Pyramid complex at Saqqarah

the usual oblong shape), a one-storey tomb of common type. Even here Imhotep showed his originality, for his mastaba was square rather than oblong and hewn out of stone rather than the usual mud-brick. The mastaba was gradually transformed into a pyramid during the long reign of Djoser; the height was increased in stages until, superimposed on top of one another, the six steps emerged in their final pyramidal form. Looking at the pyramid, you can clearly see the separate interior structures where the outer casing has collapsed.

One curious small stone annexe at the rear of the Step Pyramid, known as the Serdab, contains a statue of the king (the original is in the Egyptian Museum) looking out at the world through two eyeholes cut in the wall. The strange slope of this front wall is at the same angle as the pyramid, which serves as the Serdab's back wall.

Imhotep's legacy

Until the Step Pyramid of Djoser was built, no stone had ever been used for large-scale construction and there was no architectural tradition from which to draw. But Imhotep, a brilliant innovator and builder, drew inspiration from contemporary buildings constructed of perishable materials: reeds, mud-brick and logs of wood. It is thanks to his genius that we can see today, sculpted in stone, how bundles of reeds were tied together with the heads fanning out to form the earliest capital; how logs were laid across parallel walls to form a roof; and how reed fences separated property.

In short, the detail of Saqqarah mirrors the structures of the state

Corridor under the Step Pyramid at Saqqarah

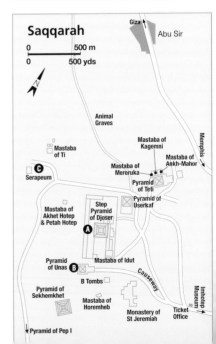

Step Pyramid of Saqqarah, the world's first pyramid

capital of Memphis, which have almost disappeared.

The Pyramid Texts

Among the other structures on the Saqqarah Plateau are several 5th- and 6th-Dynasty pyramids, which were built of poor-quality local limestone and fell to ruin when the outer casings were removed. Although unimpressive from the outside, they are of great interest and historical importance because many are inscribed with mortuary literature known as the Pyramid Texts.

Long columns of inscribed hieroglyphics, the texts include hymns, prayers and rituals for the deceased Pharaoh, as well as lists of offerings of food, drink and clothing for the afterlife. They are beautifully carved into the stone and filled with blue or green pigment. In the 5th-Dynasty

Imhotep

The exact role of Imhotep is unknown, but he is seen as the first engineer, architect and physician in history, as well as being a high priest and official of King Djoser. For the tomb of his king, Imhotep initially built a mastaba in stone blocks, not the usual mud-brick, which needed precise cutting and handling. By building it up in steps he constructed the first ever pyramid.

His achievements were recognised by later dynasties, and he was elevated to a god; later on, Greeks identified him with Asklepios, their god of medicine. Imhotep's undiscovered tomb is probably somewhere near Saqqarah and may contain many of his secrets. To cinema fans, Imhotep is better known as the inspiration for the series of films entitled *The Mummy*, showing him coming back to life and wreaking havoc.

Pyramid of Unas  (currently closed) for example, which was built about 2345BC and situated outside the southwest corner of the Djoser pyramid complex, the texts cover all the available space in the tomb chamber, apart from the walls behind and beside the empty sarcophagus, which are themselves painted to represent the facade of a building. The **Teti Pyramid** has similar texts.

The Noblemen's Tombs

It is from the **Noblemen's Tombs** (daily 8am–4pm; charge) dotted around the plateau, however, that we gain a real insight into everyday life in Ancient Egypt, especially from a group of tombs that date from the age of the pyramid builders. These are decorated with painted reliefs showing common scenes, including agricultural activities, animal husbandry, hunting and various trades, as well as family life.

The Tombs of the Apis Bulls

The **Tombs of the Apis Bulls**, or **Serapeum** (closed for restoration) as it was called in Graeco-Roman times, is a vast sepulchre of rock-hewn galleries for the internment of the sacred Apis bull of Memphis. The tombs are hewn out of solid rock, and the flanking chambers contain mighty granite sarcophagi of an average weight of 65 tonnes each, and measuring some 4m (13ft) long, by over 3m (9ft) high. Most of the lids are of solid granite.

When the discoverer of this sepulchre, the French archaeologist Mariette, first entered the galleries in 1851, he found that most of the sarcophagus lids had been pushed aside and the contents pillaged. Only one had been left intact because the robbers had been unsuccessful in their efforts to open it; Mariette succeeded where they had failed by using dynamite.

Entrance to the Tombs of the Apis Bulls

The Bent Pyramid at Dahshur

Inside the sarcophagus he found a solid gold statue of a bull that is now in the Louvre in Paris.

Dahshur

A few kilometres south of Saqqarah is the impressive but rarely visited site of **Dahshur** ❹ (daily 8am–4pm winter, until 5pm summer; charge). On the east of the site are three pyramids, built in the 19th–18th century BC, at the time of a pyramid-building revival. These pyramids are almost as impressive and considerably cheaper to visit than the ones at Giza, with fewer crowds.

The Black and Red Pyramids

The **Black Pyramid** was built of mudbrick but unused by Amenemhat III (1842–1797BC), one of Egypt's most colourful kings. The dark colour that gives it its name arises from the fact that it has been systematically stripped of its original white limestone covering. Its inscribed capstone is in the Egyptian Museum in Cairo. The view of the pyramid across the lake is one of the most charming in Egypt, worth the 5km (3-mile) drive from Saqqarah.

More interesting, however, are the two Old Kingdom pyramids, illustrating attempts at pyramid building by Snofru, the father of Khufu. The **Red Pyramid** was larger than Khafra's pyramid in Giza and is the earliest known pyramid to have been completed as a 'true' pyramid, built less than 60 years after Imhotep's great discovery.

The Bent Pyramid

Also of interest is Snofru's **Bent Pyramid** (due to open to the public in 2011) which starts at an angle of 52° and then changes to a gentler 43°, either because the architect realised that the initial angle was impossible to sustain or because such a steep pyramid would have put tremendous pressure upon the internal chambers.

The Bent Pyramid has the most intact casing of any Egyptian pyramid, and is unusual in having two entrances – one on the north side, like most pyramids, and the other on the west. Inside, the structure made internal use of cedar trunks imported from Lebanon, still intact, as beams, and externally it is the best-preserved of all the pyramids, thanks to an ingenious construction method that made stripping its surface particularly difficult. On the south side of the Bent Pyramid is a smaller pyramid, possibly for Snofru's wife, Hetepheres, which still retains some of its original limestone casing at its base.

There are two other 12th Dynasty pyramids here, another from the 13th Dynasty, and a third not yet identified.

Giza, Memphis and Saqqarah

★ ANCIENT EGYPTIAN GODS

In a land where life or death could depend on the success of a single harvest, the ancient Egyptians developed a complex religion to help them make sense of their fortunes. Each element of society and nature had a god, and every god demanded appeasement in order to maintain balance in the world, with the Pharaoh – considered a living god on earth – often the most demanding of all.

The Egyptian gods were worshipped for centuries, their influence only diminishing with the arrival of Christianity in the 1st century AD. Multiple gods were responsible for individual aspects of nature and humanity, with the Pharaoh acting as the divine conduit between the mortal and immortal worlds.

Appeasing the Gods

The Egyptian people developed complex religious practices to please the gods and give reason for the gods to favour them. But the gods never rested easy or stayed happy for long. Some of their stories read like ancient soap operas filled with intrigue, murder and despair. The tale of Osiris is the most famous of them all, telling the story of how the god Osiris became king of the underworld after being killed by his brother Seth in a fit of jealousy. His body was then separated into 14 pieces and scattered across the Egyptian empire for his wife/sister, the goddess Isis, to find. Many temples

Egyptian gods and hieroglyphics seen in the Temple of Khnum at Esna

(including Philae) are located in places where a piece of Osiris was said to have been found.

Ancient Egyptians worshipped multiple gods, with the exception of a brief period during the reign of the Pharaoh Akhenaten; the new ruler abandoned the worship of some deities in favour of Aten (the sun-deity) and moved the capital to Amarna. This new religion fell out of favour on Akhenaten's death, when his son Tutankhamun took over and traditional religious practices were restored.

The stories of the gods are told on the walls of temples and obelisks throughout Egypt. While the hieroglyphs may be confusing (see p.168), you can often tell which god is being worshipped or discussed simply by looking for standard depictions. The following should help you decipher one god from another:

Guide to the gods

Amun: Human head with tall feather plumes or ram-headed Sphinx
Hathor: Woman with a sun-disc headdress and cow horns
Horus: Falcon-headed man
Isis: Woman with headdress shaped like a throne, cow's horns and sun disc
Nephthys: Woman with headdress shaped like a basket on a stand
Osiris: Man holding crook and flail
Seth: Head of a Seth animal (curved snout with square ears) holding a sceptre
Ra: The head of a falcon with a sun-disc on his head
Sobek: Crocodile-headed man

Relief of Osiris in the tomb of Horemheb, Valley of the Kings

Statue of Horus in the temple at Edfu

ACCOMMODATION

Despite the fact the Pyramids are Egypt's best-known sight, the choice of hotels in Giza is incredibly limited and almost non-existent further south. This is due to the fact that most tourists choose to be based in Cairo, heading to Giza on a day trip and returning to their accommodation in the evening. Once the new Egyptian Museum opens on the Giza Plateau, accommodation options will improve. But until that time, choice is limited and prices remain high.

Cataract Pyramids Resort
Al Haraneya, Saqqarah Road, Giza
Tel: 02-3771 8060
www.cataracthotels.com
Located south of the Giza Pyramids along the road to Saqqarah, this is a popular local resort in the midst of lush countryside, with a huge swimming pool, its own health club and disco. 🏨 $$$

Europa
300 Pyramids Road, Giza
Tel: 02-3779 5940
An older-style concrete block with 240 rooms over eight floors. Popular with groups and great value considering the location. Restaurant on ground floor. $

Four Seasons Cairo
35 Shari' Al Gizah, Giza
Tel: 02-3573 1212

www.fourseasons.com
The large, airy and elegant rooms command glorious views over the Pyramids, Cairo's Zoo and the Nile. Spa, wellness centre with wide range of treatments, sauna, sophisticated exercise room and outdoor swimming pool. $$$$$

Mena House Oberoi
End of Shari' Al Haram, Pyramids Road, Giza
Tel: 02-3377 3222
www.oberoihotels.com
A historic landmark refurbished by the Oberoi chain, this is the place to stay if you want to be close to the Pyramids. Rooms in the 19th-century khedival hunting lodge are particularly recommended, as they are tastefully decorated with antiques. Even if you are not a guest here, lunch by the pool is strongly recommended after a visit to the Giza Pyramids. $$$$$

Mena House Oberoi hotel

RESTAURANTS

From simple to sensationally expensive and everything in between – all kinds of eateries can be found in the Giza area and, although it's packed with tourists, the food here is surprisingly good. There's plenty of street food to savour, budget options such as Andrea's, known for its spit-roasted chicken, and five-star hotels like the Mena House Oberoi which cater to blow-the-budget spenders who want fine dining.

Andrea's Chicken and Fish Restaurant
(on the left bank of the Mariyutiyah Canal at number 59 heading towards Kirdasah, Giza)
Tel: 02-3383 1133
Some of the best meze in town and certainly the best grilled chicken, served with hummous and freshly baked bread. Seating is mostly outdoors in a large garden, with simple wooden and bamboo furniture. There's also a small pool and playground to keep the children happy. Recommended.
$$

Barry's
2 Shari' Abu Aziza, next to the AA stables, in the village near the Sphinx, Nazlet Al Seman
Tel: 02-3388 9540
The food is traditional Egyptian with good meze, grills and tagines (stews), but the best thing is the cold beer and superb views over the three Giza Pyramids. **$$**

Fish Market
Americana boat, 26 Shari' An Nil, Giza
Tel: 02-3570 9693
The best fish restaurant in town, on the upper deck of a permanently moored boat, so the views are excellent too. Choose from the catch of the day and it will be weighed and cooked to perfection and served with Middle Eastern salads. **$$**

Moghul Rooms
Mena House Oberoi, Pyramids Road, Giza
Tel: 02-3383 3222
This may be the most expensive place in town, but one look at the luxurious interiors and you'll know where your cash is going.

Fresh broad bean salad, a favourite Middle Eastern dish

The authentic Indian food melts in your mouth and the entertainment is surprisingly sophisticated. **$$$**

Seasons Restaurant
Four Seasons First Residence Hotel
35 Shari' Al Giza
Tel: 02-3567 1600
With views of the Nile, first class food and service, an elegant dining room and live jazz, the Seasons Restaurant is where to go for a real treat. This is where movie stars, sheikhs and heads of state stay when they come to Cairo. **$$$$**

NIGHTLIFE AND ENTERTAINMENT

With the bright lights of Cairo merely a few miles away, nightlife in Giza tends to be restricted to a few hotel-based culture shows of dubious quality and belly dancers hired to perform to large tour groups. There are occasional exceptions though, especially in October when the Cairo Opera House arrives with a month-long series of performances of *Aida* on the Giza Plateau. Check with your hotel concierge to see if other productions have been added to the schedule of entertainments in the area.

Cinemas

Cairo Sheraton Cinema
Shari' Al Gala, Giza
Tel: 02-2760 6081
Hollywood blockbusters can be seen at the cinema in the Cairo Sheraton.

Sound and Light Show

Every evening two or three performances of the sound and light show (1 hour) are held on the Giza Plateau in front of the Sphinx. Dramatic lighting and a voice-over soundtrack tell the story of the Plateau using the 'voice' of the Sphinx as the narrator. It's a little cheesy but worth attending to see the Pyramids illuminated at night.

For further information, tel: 02-3385 2880; www.soundandlight.com.eg. 🏚

SPORTS AND ACTIVITIES

Cairo doesn't have a lot of space available for outdoor activities. Instead, sporting facilities are located in the suburbs, around Giza, Memphis and Saqqarah, including a number of top-notch golf courses and riding centres.

Fitness Centres

Gyms and fitness centres are becoming very popular in Egypt, although not all are as sophisticated as their Western counterparts, so it is advisable to check facilities first. The best facilities can be found at the Spa and Wellness Centre in the Four Seasons Hotel at the First Mall in Giza (tel: 02-3573 1212).

Golf

There is a nine-hole golf course at the Mena House Oberoi hotel (tel: 02-3377 3322; www.oberoihotels.com) with the Pyramids as a backdrop. A championship 18-hole course can be found at Dreamland Golf and Tennis Resort (6th of October City Road, Dreamland City, south of Cairo; tel: 01-0177 3410; www.dreamlandgolf.com). But the granddaddy of them all is the Pyramids Golf and Country Club (tel: 049-600 953), where guests can play various courses with a total of 99 holes.

Riding

Horses and camels are on offer in the village near the Sphinx, Nazlet Al Seman. The most reputable stables are AA (tel: 012-153 4142) and MG (tel: 02-2385 1241). The favourite stable of the expat community, particularly for riding lessons, is the well-organised International Equestrian Club (on Saqqarah Road at the end of the Al Moneeb Ring Road; tel: 02-2742 7654). The Saqqarah Country Club (Saqqarah Road to Abu Al Nomros; tel: 02-2384 6115) has good facilities and offers temporary membership. 🏚

Rowing

There are several rowing clubs in Cairo, congregating on the east bank of the Nile between Giza and Imbaba. It is possible to join a crew at the An Nil Sporting Club, near Kubri 'Abbas on the Corniche at Giza (tel: 02-2393 4350).

TOURS

For many visitors, the area itself is one long day trip. A combined visit to Giza, Memphis and Saqqarah is easy to do and can be arranged either through a tour operator or by negotiating a rate with a taxi driver. Once the Grand Egyptian Museum opens in Giza, estimated to be in 2013, more travellers will choose Giza as their full-time base.

Riding Tours

For information on camel and riding tours, head for one of the local stables. *A listing of recommended stables can be found on p.116.* Avoid hiring a horse or camel from the touts around the Pyramids.

FESTIVALS AND EVENTS

While Giza, Memphis and Saqqarah are growing in population thanks to migration from other points in Egypt, they are still considered suburbs of Cairo. As such, most of the big festivals and events take place in the capital and residents go there if they want to join the celebrations. A few exceptions are listed below.

October

Aida at the Pyramids
Tel: 02-2736 7314
The Cairo Opera House presents its annual series of performances of the Verdi opera *Aida* using the Pyramids as a backdrop. This is a truly awesome spectacle.

Pharaohs' Rally
www.rallyedespharaohs.it
Three-week cross-country endurance-driving rally across the Sahara, kicking off from the site of the Sphinx on the Giza Plateau and ending in Cairo.

December

Sphinx Festival
www.sphinxfestival.com
Held in Le Meridien Pyramids, Giza Plateau, this annual festival celebrates the fusion of art and science with dance shows, music performances and seminars on topics ranging from Egyptian cosmology to sacred geometry.

Aida at the Pyramids

Middle Egypt

A rise in security fears in the mid-1990s essentially shut down Middle Egypt to all but the most intrepid. But the region has recently been reopened to tourists as travel restrictions have been lifted. Visitor numbers remain small, meaning that if you time your visit carefully you may have the celebrated temples at Abydos and Dandarah to yourself.

 Population: Al Mennyah 221,500; Asyut 400,000

 Local dialling code: Al Mennyah 86; Asyut 88

 Local tourist office: Al Mennyah: Shari' Corniche An Nil; tel: 86-237 1521.
Asyut: 1st Floor, Governorate Building, Shari' At Thawra; tel: 88-231 5110.

 Main police station: Al Mennyah: Amarat Al Gama'a; tel: 86-236 4527.
Asyut: Shari' Farouq Kidwani; tel: 88-232 2225.

 Main post office: Al Mennyah: Shari' Corniche An Nil.
Asyut: Shari' Nahda'

 Banks: Al Mennyah: many banks are located along Shari' Al Gomhureyya.
Asyut: banks can be found on Meadan Talaat Harb.

 Hospitals: Al Mennyah: University Hospital, Meadan Suzanne Mubarak; tel: 86-236 6743.
Asyut: Gama'a Hospital at University of Asyut; tel: 88-233 4500.

At first glance, the stretch of the Nile between Luxor and the southern suburbs of Cairo seems sleepy, dotted with farmers toiling the fields just as generations have before them. But this area has seen revolution and intrigue from as far back as the 18th Dynasty, when the Pharaoh Akhenaten moved his power base to Al Amarnah, south of the modern city of Al Mennyah, in support of his new religion worshipping the power of the Aten (sun disc).

Revolutionary thoughts returned over three millennia later when outbreaks of violence broke out in the 1990s, making much of the region a virtual no-go area for tourists.

While security remains tight, the travel restrictions of the past decade have recently been removed as tensions have decreased. The incomparable temples of Abydos and Dandarah dedicated to the god Osiris and goddess Hathor respectively, are rapidly returning to 'must-see' itineraries.

Al Mennyah and Region

The provincial capital of **Al Mennyah** ❶ lies at the cusp of Lower and Upper Egypt on the west bank of the Nile,

245km (153 miles) south of Cairo. There is little of tourist interest in the city, but this is a good base for visiting the historic sights in the region.

Zouhreyyet Al Mayteen

Just as the Pharaohs of old were believed to travel by boat across the sky and through the netherworld after their death, so too did the dead of Al Mennyah rely on boats to take them to their final resting place. Until the recent construction of a bridge across the Nile, *feluccas* provided the main means of transport along and across the river – the most notable journey being to **Zouhreyyet Al Mayteen** (Corner of the Dead), the cemetery that serves the region.

Vast numbers of Coptic crosses and mud-brick domes mark the graves of

Feast of Assumption, a Christian festival at Dayr Al Adhra

the deceased of Al Mennyah's Christian and Muslim communities. This is a huge site, said to be one of the largest cemeteries in the world.

Christian culture

Twenty-one km (12 miles) north of Al Mennyah on the east bank of the Nile is the Monastery of the Virgin known as **Dayr Al Adhra** ❷ (daily 7am–4pm), where it is said the Holy Family rested on their flight from the Holy Land. The magnificent cliff-side location is approached by 66 steps hewn into the rock, which is filled with pilgrims during the week-long feast of the Assumption in August.

Rock chambers

Beni Hasan ❸ (daily, Oct–Apr 7am–4pm, May–Sept 7am–5pm; charge) is famous for its Middle Kingdom tombs, dating from around 2000BC.

The tombs comprise a long series of rock-hewn chambers about 200m (655ft) above the floodplain, extending for several kilometres along the face of the cliff. The most interesting group belongs to noblemen who governed

The cemetery of Zouhreyyet Al Mayteen outside Al Mennyah

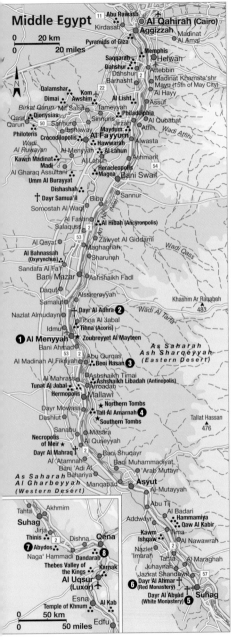

Middle Egypt

the province 4,000 years ago.

Inside, the walls are adorned throughout with vivid scenes, preserving much of their original colour. They represent men hunting, fishing and wrestling, and women weaving, and present a panorama of the everyday life of governors, courtiers and princes who lived in Upper Egypt during the Middle Kingdom.

Tall Al Amarnah

The most important site of the province, notable more for its historical significance than the quality of the remains that exist today, lies 58km (38 miles) south of Al Mennyah. Capital of the Egyptian empire for just 30 years, the city of Akhenaten at **Tall Al Amarnah 4** (daily 8am–5pm; charge) was built by the Pharaoh Akhenaten to escape the establishment. This is the site he chose to found a city dedicated to the worship of a single god, the Aten (literally the sun's disc), rather than the whole pantheon of gods worshipped by his predecessors.

While the grounds of the city are extensive, the city was razed to the ground after Akhenaten died. You can visit the tombs of the noblemen and Akhenaten's own tomb, which give an insight into life during Akhenaten's short rule. Despite the fact there is not a lot to see here, the tombs, the dusty plain and secluded nature of Al Amarnah are truly atmospheric.

Asyut

The biggest city in Middle Egypt is **Asyut**, a workaday place that once boasted great wealth due to the strength of the cotton trade in the late 19th century. Today, it is home

City of the Dead near Asyut

Middle Egypt Transport

As Middle Egypt was the main location for Islamic insurgency in the 1990s, the region was heavily restricted to tourists until changes to government policy relaxed travel options in late 2009.

Today, visitors have more freedom, but you may face delays at checkpoints and verification of your itinerary by the authorities. Carry a copy of your passport details at all times in case you are asked for identification, and be aware that you may need to add extra time to compensate for any security checks.

 Trains: The best way to travel in the region is on one of the three approved trains that leave Luxor and Cairo each day. Ask at the tourist office or train station for daily schedules.
Al Mennyah train station: Meadan Al Mahatta; no phone. Asyut station, Shari' Al Geish; tel: 233 5623.

 Airport: Asyut: 10km (6 miles) northwest of town, no phone.

 Buses: The main bus company is Upper Egypt Bus Co in Al Mennyah, tel:
086-232 6820.
Main bus stations: Al Mennyah: Shari' Sa'd Zaghlul; no phone. Asyut: Shari' Al Geish; tel: 233 0460.

 Car hire: Foreigners are advised not to drive independently in the area due to security fears.

 Taxis: Taxis are not allowed to take tourists north of Abydos (if travelling from Luxor).

to the largest population of Coptic Christians in the country. The closest Coptic site to the city is **Dayr Al Mahraq** (Burnt Monastery), 12km (7½ miles) north of Asyut. The location is believed to be where the Holy Family stayed for six months, their longest stay in Egypt. To the south, 115km (71 miles) from Asyut, are two of Egypt's most visited monasteries. The **Dayr Al Abyad** ❺ (White Monastery; daily 7am–dusk), founded in the 5th century by St Shenuda, has many striking similarities with Pharaonic temple design. Nearby **Dayr Al Ahmar** ❻ (Red Monastery; daily 7am–midnight) was founded by Besa, one of Shenuda's disciples, and is dedicated to St Bishoi.

Abydos

Abydos ❼ (daily, winter 7am–5pm, summer 7am–6pm; charge) was one of Ancient Egypt's most important cities. Believed to be the burial ground of the god Osiris, it was used as a necropolis from the earliest

Praying outside the Temple of Hathor at Dandarah

celebration of Sety's power and as an affirmation of the Pharaoh's adherence to the traditional gods, following the collapse of the monotheistic regime of Akhenaten at Al Amarnah *(see page 120)* just 40 years earlier. Each of the main gods of the traditional faith is represented in rooms towards the rear of the temple, specifically Osiris, his wife/sister Isis, their son Horus, Amun-Ra, Ra-Horakhty and Ptah.

The temple is entered via the First Hypostyle Hall, which was completed by Sety I's son Rameses II. Beyond this is the Second Hypostyle Hall, with 24 papyrus columns and decorated with perhaps the best-preserved reliefs in the country.

Dandarah

The goddess of women and beauty, the cow-goddess Hathor, is celebrated

period of Egyptian history (*c.*4000BC) to Christian times. This was the cult centre of Osiris, Egypt's most beloved god *(see right and p.112)*, whose legend is depicted in the wall reliefs of many Egyptian temples.

A place of pilgrimage

Ancient Egyptians aspired to make a pilgrimage to the revered city at least once in their lifetime (just as Muslims try to get to Mecca today). Hoping to impress Osiris, who was also known as the Judge of the Court of the Hereafter, pilgrims would leave offerings, monuments and tokens in his honour, with the ultimate gift being the **Great Temple of Sety I**, built by the New Kingdom Pharaoh (1291–1278BC).

The temple was built both as a

The Cult of Osiris

Legend relates how the much-loved ruler Osiris was killed by his evil and jealous brother Seth. Isis, the wife/sister of Osiris, faithfully searched the banks of the Nile for his dismembered body, then buried the pieces throughout Egypt, with his head believed to be buried at Abydos. Isis used her magical powers to revive her husband just long enough to conceive their son Horus.

It was at Abydos that Osiris was resurrected and assumed his powers as lord and judge of the afterlife and king of the underworld. Horus grew up and took over the terrestrial throne, avenging his father's death by slaying Seth.

at the beautiful **Temple of Hathor** at **Dandarah** ❽ (daily, winter 7am–4pm, summer 6am–5pm; entries stop one hour before closing; charge), approximately halfway between Abydos and Luxor. Dating from the Ptolemaic period, the temple is one of the best-preserved and most lavishly decorated in Egypt.

The Pronaos

The temple was begun by Ptolemy IX (116–107BC) and completed in the Roman era 250 years later. In dedicating a temple to Egypt's cow-goddess, the Ptolemaic kings were honouring one of Egypt's best loved deities. You can see images of Hathor, usually portrayed as a female figure with the head of a cow, in most Egyptian temples.

The most distinctive feature of the temple is the great Pronaos (vestibule), with 24 Hathor-headed columns and a depiction of Nut, the sky-goddess swallowing the sun in order to give birth to it again the next morning. The remarkable astrological scenes depicting the six signs of the Egyptian zodiac (the crab, the twins, the bull, the ram, the fishes and the water-carrier), the stars and the phases of the moon can all be seen in their true glory following an ongoing conservation project.

As befits a temple dedicated to the goddess of beauty, the temple of Hathor was known as a place of worship for the great Cleopatra. In fact, the rear facade of the temple features the only identified representation of her made during her lifetime.

Christian site

While not kept to the same standard as the temple, two other places of note are a Roman-era **birth house** (Mammisi) and the ruins of an early **Christian basilica**, one of the oldest Christian sites in the country.

The birth house at the Temple of Hathor

ACCOMMODATION

A lack of tourists over the past decade has meant that the hotels in Middle Egypt seem to be stuck in a time warp. Hopefully, the change in security status for the nation and relaxation of travel requirements in neighbouring regions may mean an increase in numbers (and subsequently an increase in investment). Despite the dearth of tourists, rooms are at a premium, simply because there are very few decent-quality options. Don't let that dissuade you from coming, though, as the combination of relatively few tourists and a wealth of great sights means you will often have stunning locations available to yourself.

Accommodation Price Categories

Prices are for one night's accommodation in a standard double room in low season.

$ = below E£200
$$ = E£200–E£450
$$$ = E£450–E£750
$$$$ = E£750–E£1,250
$$$$$ = over E£1,250

Al Mennyah

Lotus
1 Shari' Port Said
Tel: 086-236 4500
Clean rooms with fans and a good bar-restaurant frequented by beer-drinking locals. **$$**

Mercure Nefertiti/Aton
Shari' An Nil
Tel: 086-233 1515
Most upmarket hotel in the area, with restaurant and bar, comfortable rooms, some facing the Nile, and a swimming pool in the garden. **$$$$**

The Palace
Meadan At Tahrir
Tel: 086-236 4071
Small and simple hotel with colonial-style furniture and high ceilings. Some rooms have air conditioning and private baths. **$**

Asyut

Assiutel Hotel
146 Shari' An Nil
Tel: 088-232 9022
Two levels of room to choose from: the faded standard or the recently refurbished luxury. Standards have balconies and tired interiors. Luxury rooms come complete with flat-screen TVs and new beds. **$$$**

Casa Blanca Hotel
Shari' Moh, Tawfik Khashaba
Tel: 088-233 7662
Basic three-star hotel with clean rooms but very little atmosphere. **$$$**

Youth Hostel
03 Shari' Al Walideyya
Tel: 088-232 4846
Asyut's best budget option. Try to avoid it during Egyptian school holiday periods when the place can get packed. **$**

Typical conical-roofed houses in Al Mennyah

RESTAURANTS

In Middle Egypt, fine dining is a foreign concept. Hotel restaurants serving Egyptian dishes and basic Western options are the best options. However, you shouldn't miss out on the street food; vendors and small eateries serve up some of the best examples of Egyptian staples like *koshari* and *fu'ul*.

Restaurant Price Categories

Prices are for a two-course meal for one, not including a drink or tip.

$ = below E£15
$$ = E£15–E£40
$$$ = E£40–E£75
$$$$ = over E£75

Al Mennyah

Banana Island Restaurant
Shari' An Nil
Tel: 086-234 2993
The main restaurant of Al Mennyah's Aton Hotel has an indoor section and a pleasant outdoor terrace. The food is simple but tasty Egyptian fare. **$$**

Kushari Nagwa
Shari' Al Gomhureyya
This restaurant specialises in the popular Egyptian staple *koshari*, which is a mixture of pasta, rice, chickpeas and brown lentils topped with fried onions and spicy tomato sauce. It is usually vegetarian, although in some places meat is added. **$**

Savoy
Meadan Al Mahatta
A popular restaurant with locals and visitors alike, the Savoy serves Egyptian fast food such as kebabs, sandwiches and rotisserie chicken with salads. **$**

Asyut

Assiutel
146 Shari' An Nil
Tel: 088-231 2121
This hotel restaurant beside the Nile doesn't have a lot of atmosphere but it is one of the best places in Asyut to eat and one of the town's only bars. **$$**

Casablanca Sweets
Shari' Muhammad, Tawfik Khashaba
Tel: 088-233 7762
This is a good place to order Egyptian *fiteer*, a tasty cross between a pizza and a pancake, which comes with a range of sweet or savoury fillings. **$**

Kushari Galal
Shari' Talaat Harb
This bustling café situated in the centre of town is packed with locals from midday through to the evening. Good for a cheap, tasty and filling meal. **$**

Koshari, a favourite Egyptian dish

NIGHTLIFE AND ENTERTAINMENT

As Middle Egypt is one of the most conservative regions in the country, nightlife and entertainment options for tourists are severely limited. Alcohol is difficult to find at the best of times, and there are no performance venues hosting theatre or live music that a foreigner would feel welcome at. In fact, there are still restrictions for travellers in the region after dark, and you may experience hassle from the police if you attempt to leave your hotel in the evening.

SPORTS AND ACTIVITIES

There are no sports or activity options available to tourists in Middle Egypt. If you want to be sporty while you're here, then the Mercure Nefertiti is recommended. as it offers the only hotel gym (very small) and swimming pool in the area. There is a football team (Asyut Petroleum) with strong local support, although foreigners rarely attend matches and might create a stir of interest amongst the stands. Asyut Petroleum plays at Asyut University Stadium during the season and is currently ranked in the second division.

TOURS

Due to travel restrictions in place until recently, tour operators largely steer clear of Middle Egypt, and there are few independent travellers who attempt to visit the area. To tour the region, you will need to arrange for a car and driver and you may be stopped frequently by police at checkpoints to ask your itinerary. Your driver should be able to answer questions on your behalf, but you should bring your passport with you as identification.

For a tour of the temples at Abydos and Dandarah, visits are arranged by booking a car and driver or, more commonly, by using tour operators based in Luxor. *A full listing of operators in Luxor can be found on pp.150–51.*

FESTIVALS AND EVENTS

With one of the largest concentrations of Coptic Christians in Egypt, Middle Egypt is a great place to be during important festivals such as Coptic Easter. If you can get an invitation to a Coptic church, do try to go, as the service is filled with hymn-singing and incense-burning. Afterwards, Copts then return home to enjoy meat and special festive dishes for the first time in two months, following a long period of fasting.

August
Assumption (Virgin Mary Festival)
Dayr Al Adhra, 21km (13 miles) north of Al Mennyah

Dates change according to Coptic calendar. Pilgrims come to climb the steps of this monastery to pay tribute to the Virgin Mary. Some crawl up the steps.

Luxor

Capital of Egypt during the New Kingdom, the city of Thebes was designed to impress and inspire. The monumental temples were famed throughout the ancient world and have attracted tourists since Greek and Roman times. Today Thebes has become Luxor – one of Egypt's biggest tourist destinations, attracting thousands of visitors each year to its ancient sights and sun-drenched Nile shores.

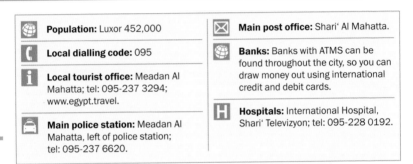

Population: Luxor 452,000

Local dialling code: 095

Local tourist office: Meadan Al Mahatta; tel: 095-237 3294; www.egypt.travel.

Main police station: Meadan Al Mahatta, left of police station; tel: 095-237 6620.

Main post office: Shari' Al Mahatta.

Banks: Banks with ATMS can be found throughout the city, so you can draw money out using international credit and debit cards.

Hospitals: International Hospital, Shari' Televizyon; tel: 095-228 0192.

Combining the grandeur of ancient Thebes with a bustling modern town, Luxor (Al Uqsur) offers a bit of everything: an extraordinary wealth of history, accommodation to suit all budgets and plenty of sunshine – even adventurous types are catered for with balloon rides, cycling and donkey treks through the mountains.

On the east bank lies the modern city, with Luxor Temple acting as the unofficial centre. Here you will find the bulk of the hotels and restaurants, the souq, shops and museums. A couple of kilometres to the northeast is the Temple of Amun-Ra at Karnak, the finest temple complex constructed in Egypt.

Across the river on the west bank, in the necropolis of ancient Thebes, are the Valley of the Kings, the Valley of the Queens, hundreds of tombs of noblemen, and a semicircle of grand mortuary temples along the edge of the floodplain.

East Bank

Today, the east side is the hub of the modern-day action, packed with taxis and horse-driven calèche drivers honking and hissing to get the attention of unsuspecting tourists. Despite the number of tourists, the east bank retains its rural, provincial flavour, especially if you leave the wide boulevards and head down the backstreets.

Temple of Luxor

The city of Luxor spreads along the banks of the Nile, and at its centre is the **Temple of Luxor** ❶ (daily, winter

6am–9pm, summer 6am–10pm; charge), an architectural masterpiece standing in complete contrast to its surroundings – a car-clogged roundabout lined with fast-food joints, souvenir shops and bookstores.

Largely built by Amenhotep III in the 18th Dynasty (*c.*1350BC) and embellished by Rameses II in the 19th Dynasty, the temple is remarkably well preserved, particularly the wall reliefs, as it was covered in sand and built over by the town until excavations started in 1885. The temple sits on the site of an older sanctuary built by Hatshepsut which was dedicated to Amun, the most important god of Thebes, mother-goddess Mut and their son, moon-god Khons.

From the ticket office, a path leads to the temple complex and an avenue of ram-headed sphinxes which once

Calèche ride in Luxor

connected with Karnak Temple to the north. In front of the temple's great pylon (entrance) are majestic statues of Rameses II and baboons supporting a large granite obelisk – one of an original pair. The other, presented to France in 1831 by Muhammad Ali, stands in the Place de la Concorde in Paris.

The pylon leads to the **Great Court**

Temple of Luxor

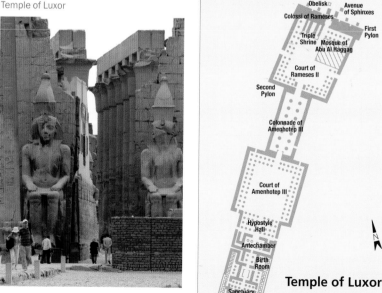

Temple of Luxor

Obelisk
Avenue of Sphinxes
Colossi of Rameses
First Pylon
Triple Shrine
Mosque of Abu Al Haggag
Court of Rameses II
Second Pylon
Colonnade of Amenhotep III
Court of Amenhotep III
Hypostyle Hall
Antechamber
Birth Room
Sanctuary

0   100 m
0   100 yds

N

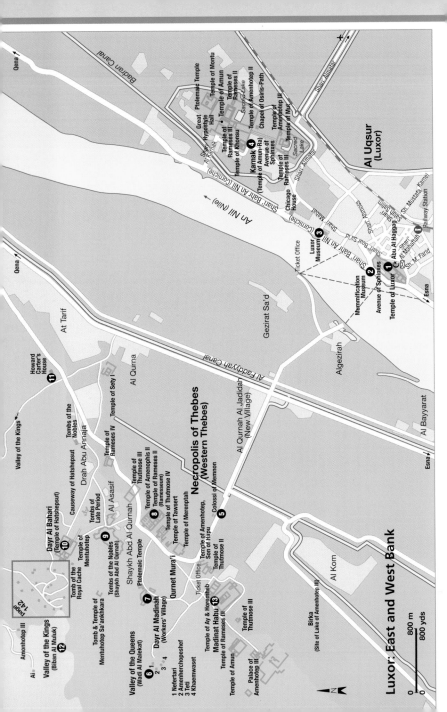

Luxor: East and West Bank

Al Uqsur (Luxor)

Temple of Montu
Ptolemaic Temple
Great Temple of Amun
Hypostyle Hall
Temple of Ramesses II
Temple of Ramesses III
Temple of Khonsu
Temple of Amenhotep II
Chapel of Osiris-Path
Karnak (4)
Avenue of Sphinxes
Temple of Amenhotep III
Temple of Mut
Sacred Lake

Chicago House

Mummification Museum
Luxor Museum (3)
Ticket Office
Avenue of Sphinxes (2)
Temple of Luxor (1)

Shari' Al Mahattah
Railway Station

Shari' An Nil (Corniche)
Shari' Bahr An Nil
Shari' Al Karnak
An Nil (Nile)

Necropolis of Thebes (Western Thebes)

Howard Carter's House
At Tarif

Tomb of the Royal Cache
Temple of Mentuhotep
Dayr Al Bahari (Temple of Hatshepsut) (10)
Causeway of Hatshepsut
Tombs of the Nobles
Drah Abu Annaja
Temple of Rameses IV
Al Qurna

Tomb & Temple of Mentuhotep Sa'ankhkara
Tombs of the Nobles (Shaykh Abd Al Qurnah) (9)
Tombs of Late Period
Al Asasif
Temple of Thutmose III
Temple of Amenophis II
Temple of Rameses II (Ramesseum)
Temple of Thutmose IV
Temple of Tawsert
Temple of Merenptah
Temple of Sety I
Shaykh Abd Al Qurnah

Ptolemaic Temple (8)

Amenhotep III
Ai
Valley of the Kings (Biban Al Muluk) (12)
Valley of the Kings

Tomb of the Royal Cache
Dayr Al Madinah (Workers' Village) (7)
Qurnet Mura'i

Valley of the Queens (Wadi Al Malekat) (6)
1 Nefertari
2 Amenherchopeshef
3 Teti
4 Khaemwaset

Ticket Office
Colossi of Memnon (5)
Temple of Amenhotep, Son of Hapu
Temple of Thutmose II
Temple of Ay & Horemheb
Madinat Habu (13)
Temple of Rameses III
Temple of Amun
Temple of Thutmose III
Palace of Amenhotep III
Al Kom
Birka (Site of Lake of Amenhotep III)

Gezirat Sa'd
Algezirah
Al Qurnah Al Jadidah (New Village)
Al Bayyarat

Al Faddiyah Canal
Badran Canal
Qena
Esna

0   800 m
0   800 yds

N

Avenue of Sphinxes, Temple of Luxor

of Rameses II, and in the southeast is the 14th-century **Mosque of Abu Al Haggag**, protecting the tomb of a 12th-century holy man, Luxor's patron saint. When the site was excavated, the mosque was the only building left undisturbed and now hangs about 13m (40ft) above ground level.

Beyond the court is the **Grand Colonnade of Amenhotep III**, with massive papyrus columns, which were the prototype for the Great Hypostyle Hall at Karnak. This leads to the **Sun Court of Amenhotep III,** where a cache of statues was found in 1989, now in the Luxor Museum. Wall carvings depict Amenhotep making offerings to the gods in thanks for his divine power.

Because of its location in the town centre surrounded by traffic, Luxor Temple doesn't offer a sound and

---

Luxor Transport

 Airport: Located 7km (4 miles) east of town and served by Egyptair along with numerous international charter flights.

 Buses: Main bus station is situated on the airport road, on the outskirts of town, 1km ($^2/_3$ mile) before the airport; tel: 095-237 2118. Upper Egypt Bus Company; tel: 095-232 3218.

 Trains: Main train station is at Meadan Al Mahatta; tel: 095-237

2018; www.egyptrail.gov.eg. Abela Egypt Sleeping Train; tel: 095-237 2015; www.sleepingtrains.com.

 Car hire: Independent driving is not recommended in Luxor. Drivers can be erratic, and regular government checkpoints may turn away foreigners due to ever-changing security concerns.

 Taxis: Taxis can be hailed from anywhere in the city. Negotiate a price before you get in.

Luxor women enjoying the shade

light show, but it is one of the only temples in Egypt open to visitors after dark. A stroll through the spotlit treasures is highly atmospheric and well worth undertaking.

Along the Corniche

Between the Temple of Luxor and the Nile is the Corniche (Shari' Bahr An Nil), a tree-lined avenue leading to Karnak. A wide path follows the riverbank, ideal for a shady stroll. The *felucca* captains gather here, hoping to attract tourists onto a boat trip, but the day trips aren't as inspiring as those from Aswan. If Aswan is on the itinerary, it's best to wait until then for a jaunt on the river.

Further on, the bustle increases as Nile cruisers disgorge their passengers for tours or shopping trips. Horse-drawn carriages ply the Corniche offering trips to Karnak, or a ride back to hotels and restaurants.

Luxor's museums

Also on the Corniche, on the same side of the river, is the **Mummification Museum ❷** (daily, winter 9am–9pm, summer 9am–10pm; Ramadan 1–4pm; charge 🏛), which has well-presented displays explaining the process of mummification, as well as an array of tools and materials used in this ancient and peculiar art.

To the north, the excellent **Luxor Museum ❸** (daily, winter 9am–3pm, 4–9pm, summer 9am–3pm, 5–8pm; Ramadan 1–4pm; charge), designed by one of Egypt's leading architects, the late Mahmoud Al Hakim, displays important finds from the temples, the Valley of the Kings and other local sites.

Among the highlights are a magnificent cow-head of the sky-goddess Mehit Weret, covered in gold leaf, found in Tutankhamun's tomb, and two royal mummies: that of Ahmose I, founder of the 18th Dynasty,

The Art of Mummification

The belief in life after death by the Ancient Egyptians prompted priests to determine that preservation of the body was necessary in order to ensure eternal life. Mummification began as a practice around 3000BC as a simple procedure whereby internal organs were removed from the body to prevent putrefaction before the corpse was wrapped up in linen cloth and placed in carved wooden coffins.

The process became more elaborate with each and every generation. As mummification developed, natron was used to remove moisture from the body and preserve the internal organs. Spices and oils were then used to anoint the organs, after which the body was wrapped with amulets as prayers were uttered by the priests in order magically to 'recharge' the corpse's limbs and organs in the afterlife.

Luxor can be a good place to pick up a few bargains if you know what you're looking for and are prepared to haggle. Alabaster especially is a good buy (see p.143), as it is quarried and carved locally. And if you really want to be left alone, avoid using English while wandering around the stalls, and tell the merchants you are from Iceland whenever they ask. The shocked silence and pause should be long enough to allow you to move on.

Temple of Karnak

The **Temple of Amun-Ra at Karnak** ❹ (daily, winter 6am–5.30pm, summer 6am–6.30pm, last tickets sold one hour before closing; charge), lying 2km (1¼ miles) from the centre of Luxor, is a vast complex extending over 3 sq km (1 sq mile) comprised of sanctuaries, kiosks, pylons and

Sunset on the Nile, Luxor

and one mummy identified recently as being of Rameses I, founder of the 19th Dynasty. Displayed in darkened rooms without their wrappings, they make a gruesome sight (children may find them frightening).

Nearby is a statue of Thutmose III, one of the best-preserved statues of this famous ruler and a masterpiece of Ancient Egyptian art.

Luxor's souq

Lying a few streets parallel to the Corniche is Luxor's busy souq. The merchants of Luxor are known as being the most aggressive in the country, and the ones who drive the hardest bargain. Despite the annoyance,

🚶 LUXOR'S EAST BANK

The monumental temple complexes of Karnak and Luxor rank among the world's greatest ancient sites. In terms of artistic achievement, they are Egypt's finest; in scale, its most impressive.

Thebes, Luxor's famous ancestor, was one of the greatest cities of the ancient world. Serving as Egypt's capital during the Middle and New Kingdoms, (2040–1070BC), the city benefitted from the lavish patronage of some of Egypt's most powerful Pharaohs, among them Queen Hatshepsut, Sety I and Rameses II.

Then, as now, the city straddles both banks of the Nile. The east bank, where the sun rises, is the site of temples and palaces – the land of the living. The west, where the sun sinks,

has tombs and necropoli – the land of the dead (see p.139).

Covering around 40 hectares (100 acres), **Karnak Temple** (Shari' Al Karnak; daily 6am–5.30pm, summer to 6pm; charge) was Egypt's most important religious and intellectual centre for over 1,500 years. Every Pharaoh wished to leave his mark, building, embellishing, enlarging or restoring the complex's temples.

From the ticket office, the avenue of ram-headed sphinxes (representing Amun) lining the Processional Way leads to the unfinished First Pylon.

To the left of the large Forecourt is Sety II's shrine (1199–1193BC); to the right the beautiful Temple of Rameses III (1182–1151BC).

A colossus of Rameses II guards the Second Pylon. Next door, the Great Hypostyle Hall, begun by Amenhotep III (1386–1349BC), continued by Sety I (1291–1279BC) and finished by

Decorated wall, Karnak Temple

Tips

- Distance: 7.5km (5 miles)
- Time: a full day
- Head out as early as possible to take advantage of the relative cool and tour group-free peace of the morning.
- Karnak lies only around 2.5km (1½ miles) north of Luxor centre, so you can walk around the sites or take a calèche (from E£20–40 per hour; negotiate the price before jumping in) or a taxi (E£5–10).
- Wear a hat, apply sunscreen and drink lots of water.

his son Rameses II (1279–1212BC), is considered one of Ancient Egypt's architectural masterpieces. The hypostyle hall contains 134 columns spreading over 5,500 sq m (59,000 sq ft).

Beyond lie the obelisks of Thutmose III (1504–1450BC), and Queen Hatshepsut (1498–1483BC) and the Sanctuary of Amun.

Also dedicated to Amun, Mut and Khonsu, the **Temple of Luxor** (daily 6am–9pm, summer to 10pm; charge) was built principally by Amenhotep III (1390–1352BC) and Rameses II (1279–1212BC).

Until 1885, Luxor's temple lay buried under the modern town of Luxor. After relocating its inhabitants, just one building was allowed to remain: the **Mosque of Yusuf Abu Al Haggag**, perched on top of columns in the courtyard of the temple.

The 3km (2-mile)-long processional **Avenue of Sphinxes** is currently under restoration and will eventually link Luxor and Karnak again.

In front of the First Pylon, built by Rameses II, stands an obelisk and several colossi. Surrounded by two rows of columns and further colossi is the Court of Rameses II. The barque shrine to the right was built by Thutmose III.

Beyond the Second Pylon lies the **Processional Colonnade of Amenhotep III**, with walls decorated during Tutankhamun's reign. Nearby is the Great Sun Court of Amenhotep III, and behind, the Inner Sanctuary of Amun's Barge, built by Alexander the Great; to the left is Amenhotep III's Birth Room.

Near the Temple of Luxor lies the diminutive but imaginatively designed

The Temple of Luxor

Mummification Museum (tel: 095-238 1501; daily, winter 9am–1pm and 4–9pm, summer 9am–1pm and 5–10pm; charge).

Further along the Corniche, the outstanding **Luxor Museum** (tel: 095-238 0269; daily, winter 9am–9pm, summer 9am–1pm and 5–10pm) contains stunning ancient artefacts discovered in the area.

135

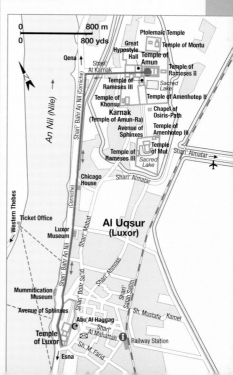

obelisks dedicated to the Theban gods, principally Amun, the most powerful of all. At the height of Theban power, the temple was known as Ipet-Isut, 'the most perfect of places'.

Try to visit Karnak at the beginning of the day as the complex opens, or towards the end of the day just before closing time in order to avoid the vast crowds. Children may appreciate the sound and light show as an alternative, especially on hot days when the overwhelming number of people and lack of shade can make it hard to appreciate the site.

Begun during the Old Kingdom, it became the national shrine from the 11th Dynasty, c.2134BC. The temple complex was expanded during the following centuries, with each of the Pharaohs adding their own ever more splendid shrines and monuments. The continued expansion makes Karnak an invaluable location

for contemporary scholars as they can witness the development of Egyptian architecture, design and construction simply by wandering through the complex.

The **Avenue of Sphinxes**, topped with ram's heads topped with sun discs, marks the route from the Nile to the temple entrance. This was used for ceremonies, when statues of the gods were carried to the river for journeys to the west bank, or to the Luxor Temple. The ram was the sacred animal of the god Amun.

The temple is entered through a colossal pylon, one of the most recent structures on the site and, though never actually finished, the largest to be built in Egypt during the Ptolemaic period.

The gateway leads to the **Great Court** , an immense temple court-yard. To the left is the diminutive **barque shrine of Sety II**, dedicated to

Karnak Temple

Detail of columns in the Hypostyle Hall

the Theban triad of Amun, Mut and Khons, and further along on the right is a larger structure, the **Temple of Rameses III**.

Behind a second smaller pylon, fronted by statues of Rameses II, is Karnak's masterpiece, the **Great Hypostyle Hall B**. Its 134 immense columns represent the papyrus forests of the sacred island from which all life sprang. This mighty work, the largest hall of any temple in the world, was started by Amenhotep III. Sety I (1291–1279BC) built most of it and decorated the northern half in fine raised reliefs, mostly of his battles in Syria and Lebanon, and Rameses II added the rest of the relief work, and placed the colossi of himself at the entrance.

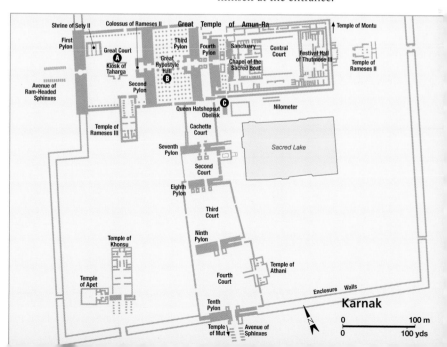

Karnak

Behind the third pylon is one of the two obelisks raised by Thutmose I, still standing. Beyond the fourth pylon is the oldest preserved part of the temple, constructed by Thutmose III around the splendid obelisks erected by his stepmother Hatshepsut. Her pink-granite **obelisk**  is the tallest in Egypt, measuring 30m (97ft) high. Originally the point was topped by a cap of pure gold, which reflected the sun and acted as a beacon.

South of the temple, the Sacred Lake was used for ceremonies. Today it forms the setting for the second part of the popular sound and light show. The giant granite scarab to the northwest of the lake is worth a look. Originally it was placed in front of the temple of Amenhotep III on the west bank. Egyptians claim it brings you luck if you walk three times counter-clockwise around the scarab before touching it and making a wish.

Luxor Temple floodlit at night

West Bank

The mountains of the west bank made for an evocative final resting place for the Pharaohs of the New Kingdom. Hoping to be near the god Amun-Ra (symbolised by the setting sun in the west) in the afterlife, they carved out elaborate tombs from the dusty and hot cliffs and built stunning tributes to honour both their own supreme power and the power of the immortal gods.

Crossing to the Colossi

There are no bridges crossing the Nile from the centre of Luxor. Instead, taxis must drive out of town to the north or south. To avoid this added time to the journey (and added expense), head to the ferry docks in Luxor to cross to the west bank. From here, a road leads to the low hills that hide the tombs. Taxis are plentiful from this point, or you can hire a guide with a horse or donkey *(see below)*.

The first major monuments you see on the west bank are two huge weathered stone sentinels standing watch over the plain, facing the Nile. Standing at a height of 21m (68ft), these are the **Colossi of Memnon** ❺, all that remains of what was once the largest mortuary temple, that of Amenhotep III.

The ticket office for the sites of the **west bank** (daily, summer 6am–6pm, winter 9am–5pm) is just past the Colossi of Memnon, at the crossroads. While you can sometimes buy tickets at individual sites, it's not always the case. To avoid disappointment, try to pick up as many tickets as possible at this point.

Colossi of Memnon

Where the road divides, the road to the left goes to the temple complex of **Madinat Habu** and the road straight ahead leads to the **Valley of the Queens** ❻. Queens and royal children were buried in a valley separate from their husbands and fathers. The renowned Theban Queen Nefertari, wife of Rameses II, has the most ornate tomb (No. 66), but the tomb is closed to preserve it.

Dayr Al Madinah

East of the Valley of the Queens are the remains of the town of the artisans, called **Dayr Al Madinah** ❼, home to generations of painters, masons and builders who worked on the royal tombs. Simple homes made of stone stand row upon row, and a wealth of everyday artefacts was found here, notably cooking utensils and work tools. Also excavated were simple tombs where the artisans buried their dead. Those of Sennedjem (No. 1) and Inherka (No. 359) are worth exploring.

Ramesseum and the Tombs of the Nobles

A right turn at the ticket office junction leads along the valley floor past the modern artisan village of Sheikh Abd Al Qurnah, known for its alabaster and onyx objects. The simple brick buildings faced with ochre-and-blue stucco, though larger than those at

Inside the Tombs of the Nobles

Dayr Al Medinah, are similar in style. Here, too, tombs and temples are scattered along the desert edge, the oldest being the **Ramesseum** ❽, the mortuary temple of Rameses II. Built to celebrate the cult of the dead king, the Ramesseum was decorated with majestic statues of the Pharaoh, and the pylon depicts him triumphant at the Battle of Qadesh, when he quashed the Hittites. Sadly, much of the temple lies in ruins.

On the opposite side of the road lie the **Tombs of the Nobles** ❾ and the site of the village of Qurnah. Stopping at the Tombs of the Nobles is worthwhile in order to examine some fine examples of 18th Dynasty artwork, painted when creativity had reached a peak in the empire. The paintings give a fascinating insight into the everyday life of important officials in the New Kingdom.

Qurnah is of more contemporary interest, bulldozed in 2010 following years of dispute between the government and villagers. Officially, it was said the villagers had to be moved in order to avoid water seepage into the nearby Tombs of the Nobles. Unofficially, ancient treasures had been plundered by Qurnah's residents for thousands of years and the government wanted to put an end to the lucrative black market trade in antiques and artefacts.

The Temple of Hatshepsut

Before turning away from the floodplain towards the Valley of the Kings, one of the most impressive Theban temples comes into view on the left, that of Queen Hatshepsut. A remarkable woman, she ruled as co-regent with her brother Thutmose II, and then her stepson Thutmose III. The **Temple of Hatshepsut** ❿ (Dayr Al Bahari), dedicated to the goddess Hathor, is a vast three-tiered structure, carved into the base of the rose-coloured hillside, facing out towards the river. Each level has a colonnade facade, and it is only as you approach that you appreciate its monumental scale.

A wide ramp, once lined with sphinxes and obelisks, on the Lower Terrace leads to a large courtyard at Middle Terrace level. A smaller ramp leads to the Upper Terrace. Behind the colonnades on the Middle Terrace, to the left of the ramp, carved scenes depict a trade mission bringing myrrh and incense from Egypt's neighbour Punt, present-day Somalia. A small temple dedicated to Hathor, to the left of the colonnade, has columns representing her with a cow's head,

The Temple of Hatshepsut

symbol of fertility. To the right, wall carvings relate scenes from the life of Queen Hatshepsut, including her divine birth: her mother is shown being attended by Heqat, the frog-headed midwife-god, watched over by Amun himself. A small temple is dedicated to the jackal-headed Anubis, god of the dead and of mummification.

Most of the carvings of Hatshepsut at the temple were destroyed, as Thutmose III removed all traces of her existence when he became Pharaoh after her death. But this does not spoil the formidable architectural achievement of the temple itself.

Carter's House

The latest addition to the wealth of sites on the West Bank is the restored home of explorer Howard Carter. Situated where the road to the Valley of the Kings meets the road to the Temple of Sety I, the **house** ⓫ (daily 6am–5pm; free) was reopened to the public in November 2009. The property features displays that chronicle Carter's life and work, and recreations of the home as it would have been during the time of the discovery of Tuthankamun's tomb.

The Valley of the Kings

The practice of burying the pharaohs away from the capital began c.1490BC when Thutmose I carved his tomb deep into the rock in a narrow valley in the dusty hills of the west bank. He felt that by moving his tomb away from the city, his tomb and treasures would be better protected from tomb

Decoration at the Temple of Hatshepsut

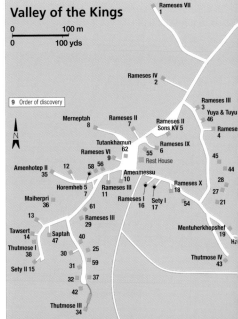

Valley of the Kings

0   100 m
0   100 yds

9   Order of discovery

N

Rameses VII 1

Rameses IV 2

Rameses III 3

Yuya & Tuyu 46

Merneptah 8

Rameses II 7

Rameses II Sons KV 5

Rameses IX 6

Ramese 4

45

44

Tutankhamun 62

Rameses VI 9

55

Rest House

Amenhotep II 35

12

58

56

Amenmessu 10

28

27

21

Horemheb 5 7

Rameses III 11

Rameses I 16

Sety I 17

Rameses X 18

54

Maiherpri 36

61

13

Rameses III 29

Mentuherkhopshef 19

Ha

Tawsert 14

Saptah 47

40

25

Thutmose I 38

30

59

Thutmose IV 43

Sety II 15

31

32

37

42

Thutmose III 34

Getting to and from the Valley of the Kings

raiders. Others followed his example, creating a veritable 'city of the dead', now with each tomb more elaborate or brightly decorated than the last.

A ticket for the **Valley of the Kings** ⑫ includes a visit to three tombs – to visit more requires the purchase of additional tickets at the entrance. To date, 63 tombs have been discovered in the valley, dating from *c*.1490–1100BC, but only a few of these are open to the public, on a rotational basis.

The **Tomb of Tutankhamun** (No. 62; additional charge) is certainly the best known, but perhaps surprisingly the most disappointing. The king died very young, and artisans had only just begun to dig the chambers. His tomb is therefore small and sparsely decorated. Nevertheless, the extraordinary discovery in 1922 of the tomb with its vast treasure trove virtually intact is what continues to draw visitors. Also, Tutankhamun's mummy is the only

Buying Alabaster

If touring the west bank by private taxi, then your taxi driver will probably mention a 'lovely alabaster factory offering good price'. The west bank is one of the few places in the world where top-quality alabaster is quarried, and many factories continue to fashion vases and trinkets out of the creamy stone using the same methods as practised thousands of years ago.

Hand-carved alabaster should have a rough, waxy feel and be translucent when held up to the light. It is also surprisingly light. Cheap alabaster found in the city souq is usually machine-finished, with a heavier weight and smooth surface.

Try to visit an alabaster factory independently (if possible), as taxi drivers and tour guides invariably get a percentage of the purchase price as an 'introduction' fee, which is then included as a mark-up in the final amount.

one still to be found *in situ* – many others are on display in the Egyptian Museum in Cairo *(see p.68)*.

Other tombs in the Valley of the Kings are much more instructive about Egyptian life, death and the afterlife. They are also considerably larger and more brilliantly decorated.

The **Tomb of Rameses VI** (No. 9) reopened in 2000 after major renovations. The long tomb shaft is decorated with superb frescoes illustrating chapters of the Book of the Dead – the 'manual' of rituals to be performed in order to reach the afterlife. A magnificent painting of Nut adorns the ceiling, showing the sky-goddess swallowing the sun each evening to give birth to it each morning, a cycle designed to revive the souls of the dead Pharaohs.

Exquisite frescoes in the **Tomb of Rameses III** (No. 11) depict scenes of boats sailing on the Nile, weapons of war including spears and shields, and two harpists singing the praises of Rameses before the deities – hence the temple's alternative name, 'Temple of the Harpists'.

Although the paintings in the **Tomb of Rameses IV** (No. 2) have deteriorated, the colours are still bright and impressive, and the huge red-granite sarcophagus is covered with texts and magical scenes. Graffiti on the walls dates back to 278BC.

One of the longest and most beautiful tombs in the valley is the **Tomb of Sety I** (No. 17; closed to the public), decorated with raised, painted relief scenes on the walls and vivid astronomical figures on the vaulted ceiling.

The deepest tomb (90 steps down) is the **Tomb of Amenhotep II** (No. 35). Several mummies were found here, leading to a much-improved understanding of the genealogy of the dynasties.

Tomb of Rameses VI

ACCOMMODATION

When it comes to value, no city in Egypt offers more than Luxor. A surfeit of rooms combined with an industry that is still recovering from the effects of the terrorist attacks of the 1990s mean that it's a buyer's market for accommodation. It is possible to enjoy a break in a three-star hotel with a swimming pool and Nile views (you might have to crane your head a bit) for as little as E£170 per night. Boutique hotels have only just arrived on the scene in Luxor – and the west bank is where to look for them. While you will be away from the city hubbub, the access to the historic sites of Thebes and the tranquillity will make up for any inconvenience.

East Bank

Emilio Hotel
Shari' Yusuf Hassan
Tel: 095-237 3570
This is a very good mid-range hotel with comfortable rooms equipped with all mod cons. There is a rooftop pool and sundeck. Book in advance in winter, as it is popular with tour groups. **$$$**

Luxor Sheraton Resort
Shari' Al Awameya
Tel: 095-237 4544
www.sheraton.com
Faded luxury hotel that nevertheless offers spacious rooms overlooking the Nile or bungalows in a shaded garden. The Italian restaurant in the garden, with a pond inhabited by pelicans and flamingos, is a popular place to eat in Luxor. **$$$$$**

Maritim Jolie Ville Luxor
Crocodile Island, 6km (4 miles) out of town
Tel: 095-227 4855
www.jolieville-hotels.com
The best hotel on this side of town occupies its own island. European-managed, with excellent service, good food and a relaxed atmosphere. The comfortable bungalow rooms are set in a splendid garden with its own swimming pool. Most have views of this beautiful stretch of the Nile. **$$$$$**

Mercure Hotel
Shari' An Nil
Tel: 095-237 4944
www.mercure.com
This hotel offers clean, modern rooms in a really central location. The shaded gardens are a very pleasant spot to cool down and have a drink. **$$$$**

Mina Palace
Shari' An Nil
Tel: 095-237 2074
Good-value and friendly hotel on the Corniche, with slightly run-down air-conditioned rooms and private bathrooms. Some corner rooms have balconies overlooking the Nile and Luxor Temple. **$$**

New Philippe
Shari' Dr Labib Al Habashi
Tel: 095-237 2284
Excellent three-star hotel offering spotless air-conditioned rooms, TV, fridge and some balconies. The pleasant roof terrace has a small pool and bar. Recommended, but book ahead, especially in winter. **$$$**

Saint Joseph
Shari' Khaled Ibn Al Wallid
Tel: 095-238 1707
Popular spot with budget-minded Brits, this nondescript hotel offers great value, clean rooms and a great rooftop pool with views of the (slightly obscured) Nile. **$$**

Sofitel Old Winter Palace

Sofitel Old Winter Palace
Shari' An Nil
Tel: 095-238 0422
www.sofitel.com
Old-style hotel, refurbished to some of its former splendour. The rooms in the old building have more character than the new garden wing, but service everywhere can be slow at times. **$$$$$**

Sonesta St George
Shari' An Nil
Tel: 095-238 2575
www.sonesta.com
One of the newer luxury options in Luxor; perhaps not the most handsome building, but offering good value for money, as well as good views over the Nile and all modern conveniences. **$$$$$**

West Bank
Al Gezira Hotel
Al Gezira, near the ferry landing
Tel: 095-231 0034
www.el-gezira.com
Very friendly budget hotel with views over the Nile and the east bank, and perfectly clean rooms. **$**

Al Moudira
Daba'iyya, 15km (9 miles) south of ticket office on the west bank
Tel: 012-325 1307
www.moudira.com
Palatial desert resort designed by French-Egyptian architect Olivier Sednaoui. The vast rooms are sumptuously decorated with locally made furniture, Ottoman fabrics and antiques. **$$$$$**

Amoun Al Gazira
Geziret Al Bairat (near the ferry landing, left at the Mobil petrol station)
Tel: 095-231 0912
Pleasant family-run hotel in a standard modern building overlooking the Theban hills and fertile countryside. The rooms are simply furnished, but spotless and comfortable, some with private bathroom. **$**

Marsam Hotel
Also known as Sheikh Ali's Hotel, opposite the Tombs of the Nobles
Tel: 095-237 2403
In 1881 the Abdul Rassoul family discovered the Dayr Al Bahari cache of royal mummies, now in the Cairo Museum. The late Sheikh Ali, a descendant of the family, established this simple hotel, now run by his son. The tranquil garden has views over green fields. **$**

El Nakhil
Geziret Al Bairat (near the ferry landing, 200m/yds from village mosque)
Tel: 095-231 3922
Well-run establishment with a nice adjoining restaurant. Particularly good for mobility-challenged tourists as it features ramps for wheelchairs and accessible bathrooms. **$**

Nour Al Gourna
Opposite the ticket office, Gurna
Tel: 095-231 1430
Delightful small hotel run by French woman Eléonore and her Egyptian partner, with large, simple but stylish rooms overlooking the sugar-cane fields or pretty palm grove; all have fans and mosquito nets. **$$$**

Pharaoh's
Near the ticket office on the west bank
Tel: 095-231 0702
One of very few mid-range hotels on this side of the Nile, with clean rooms, some with private bathrooms and a pleasant garden bar/restaurant. **$$**

RESTAURANTS

If you're arriving in Luxor following a cruise, then you'll find the city a delightful change of pace. This Nile-side town offers a bit of everything, including Japanese, Chinese and Italian eateries for those who want to break up a holiday filled with *fu'ul* and *ta'amiyah*. While quality levels can be up and down, prices are generally fair. Reservations are recommended at some of the more high-end or celebrated venues such as Sofra, as tour groups often fill the popular spots.

East Bank

The 1886
Old Winter Palace, Shari' An Nil
Tel: 095-238 0422
You won't feel like you're in Egypt any more at Luxor's leading French restaurant, complete with Venetian glass chandeliers and white-gloved waiters. **$$$**

Al-Kebabgy
New Lower Corniche opposite the Old Winter Palace
Tel: 095-238 6521
Good Egyptian fare including tagines, grilled meats and duck, all served with salads and rice. The stuffed pigeon is a speciality, and so is the duck with orange. Slightly more expensive than most, but great to sit out on the river. **$$$**

A Taste of India
Shari' St Joseph Hotel
Tel: 010-214 8079
Bangladeshi and North Indian favourites that have proven a hit with the British expat and tourist population. May be spicier than what you're used to, so ask them to tone it down if you can't take the heat. **$$**

El Tarboush
Old Winter Palace, Shari' An Nil
Tel: 095-238 0422
Elegant Egyptian restaurant serving great versions of classic dishes. The location in the garden of the Winter Palace adds to the allure. Jacket and tie required. **$$$**

Jewel of the Nile
Shari' Al Rawda Al Sherifa
Tel: 016-252 2394
Egyptian dishes meet English favourites such as cottage pie and apple crumble. All items on the menu are made using organic produce when available. **$$–$$$**

Miyako
Sonesta St George, Shari' An Nil
Tel: 095-238 2575
Luxor's one and only Japanese restaurant is pretty good considering the lack of competition. While the sushi and sashimi are tasty, it's the teppanyaki that stands out. **$$**

Oasis Café
Shari' Dr Labib Al Habashi
Tel: 095-237 2914
In Luxor you have your choice of cheesy budget restaurant or over-priced hotel eatery. The Oasis makes a pleasant change by bucking the trend. A sleek and sophisticated place for a light bite or coffee. **$**

Fresh bread

Negotiate with the driver before taking a ride in a calèche

Sofra
90 Shari' Muhammad Farid
Tel: 095-235 9752
Classic versions of Egyptian favourites served in a beautifully restored 1930s home with open terraces. The menu offers great descriptions that will make you want to try them out at home. **$$**

West Bank
Aux Trois Chacals
Opposite Colossi of Memnon
Tel: 010-192 3130
French home cooking, Italian coffee and Egyptian staples – the best of three nations in one home-style eatery. **$$–$$$**

Maratonga Cafeteria
In front of Medinat Habu, Kom Lolah
Tel: 095-231 0233
Light Egyptian bites and cold drinks – ideal after a morning of temple-hopping. **$**

Nur Al Qurna
Opposite the ticket office on the west bank
Tel: 095-231 1430
Peaceful restaurant set in a beautiful garden with long tables in the shade of palm trees. Good simple Egyptian fare; no alcohol. **$**

Tutankhamun
At the public ferry landing on the west bank
Tel: 095-231 0918
Simple but clean restaurant, serving very good food. Worth crossing the Nile for. **$**

NIGHTLIFE
If you're travelling to Luxor with a plan to hit the clubs, then you might want to rethink your destination. Nightlife in Luxor is very much of the 'cold beer and sunset' variety. People come here to visit the extraordinary tombs and temples and the best time to head out is first thing in the morning, so late nights tend to be avoided. There are still fun spots to be enjoyed though, including a number of expat-favoured pubs. But if it's late nights you're after, Hurghadah and the Sinai would be better points to head for.

Cocktail Sunset
Shari' An Nil, opposite Luxor Museum
Tel: 095-238 0524
After enjoying the sound and light show at Karnak, stop at this bar for a cocktail on your way back to the city centre.

King's Head Pub
Shari' Khalid Ibn Al Walid
Tel: 095-238 0489

Great selection of lager and wide-screen TVs are perfect for sports fans.

Nile Terrace
Shari' An Nil, in front of Old Winter Palace
Tel: 095-239 0422
Fancier than other drinking spots due to its location, this elegant terrace caters more to sippers than those who love a few pints.

ENTERTAINMENT

When it comes to entertainment in Luxor, most activity occurs in the larger resort hotels. Expect a selection of evenings catering to the demands of Western tourists, including karaoke nights, folklore shows, live music and belly dancing. While the performances are far from authentic (and the quality varies a good deal), they are a fun way to pass an evening if you don't mind a bit of kitsch.

Temple illuminated at night

Folklore Shows

Most of the large hotels on the east bank offer some sort of folklore or cultural show every evening. Schedules change weekly, so it is best to call ahead or drop in to see what's on. Some element of belly dancing and 'Sufi-style' spinning is often involved along with music performance, all of which is very much geared to tourists.

Sound and Light Shows

The sound and light show at Karnak is probably the most popular in Egypt. Some find it cheesy, others enjoy the new perspective it gives to the temples. English language performances at Karnak occur 3–4 times nightly and last about 90 minutes. Tel: 02-385 2880; www.soundandlight.com.eg.

SPORTS AND ACTIVITIES

The focus here is on history and architecture not keeping fit, but there are opportunities for active types. Cyclists should consider visiting the west bank by bike. *Details on what to expect can be found on page 150.* Joggers tend to congregate on the Corniche during the early hours of the morning before temperatures get too hot for comfort. And if you would like to cool down, many hotels offer access to their swimming pools for a small fee if you aren't staying with them. Try the Sonesta, Saint Joseph or Emilio, where prices range from E£20 to E£50 per person for a day of swimming.

TOURS

Luxor offers the most dynamic range of tour options in the country, and on the whole you get what you pay for, with safety usually being the first thing struck off the list when dealing with a cheap operator. The new tourist office next to the train station is a valuable resource to consult in order to determine fair prices and get recommendations. While organised tours do cost more than doing things independently, the amount of hassle tourists receive in Luxor makes booking through a tour operator appealing. Consider paying the extra pounds if you want to avoid haggling over taxi costs, endless requests for baksheesh and unexplained stops at alabaster and souvenir shops.

Take a balloon ride over Karnak

Balloon Rides
If you have the money, then a balloon ride is an amazing way to see the Valley of the Kings and west bank. Prices start from E£600 per person and go up, up and away depending on the number of extras you book (champagne, breakfast, roses, you name it). Recommended operators include:

Hod-Hod Soliman
Tel: 095-227 1116
hodhodoffice@yahoo.co.uk **(no website)**
Sindbad Balloons
Tel: 010-330 7708
www.sindbadballoons.com
Sky Cruise of Egypt
Shari' Khalid Ibn Al Walid
Tel: 095-237 6515

Bike Tours
Bikes can be rented from most hotels on both sides of the river, although it's not recommended in the summer when it's far too hot to cycle. While bike-riding on the east bank isn't advised due to the high traffic, the west bank offers ideal touring conditions with relatively flat runs between the sights. There are plenty of villages and tourist cafés lining the roads in case you need a break. Try to head off in the early morning or late afternoon to avoid the heat.

Calèche Tours
Calèche (horse-drawn carriage) operators will hiss at you from every corner in the east bank offering their transport services around the city. Typical trips will involve stops at Karnak, the Luxor Museum, Luxor Temple and the souq. Negotiate your trip cost in advance and be sure to tell the driver that stops and waiting time need to be included in the cost. Expect to spend about E£10 per hour. 👬

Felucca Tours
*Felucca*s from Aswan don't tend to come as far as Luxor due to the delays formed by the lock at Esna. Half-day trips are, however, a possibility, with Banana Island the most popular destination. A trip to Banana Island costs about E£10 per person or E£60 per boat if there are just a few of you going on the journey. The full journey takes about two hours round-trip, with many choosing to travel there about one hour before sunset to enjoy the natural light show in all its glory. To get the best rates, negotiate directly with the *felucca* captains. You'll find them punting for business along the Corniche.

Riding Tours
Donkey-, horse- and camel-riding tours of the west bank are best booked through one of the boys who greet tourists at the ferry docks on the west bank side of the river. There have been reports of tourists being denied assistance if they don't pay extra at the end of the tour and of single females receiving unwanted attention, so it's best to negotiate as part of a group if possible. Prices start from about E£30 per person, per hour. One recommended stable for horse, camel and donkey rides is:

Quest for Egyptian Adventure
QEA House, Gezira Al Bairat, West Bank
Tel: 010-294 3169
www.questforegyptianadventure.com

Tour operators
Most of Luxor's tour operators are clustered on the Corniche near Luxor Temple or the Old Winter Palace.

Eastmar Travel
Shari' An Nil, Old Winter Palace
Tel: 095-237 3513

Tour operator with multiple branches across the country. Specialist in Abydos and Dandarah day-trip excursions.

Nawas Tours
Near Luxor temple on the Corniche
Tel: 095-237 0701
Known as the budget operator. Expect larger groups and less flexible itineraries. A good choice for coach transfers to the Red Sea coast and ferry tickets onwards to the Sinai.

Thomas Cook
Shari' An Nil, next to Old Winter Palace
Tel: 095-237 2402
Thomas Cook was the first to bring tourists here, and he would now be amazed at the range of tours offered in his name.

FESTIVALS AND EVENTS

Luxor offers a few unique festivals and events in addition to the collection of high holidays on the Islamic calendar. By far the most important (and most fun) is the Mouled of Abu Al Haggag, a celebration of the city's patron saint that brings in merchants and visitors from across the country every year. Book your hotel room well in advance if you plan on joining the action.

January/February
Luxor Marathon
www.egyptianmarathon.com
International competitors are drawn to this annual race that passes by some of Thebes' most celebrated monuments, including the Colossi of Memnon and Ramesseum.

October
Pharaonic Wedding Festival
www.luxor.world-guides.com
Forty couples are invited to be married at Karnak Temple in traditional Egyptian style following ancient Pharaonic rituals. Between 15th and 20th of the month.

Dates change
Mouled of Abu Al Haggag
Throughout the east bank, with special focus on Abu Al Haggag Mosque in Luxor Temple. Held two weeks before the start of Ramadan, this two-day street fair honours the patron saint of the city with parties, dancing, music and special foods.

Children accompany Luxor marathon runners

Upper Egypt

The lush views of cane and cotton fade away between Luxor and Aswan as desert encroaches. To the south, Nubia awaits – once an empire, now covered by Lake Nasser following the completion of the Aswan High Dam. You can explore by land or take a cruise along the Nile just as the Egyptians did centuries ago; the riverbanks are peppered with Ptolemaic temples.

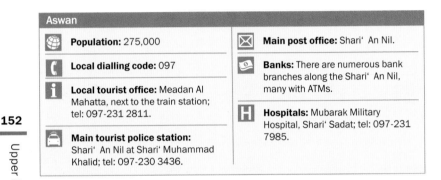

Aswan

Population: 275,000

Local dialling code: 097

Local tourist office: Meadan Al Mahatta, next to the train station; tel: 097-231 2811.

Main tourist police station: Shari' An Nil at Shari' Muhammad Khalid; tel: 097-230 3436.

Main post office: Shari' An Nil.

Banks: There are numerous bank branches along the Shari' An Nil, many with ATMs.

Hospitals: Mubarak Military Hospital, Shari' Sadat; tel: 097-231 7985.

For Nile cruise passengers, the stretch of the river lying between Luxor and Aswan is home for the bulk of their trip. Sunset over the west bank while sipping a gin and tonic, splashing children waving to you as they dip in the Nile's fast-flowing waters, farmers taking a break from their harvest – these are just some of the images of this quiet, pastoral landscape.

But this part of the Nile is more than just a pleasant place for a cruise; it's also home to three important temples built along the caravan routes from Nubia to ancient Thebes. Aswan itself is the most important city in the region and retains a certain sleepiness that belies its size. For many visitors, Aswan marks a

delightful change away from the hard-sell, hard-nosed atmosphere found in Egypt's other main cities, arguably due to the Nubian influence found in the region. Nubians are known for their warm welcome and charm, despite the harsh hand dealt to their people. For Nubia, as an area, no longer technically exists, covered by the man-made lake formed following the completion of the Aswan High Dam in 1970.

Treasures such as the great Temple at Abu Simbel and Philae were threatened by this modern-day piece of engineering, as it was clear that the waters formed by the man-made reservoir would quickly submerge the structures. It was only through the intervention of Unesco that the temples were dismantled piece by piece and relocated to high ground away from the lake's shoreline. However, around 800,000 Nubians lost their land, much of their culture and their ancestral homes.

Luxor to Aswan

The Nile Valley begins to change south of Luxor as the area gets more arid and desert-like. Sand begins to creep its way to the river shores, interspersed with small villages dotted with palm trees. This region is Egypt at its most relaxed, enjoyable either seen from the deck of a cruise-ship or *felucca* or as part of a taxi transfer between the two cities, stopping at any of three major temples along the way.

Painted relief in the Temple of Knum, Esna.

Life on the road

Esna

Lying 50km (30 miles) south of Luxor on the west bank of the Nile, is the small town of Esna, built over the ruins of the **Temple of Khnum**  (daily, winter 7am–4pm, summer 7am–5pm; charge). While Esna is the largest town between Aswan and Luxor, its days of prominence are long gone and most of the contemporary buildings are largely uninspiring. The temple, however, was one of the most important places of worship in Upper Egypt, notable for its Roman-era Pronaos, which contains 24 columns and a number of high-quality reliefs and inscriptions showing scenes of Roman emperors depicted as Egyptian Pharoahs.

Edfu

A further 20km (12 miles) south is the market town of **Edfu** ❷, home to the best-preserved temple in Egypt. The town is almost always included as a stop for *felucca* and cruise-ship passengers. Multiple calèches wait by the docks to transport visitors the short journey up to the temple. On hot days, this is a good option.

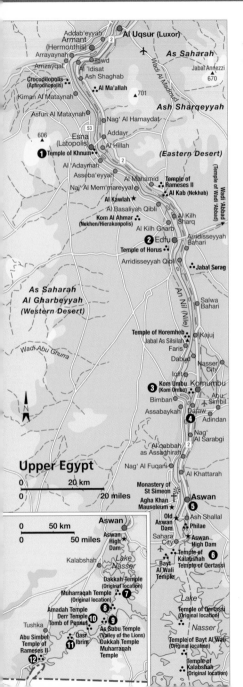

The **Temple of Horus** (daily, winter 7am–4pm, summer 7am–5pm; charge) lay buried beneath the town until the 1860s, which explains its near-perfect conditon, its great pylon, exterior walls, courts, halls and sanctuary all still intact. It was dedicated to Horus because of an ancient belief that the structure stood on the location where the god Horus defeated Seth in a battle to avenge the murder of his father Osiris.

The outer walls tell the story of the temple, with hieroglyphs recording that construction began in 237BC during the reign of Ptolemy II Euergetes, continuing until decoration of the outer walls was finished in 57BC. The dates confirm that the temple was one of the last to be built on a grand scale honouring the ancient gods.

Guarding the First Pylon and in the courtyard are the two famous and beautiful granite statues of Horus in his falcon form. The carvings inside the walls and up the staircase illustrate the Festival of the Beautiful Meeting, in which the statue of Horus was carried to Hathor's temple in Dandarah. The festivities took place in the Festival Hall, and every year the statue of Horus was carried up to the roof to be revitalised by the sun. The birth house outside the temple has fine carvings of Horus' divine birth and of Isis suckling her son, as well as the Ptolemaic ruler.

Kom Ombo

Around 40km (24 miles) north of Aswan, the river now takes a turn to the west, and standing on a promontory on the eastern bank is **Kom**

Statue of Horus, Edfu

Ombo (daily, Oct–May 7am–4pm, June–Sept 7am–5pm; charge). The temple is unique in that it is dedicated to not one but two gods – Horus and Sobek (the local crocodile god).

The temple is divided down the middle, with the falcon-headed god Horus worshipped to the north and Sobek to the south. It is believed that temple priests kept crocodiles on site for devotees to worship.

South of the temple wall, near the entrance, is a small shrine to Hathor, in which are stored some mummified crocodiles found in a sacred animal necropolis nearby. A double entrance leads into the inner Hypostyle Hall with its blooming floral columns and vulture-covered ceiling, and on into

Upper Egypt Transport

You are not allowed to travel from Aswan to Abu Simbel under your own steam; you have to join a convoy, which departs twice daily (4.30am and 11am). *For more on convoys, see p.171.*

 Airport: Located 25km (15½ miles) southwest of Aswan. The easiest way to get to Abu Simbel from Aswan is by plane – the journey takes about 40 minutes. Flights get booked up quickly, so book in advance.

 Trains: The train station is at Meadan Al Mahatta, Aswan; tel: 097-231 4754.
Trains to and from Cairo: Abela Egypt Sleeping Train; tel: 097-230 2124; www.sleepingtrains.com.

 Buses: The bus station is situated 3.5km (2 miles) north of Meadan Al Mahatta, Aswan; however, there are currently no departures available for tourists going northbound to Luxor.

 Ferries: *Feluccas* and cruise ships are available northbound. Passage can be negotiated with the captain or ship manager directly, or contact one of the tour operators (*see p.176*). One passenger ferry departs each week from Aswan for Wadi Halfa in the Sudan. Tickets are available from the Nile River Valley Transport Corporation office behind the tourist police station; tel: 097-303 348.

 Car hire: Renting a car is not advised in Aswan, as security restrictions prevent tourists from travelling outside city limits without police support.

 Taxis: All drivers are independent and can be hailed from the street.

two symmetrical sanctuaries. Take a look at the seven chapels behind the sanctuaries; they have interesting wall carvings on the outer walls, including depictions of medical instruments used to perform surgery and dental work, evidence of Ancient Egypt's advanced medical knowledge. Outside, in the centre of the northern wall is a depiction of Marcus Aurelius. Across the court is a birth house, with reliefs of Ptolemy VIII Euergetes' divine birth, and a small sacred lake where crocodiles were most probably raised.

A small new museum, the **Sobek Museum** (same opening times as temple), displays objects found in the area and many crocodile mummies.

Daraw, the camel market

The dusty town of **Daraw** ❹ on the road from Kom Ombo to Aswan is home to one of Egypt's largest camel markets (Souq Al Jemal). Although

Daraw camel market

this is a daily event, the best times to come are on Sunday or Tuesday mornings (6.30am–2pm), when there are hundreds of camels. Try to visit the market early, before 10.30am, when the trading is at its liveliest. Many herdsmen and camels walk all the way from Sudan along the Forty Days Road that crosses the desert to a place north of Abu Simbel. From there, they are driven to Daraw where they are sold, then sometimes driven to Birqash in Cairo.

Aswan

Egypt's southernmost city owes its existence to trade. Perched at the border between ancient Nubia and the Egyptian empire, **Aswan** ❺ has long been a market town and an important stop for many African traders heading into Egypt and beyond. Following the demise of the Egyptian empire, Aswan lost much of its importance, only to return to its former prestige as tourists discover its relaxed charm. As the unofficial headquarters of the relocated Nubian people, Aswan features a unique cultural mix of Arabic and Nubian influences and arguably the best souq outside Cairo.

Elephantine Island

The origins of Aswan lie not on the east bank where the bulk of the city now sits, but to the original settlements on **Elephantine Island** ❹. The Ancient Egyptians believed this was the source of the Nile, from where it flowed both north and south. At the southern tip of the island lie the remains of the ancient settlement of Yebu, home to the small (and dusty) **Aswan Museum** (daily, winter

Ruins of Yebu, Elephantine Island

8am–5pm, summer 8.30am–6pm; charge), filled with artefacts collected from the site. The modern annexe houses an eclectic collection of exhibits relating to life on ancient Elephantine, ranging from mummies and sarcophagi to jewellery and weapons, dating from pre-Dynastic times to late Roman.

Exploring Yebu

Spread around the back of the Aswan Museum are the impressive and atmospheric remains of Aswan's first settlement, the ancient town of **Yebu** (same ticket and opening times as museum). The steep, rock-strewn paths and lack of any gates or safety fences make exploring the site difficult if you have children in tow. Sights of note include the **Temple of Khnum**, on the tip of the island, the reconstructed 18th-Dynasty **Satet Temple**, and the **Nilometers B**. From the Old Kingdom onwards a strict watch was kept on the rise and fall of the Nile, and its measurement was one of the important functions of the resident governor of Elephantine, and later Aswan, to assist farmers and tax collectors who could anticipate

Animalia

While on Elephantine Island, try to visit Animalia, home to Nubian guide Muhammad Sobhy. Housing a small museum and fixed-price shop selling Nubian crafts, Animalia is a great one-stop-shop for those looking for a bit of culture with their Coca-Cola.

Muhammad is full of fascinating details about Nubian life and culture, and will give you a personal tour of the museum for around E£10. Do make sure you have the right Muhammad by going inside the café, as fake guides have been known to hover around the bar, posing as Muhammad to capitalise on his reputation. **Animalia**, Main path, Siou; www.animalia-eg.com; tel: 097-231 4152. Hours vary according to the season and Muhammad's availability.

Booking a *Felucca*

Securing a *felucca* for a day trip or extended cruise is relatively easy – just head to the Corniche and wait for a captain to approach offering his services. To get an idea of current prices, the tourist office next to the train station can tell you the going rate. At time of press, the typical cost was about E£100–120 for a three- to four-hour cruise per boat or E£180 per person for a three-day cruise to Edfu, including meals for a minimum of six passengers.

the success of the annual crop based on the water level.

Kitchener's Island

From Elephantine Island, it's a quick sail onwards to **Kitchener's Island** ⓒ, home to the Botanical Garden (daily 8am–sunset; charge; 🏛). In return for his military achievements in Sudan, Consul-General Kitchener was presented with this island, for which he collected exotic plants and seeds from across the world. Today, it is a popular location for couples and families – especially on hot days, when the cool and inviting shade of the trees beckons to Aswan's middle classes.

The west bank

Where Aswan and the east bank are bustling and filled with activity, the west bank remains peaceful and untouched. Opposite the town centre, dug into the hillside, are the **Tombs of the Nobles** ⓓ (daily 8am–4pm, summer to 5pm; charge), accessible via a steep flight of steps.

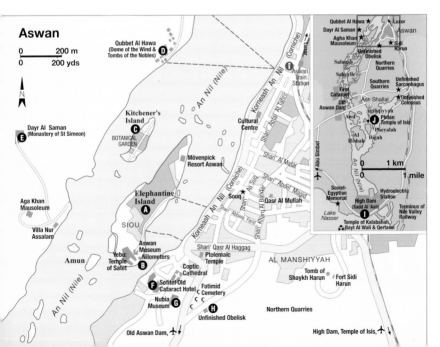

Belonging to Aswan's former Pharaonic rulers, nobles and dignitaries, most of the rock tombs date from the Old and Middle Kingdoms, although those nearest the river are Roman. Dozens dot the hillside, but just five are currently open. They depict telling scenes of everyday life, but the views alone over Aswan and the Nile are worth the steep climb.

Further inland is the **Dayr Al Saman** Ⓔ (Monastery of St Simeon; daily 7am–4pm; charge). The 6th-century monastery once provided for about 300 monks, and though it lies in ruins in the desert sands it is still an impressive sight.

The last west bank site is the **Aga Khan Mausoleum** (closed to the public), the final resting place of the Aga Khan III, distinguished leader of the Ismaili sect of Islam. The Aga Khan loved Aswan for its tranquillity and timeless quality, and had his

Tombs of the Nobles

domed mausoleum built high up on the bluffs overlooking the river, from where there are fabulous views over the city of Aswan.

Upper Egypt

Felucca captain

⚑ ASWAN AND ISLANDS

Palpably hotter than towns further north and home to the Nubian people, Aswan feels like Africa at last. Attractions include a ruined Christian monastery, a Pharaonic-era city, a garden, museum and souq.

In Pharaonic times, Aswan played a vital military and commercial role. Marking Egypt's southern boundary, it served as a launching pad for major military expeditions, a vital trade hub, and an important source of granite.

Lying on the west bank, the **Monastery of St Simeon** (Dayr Al Saman; daily, winter 8am–4pm, summer 7am–5pm; charge) dates from the 10th century. For 200 years it served as a base for the conversion of the pagan populace, until destroyed by Salah Addin in the 12th century.

Though just ruins remain, it's impressive for its size, its fortress-like appearance and dramatic desert setting.

Lying southwards is the single-domed **Aga Khan Mausoleum** (closed to visits). The Ismaili's sect 48th imam loved to winter at Aswan with his wife, until his death in 1957. Both are buried here. Close by lies their former winter villa.

Honeycombing the hillside opposite the west bank's ferry terminal are the **Tombs of the Nobles** (daily 8am–4pm, summer until 5pm; charge) which date to the Old and Middle Kingdoms. Just five are open. The interiors have been badly damaged, but in a few places the original colours remain. Though small

Aga Khan Mausoleum

Tips

- Distance: 15km (9 miles), not including boat trips
- Time: a full day
- Start early to avoid the heat, and bring a hat, sunscreen and lots of water.
- The 30–40-minute monastery trek by foot or camel can be pre-arranged through your hotel.
- Public ferries connect the east bank (opposite the Egyptair office) to the Tomb of the Nobles on the west bank, as well as to Elephantine Island.
- Another ferry departs from the other side of Elephantine Island to the centre of Aswan town, opposite the Telephone Central office.

and crude compared to the tombs of Luxor's Valley of the Kings, they're still interesting, and also afford great views over the river.

On the east bank, Aswan's **Nubia Museum** (tel: 097-231 9111; daily 9am–9pm; charge) provides a excellent introduction to Nubian history, art and culture.

On Elephantine Island, a 19th-century colonial villa (with a modern annexe) houses the **Aswan Museum** (tel: 097-230 2066; daily, winter 8am–5pm, summer 8.30am–6pm; charge) which contains an eclectic but dusty collection of artefacts found in and around Aswan.

Below the museum at the water's edge are two **Nilometers** (same ticket as museum), one dating to the 6th century BC, the other to Ptolemaic times. Behind the museum lie the remains of Aswan's first settlement, the ancient town of **Yebu** (same ticket and opening hours as museum) founded around 3100BC. Though little excavated, it's an interesting place to wander. Highlights include two temples, a finely carved granite 'throne', a Graeco-Roman necropolis of Sacred Rams, and a small step pyramid attributed to Sneferu (2613–2589 BC).

A path leading towards the Mövenpick Hotel takes you through some traditional **Nubian villages** where you may be invited for tea. The Mövenpick's ferry sails to the landing opposite.

Charter a *felucca* (from E£30 per hour) and sail west to Kitchener's Island, home to the cool and peaceful **Aswan Botanical Garden** (tel: 097-

Monastery of St Simeon

910 1838; daily 7am–5pm, summer to 6pm; charge). The small island was presented to Lord Kitchener in the 1890s in return for services in Sudan. A keen amateur botanist, Kitchener planted the island with an eclectic collection of over 400 species (many labelled), originating from India, Africa and Southeast Asia.

Back on the east bank, Aswan's souq runs along and just off Shari' As Suq and sells everything from spices and herbs to Nubian-made baskets, musical instruments, CDs of Nubian music and local charms.

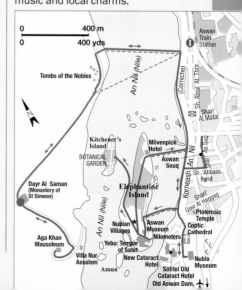

The east bank

Running the length of the city centre, the riverside **Corniche** (Shariʻ An Nil) is the place to stroll and be seen in Aswan. This busy road is lined with floating restaurants and docked cruise ships on one side and banks and budget hotels on the other.

At its southern end you will find the **Old Cataract Hotel ❺**, undergoing a complete revamp at the time of writing but harking back to the days of Edwardian elegance. It has seen such illustrious guests as Winston Churchill and Agatha Christie, who wrote her thriller *Death on the Nile* while staying here.

On the main road to the south, only a few minutes' walk from the hotel, is the imposing **Nubia Museum ❻** (daily, winter 9am–1pm and 5–9pm, summer 10am–1pm and 6–10pm; charge), inaugurated in 1997 and currently undergoing

some refurbishment. With a research facility and library dedicated to promoting Nubian traditions such as dance and music, it also houses finds rescued from several archaeological sites that were subsequently flooded by the waters of Lake Nasser. Behind the museum it's worth visiting the **Fatimid Cemetery**, a burial ground dating from the Tulunid period that is filled with beautiful domed tombs.

The Unfinished Obelisk

On the other side of the road, across from the cemetery, is one of Aswan's many quarries where the **Unfinished Obelisk ❼** (daily, winter 7am–4pm, summer 7am–5pm; charge) can still be seen, attached to the bedrock. The 42m (137 ft) long obelisk would have been the single heaviest piece of stone in Ancient Egypt had the workers not discovered a crack while hewing it out of the rock.

Old Cataract Hotel

Aswan's Souq

Parallel to the Nile is the long stretch of Aswan's souq which, despite all the tourists, still retains a strong African flavour. This is a good place to pick up souvenirs and crafts. The little shops sell cotton, *karkadeh* (hibiscus flowers for infusion, the local drink here), Nubian baskets, dates, ebony cane and crocheted skullcaps.

But for the best deals, head straight to the spice merchants. Avoid the saffron (which is usually safflower) and instead haggle for cumin, pepper and black henna, a natural dye used to create stunning temporary tattoo designs by Nubian women.

Part of the Aswan Dam

The Aswan Dam

The taming of the Nile's unpredictable moods and the year-round conservation of its waters have been at the core of Egypt's history and civilisation since its earliest beginnings. In primeval times, the unharnessed flood roared down annually from the Ethiopian highlands, swamping the valley for three months before it receded, leaving behind thousands of tonnes of fertile silt. This accumulated over the millennia, creating the 10m (33ft) thick blanket of soil which constitutes the Nile Valley and the Delta.

The flood, however, was unreliable and occasionally failed to appear, causing severe drought and hardship. In 1952, Nasser's new post-revolutionary government embarked on the construction of a high dam that would generate enough electricity for industrial and rural electrification, and provide enough water to bring millions of new acres under cultivation. During its construction, 30,000 workers laboured on the dam, eventually completing it in 1972 and ending thousands of years of annual flooding. The **Aswan High Dam ①** straddles the Nile 13km (8 miles) south of Aswan and is often included as part of an organised tour to the Unfinished Obelisk and Abu Simbel (*see p.170*).

Lake Nasser

Formed following the completion of the Aswan High Dam in 1972, Lake Nasser stretches for 800km (500 miles), deep into Sudan, submerging many ancient temples and monuments as well as most of lands that housed the Nubian people. Today, the lake is a popular destination for sport fishermen, drawn by the Nile perch, and as an alternative cruise location for those looking to visit some of the lakeside temples that are difficult to reach overland.

Philae

During the Ptolemaic period the cult of Isis moved 8km (5 miles) south of Aswan to the **Temple of Isis ❶** (daily, winter 7am–4pm, summer 7am–5pm; charge plus boat charge) near Bigah Island, identified with the burial place of Osiris. On Philae, a particularly beautiful temple was dedicated to Isis and became the most important shrine in Egypt for the next 700 years.

The construction of the first Aswan Dam in 1902 resulted in the partial submersion of Philae for eight months of the year. When the High Dam was built between 1960 and 1971, Philae was threatened with total and permanent immersion, and an international effort was launched to save it. A 1.6km (1-mile) long coffer-dam was constructed around the island, and all the water within was pumped out. Stone by stone the temples were dismantled and transported to nearby Agiliqiyyah Island, which had been levelled and remodelled so that the temple could be reconstructed on the site.

Visiting Philae

Small boats take tourists from the boat landing at Shellal in Aswan to Agiliqiyyah Island, where stairs lead from the landing to the oldest part of the Philae complex: the **Kiosk of Nectanebo I** (30th Dynasty) and the **Outer Temple Court**, flanked on both sides by colonnades. The entrance to the Temple of Isis is marked by the 18m (60ft) high towers of the First Pylon, where reliefs show the Ptolemies in traditional Pharaonic poses. To the left of the Central Court is the **Birth House of Ptolemy IV** (221–205BC), with fine reliefs depicting the god Horus rising from the marshes. A stairway inside the Inner

Cruise ships on Lake Nasser

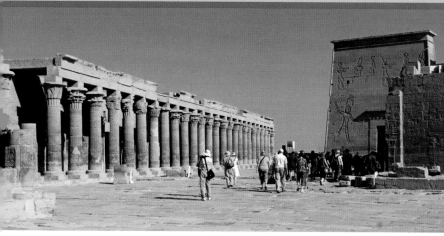

Temple of Isis, Philae

Sanctuary of Isis leads to the Osiris Chambers, decorated with exquisite reliefs illustrating the Osiris myth. Inside the sanctuary, reliefs show Isis suckling her son Horus as well as the young Pharaoh.

The most photographed part of the temple is probably Trajan's

Kiosk, (c. AD100), displaying floral columns and reliefs of the Roman Emperor Trajan making offerings to Isis and Osiris.

The Temple of Kalabshah

For most of the year, the only way to get to the **Temple of Kalabshah** ❻ (daily 8am–4pm; charge) is by boat, but sometimes, when the water is low, it can be reached via a 10-minute walk from Aswan's boatyard.

The original site of Kalabshah, ancient Talmis, was 50km (31 miles) further up the Nile, and today the temple lies somewhat forlorn in the shadow of the High Dam, where it was relocated in 1970. The temple, dedicated to the Nubian fertility god Marul (Mandulis to the Greeks), was built around 30BC during the reign of Emperor Augustus, over an older Ptolemaic temple. During the Christian era it was used as a church. An impressive stoneway leads up to the First Pylon. The colonnaded court and Pronaos beyond the pylon have

---

Nubian Specialities

Traditionally, Nubian meals are served on the ground. Diners kneel on woven mats and all dishes are covered with woven food coverings known as *kutas*. Favoured ingredients and dishes to look out for while in Upper Egypt include:

- *Fetir* – *kissira* (see below) that has been covered in burnt sugar and cooked in oil.
- *Gurusa* – a chapatti-like pancake.
- *Kissira* – a white, paper-like bread that uses *lagin* (a pounded maize beaten until it forms a smooth paste).
- *Lebere* – *kissira* left in the sun until it dries out and forms small flakes.
- *Mongolobo* – a cake made from *lagin*.

Wadi As Sabu

varied floral capitals, clearly suggesting a garden. Inside the sanctuary, the emperor is seen in the company of the entire Egyptian pantheon. A stairway leads to the roof, with magnificent views over Lake Nasser.

Dakkah, Muharraqah and Wadi As Sabu

The rest of the temples from here to Abu Simbel are difficult to reach due to the convoy system in place (*see p.171*) and are more commonly included as part of Lake Nasser cruise itineraries.

The most prominent temples are a collection of three that lie on the western shore, about 140km (87 miles) south of Aswan – Dakkah, Maharraqah and Wadi As Sabu.

Dakkah ❼ was begun 40km (25 miles) north of its present site by the 3rd-century local king Argamani, reusing stones from earlier buildings. Despite extensive additions under the Ptolemies and the Roman Emperor Augustus, the temple was never finished, as is apparent from the lack of decoration on parts of the pylon.

The nearby temple of **Muharraqah** ❽ originally stood 30km (18 miles) north of its present site at the frontier marker of Ptolemaic Egypt. It is a later building than Dakkah, constructed in the Roman period and dedicated to Isis and Serapis.

Wadi As Sabu ❾ (the Valley of Lions) is the most complete of this group. The temple, originally located 2km (1¼ miles) further southwest, takes its name from an avenue of sphinxes that lead to a temple built by the viceroy of Kush for Rameses II. Colossal figures of the Pharaoh stand at the entrance and line pillars in the court. The outer areas of the temple were built of sandstone, but the vestibule, antechamber and sanctuary were carved out of the rock.

Amadah trio

Forty kilometres (25 miles) south of Wadi As Sabu, three monuments now stand near the original west bank site of the Temple of Amadah. The small 18th Dynasty **Amadah Temple**  was built a couple of kilometres away from its present site by Thutmose III and Amenhotep II. The illustrations of planning and building the temple (in the innermost left-hand chapel) are worth finding. The nearby rock-cut **Temple of Derr** was moved 11km (7 miles) north to its present site. Like the Wadi As Sabu temple, it was dedicated to Amun-Ra and Ra-Horakhty; its figures were badly damaged by Christians using it as a church. Also here is the tomb of Pennut, a local governor (1141–1133BC), moved from Annoabah, 40km (25 miles) south.

Qasr Ibrim

About 15km (9 miles) north of Abu Simbel is **Qasr Ibrim** ⓫. Now an island, before the flooding it was situated on the eastern bank where three massive peaks of rock rose from the river. Crowning the middle peak was a ruined town, whose fortress commanded the valley for miles around in all directions.

This *qasr* (castle) is all that emerges above the level of the lake today, but it must have been a striking landmark in Pharaonic times when the first temple-fortress was built. Excavations have revealed inscriptions dating from the 16th century BC, and there are remains of a significant Byzantine cathedral.

It is known that the Romans, Salah Addin, the Ottoman Emperor Selim and Muhammad Ali all stationed garrisons here.

Relief in Amadah Temple

★ HIEROGLYPHS

Until the discovery of the Rosetta Stone in the early 19th century, the pictorial script on the walls of Ancient Egypt's temples was completely indecipherable. Decoding the hieroglyphs (meaning 'sacred carvings' in Greek) has enabled us to unlock the secrets of Egypt's history. The earliest messages, found at Abydos, date to 3250BC, making hieroglyphs man's oldest form of written communication.

While other empires from a similar time period may have reached equivalent heights, their glories have faded due to the lack of any written record of their success. Hieroglyphs not only provide the link needed to reveal Egypt's history; they also provided the means by which the state took shape: they were used by scribes working on the king's behalf to collect taxes and organise workforces. As very few people were literate, scribes were considered part of society's elite.

According to legend, hieroglyphs were given to man by Thoth, the ibis-headed god of scribes and learning. The hieroglyphs carved into temple walls were considered to be the words of the gods, conveyed through the scribes for permanent admiration. The small figures of animals, birds and symbols were thought to impart divine power. In fact, some signs were considered so powerful that they were

Interior of Temple of Derr, Aswan

separated when carved to ensure that they didn't come to life.

Over 6,000 hieroglyphs were eventually developed in the three and a half thousand years they were in use. The script is phonetic, and each symbol represents a different sound. For instance, the owl – a common sight and therefore sound in the Egyptian language – represented 'm', and the zigzag water sign 'n'.

Reading hieroglyphs

Hieroglyphs can be read horizontally or vertically, and there are no vowels, making it difficult to determine grammar. The symbols can also be read right to left or left to right, depending on the direction the characters are facing. But most writing chronicles the names of gods or Pharaohs, so repetition is common. Crack one name and many others will be revealed by using the hieroglyphs in the words you have deciphered to sound out the rest.

Tradition stated that Pharaohs had five names; however, only the two most important ones would be surrounded by a cartouche – an oval-shaped ring with a 'handle' on one side. The cartouche served to protect the Pharaoh named inside from evil as the ancients believed that reading and speaking the name of a dead Pharaoh could make him live again in the afterlife.

Names were as important to an individual's existence as their soul *(ka)*. For translators, cartouches also serve as an instant flag that the words contain the name of a Pharaoh.

Hieroglyphs on the obelisk, Temple of Luxor

Deciphering hieroglyphs at Philae's temple

Abu Simbel

The temples at **Abu Simbel** ⑫ have been marvels of architectural achievement not once, but twice. The first time they struck awe was when they were hewn into the cliffs of the Nile Valley under the orders of Rameses II. The second occurred millennia later when a Unesco-led operation carved the temples from the cliffs piece by piece and rebuilt the structures on higher ground, in order to prevent them being flooded by the waters of Lake Nasser when the Aswan Dam was created.

Most people take the regular flights from Aswan to Abu Simbel, which take around 50 minutes. For security reasons, travellers going overland to Abu Simbel are still made to travel in convoys of organised tours *(see box, opposite)*.

The Temple of Rameses II

The facade of the **Temple of Rameses II** (daily, winter 6am–5pm, summer 6am–6pm; charge for each temple) is one of the most enduring images of Egypt. The four monumental colossi of Rameses II that frame the entrance stand 20m (65ft) high and face the rising sun, to be infused with the energy of the sun-god each day. The Pharaoh is seated, imperturbable, wearing the double crown signifying his control over both Upper and Lower Egypt. At his feet are his family, represented as diminutive figures. Bas-reliefs carved on the Pharaoh's thrones depict the Nile gods. Between the two central colossi is an alcove with a small statue to Ra-Horakhty (Ra the sun-god combined with Horus), with whom Rameses shares the temple.

Statue of Rameses II at his temple at Abu Simbel

Temple of Nefertari, Abu Simbel

This temple has no forecourt, so you enter directly into the Hypostyle Hall. Carvings on the columns show Rameses (in the form of Osiris) making offerings to the gods, and the walls show scenes from his military campaigns, returning in triumph with hundreds of Hittite prisoners. The north side is almost entirely devoted to the most important victory of his reign, the Battle of Qadesh, in which the young Pharaoh overcame the Hittites near the Syrian town of Qadesh.

The Temple of Nefertari

Near the temple of Rameses II is the smaller **Temple of Nefertari**, his beloved wife. She, too, is deified, and in a facade of six colossi 11.5m (38ft) high, she stands at equal height to her husband – a rare honour for a consort in Egypt. However, of the six statues only two are of Nefertari; the other four are consecrated to Rameses, maintaining his position of superiority. Within the sanctuary

dedicated to Hathor is a room where Rameses and Nefertari made offerings to the gods, as well as carvings showing the Pharaoh himself worshipping his deified wife.

The Convoy System

Following terrorism events in the 1990s, the Egyptian government adoped a policy of herding all tourists onto dedicated convoys of tour buses accompanied by police or military protection when travelling between major cities. Thankfully, the security threat has diminished and most of the convoys have been removed, with one exception. The convoy to Abu Simbel from Aswan still stands, making private overland visits to the temples between Abu Simbel and Aswan near-impossible unless you have pockets deep enough to pay for private police protection. The convoy departs twice daily at 4.30am and 11am, returning two hours after it arrives in Abu Simbel.

ACCOMMODATION

Aswan has a wide range of accommodation options to suit the many international visitors who arrive each year. Turnover of rooms in the town is higher than average simply because many people stay here for just a day or two before embarking on a cruise. Although finding a room shouldn't be a problem, standards may

Accommodation Price Categories

Prices are for one night's accommodation in a standard double room in low season.

$ = below E£200
$$ = E£200–E£450
$$$ = E£450–E£750
$$$$ = E£750–E£1,250
$$$$$ = over E£1,250

be low, as many properties are in need of refurbishment. This should change once the Sofitel Old Cataract Hotel, Aswan's finest luxury accommodation, reopens for business. The grande dame of Aswan's hotels has been undergoing a glamorous restoration – hopefully other properties that have been riding on their reputations for too long will follow suit once the ribbons are cut.

Aswan

Basma
Shari' Abtal At Tahrir
Tel: 097-231 0901
www.basmahotel.com
A full-blown resort hotel with all the modern conveniences you would expect, including a huge swimming pool. Most rooms have excellent views over the river. **$$$$**

Isis Corniche
Shari' An Nil
Tel: 097-232 4744

Mövenpick Resort Aswan

Built on the riverbank in the centre of town, this resort hotel could do with some renovation, but its location on the Nile in the centre of town is excellent. The garden has a pool and several restaurants. **$$$$**

Keylany Hotel
25 Shari' Keylany
Tel: 097-231 7332
www.keylanyhotel.com
By far Aswan's best budget hotel, with simple but clean air-conditioned rooms, modern furniture and spotless bathrooms. The manager is extremely friendly and helpful, there is a great roof terrace for sunset drinks and an internet café. Highly recommended. **$$**

Marhaba Palace Hotel
Shari' An Nil
Tel: 097-233 0102
www.marhaba-aswan.com
Modern hotel overlooking the Nile with spacious rooms with private bathroom, air con, satellite TV and internet access. The hotel has a good restaurant with lovely views of the Nile and a heated swimming pool in the garden. **$$$**

Mövenpick Resort Aswan
Elephantine Island
Tel: 097-230 3455
www.moevenpick-hotels.com
Recently renovated (for Aswan) spa-hotel.

The huge ugly tower is still there, but the spacious rooms are great, with wide views over the Nile. It is a peaceful resort with a pool set in the garden, and a spa specialising in sand treatments for rheumatism. A free ferry transports guests in and out of town. 🏨 $$$$$

Nuba Nile Hotel
Shari' Abtal At Tahrir
Tel: 097-231 3267
Good budget hotel near the train station, with rooms of variable standards. Make sure yours has a window, as a few rooms don't have one. Popular with backpackers who also hang out in the neighbouring *ahwa* (coffee house). $

Pyramisa Isis Island Resort and Spa Aswan
Isis Island
Tel: 097-231 5100
www.pyramisaegypt.com
Huge resort hotel, owned by the Mubarak family, set on its own island upriver from Aswan. The property is very tired and in need of a renovation, but the location is the big plus, right on the river overlooking Elephantine. $$$$$

Sara Hotel
Shari' Al Fanadak
Tel: 097-232 7234
www.sarahotel-aswan.com
Modern hotel with great views over the Nile. The rooms don't have a lot of character, but are spotless and have satellite TV and air conditioning. There is also a pool and sun terrace for the days you want to take it easy. $$$

Sofitel Old Cataract
Shari' Abtal at Tahrir
Tel: 097-231 6000
www.sofitel.com
Aswan's most famous property harks back to the days of grand cruising and colonial splendour. Currently being renovated, the hotel looks like it will be closed until 2011. $$$$$

Sofitel Old Cataract Hotel before being refurbished

Abu Simbel
Eskaleh
Abu Simbel
Tel: 097-340 1288/012-368 0521
Email: fikrykachif@genevalink.com
The Nubian musician Fikry Kachif, who also works as a guide, recently opened this small but charming mud-brick hotel with just five rooms. The rooms are simple but comfortable, with very clean bathrooms, and some have their own terrace overlooking the lake. $$

Nefertari Hotel
Tel: 097-340 0510
Basic rooms are uninspiring, but the swimming pool overlooking Lake Nasser and convenient location near the Temple of Rameses II make up for the standard interiors. $$$

Seti Abu Simbel
Tel: 097-340 0720
The first and only five-star hotel in Abu Simbel, with chalet-style rooms set in a garden overlooking the lake. All modern amenities and a very relaxing atmosphere make this a very pleasant place to stay. $$$$

RESTAURANTS

Restaurants can be found in the souq and along the Corniche, almost all focusing on local and Egyptian dishes, although you will also find Western food, such as pizza, pasta and burgers. One highlight to dining in Upper Egypt is the opportunity to experience home-cooked Nubian cuisine. Aswan boasts a few Nubian restaurants located on the small islands that are scattered along the Nile at this point. A small boat will take you to a tiny speck of land where you will be greeted by a spread of Nubian dishes and a cultural floorshow.

Animalia
Main Path, Siou, Elephantine Island
Tel: 097-231 4152
www.animalia-eg.com
Friendly café with displays of Nubian history and culture staffed by the knowledgeable Muhammad Sobhy. *See the box on p.157.* **$**

Aswan Moon
Shari' An Nil
Tel: 097-231 6108
Floating restaurant on the Nile which attracts many *feluccas*. Beer, fresh fruit juices and standard Egyptian fare in a relaxing atmosphere. **$**

Chef Khalil
Shari' As Souq, near the train station
Tel: 097-231 0142
Simple but very popular fish restaurant that serves fresh fish, by the weight, from Lake Nasser or the Red Sea. The grilled or baked fish is served with salad and rice. **$**

Aswan Moon

Kenzi House
Seheyl Island
Tel: 012-415 4902
Experience real Nubian village life at this restaurant located on Seheyl Island. A good place to experience Nubian music. **$$**

Makka
Shari' Abtal At Tahrir
Tel: 097-230 3232
The best kebab and kofta in town, sold by the kilo, and served in a totally Islamic kitsch decor. No alcohol. **$**

Nubian Duka Restaurant
Essa Island, south of Elephantine, free shuttle boat from the dock opposite the Egypt Air office
Tel: 097-230 0307
The Nubian offers a three-course set menu with a folklore show of regional music and dance. The food is tasty and usually includes grilled meats and Nubian spicy stews, but you will probably be surrounded by tour groups. **$$**

Toya
Tariq Al Mahad, Abu Simbel
Tel: 012-357 7539
Popular place with tour groups, Toya serves great breakfasts to those who stick around in town during the morning hours, and local Nubian specialities the rest of the day. At night, it's a good spot for a coffee and sheesha in a town not known for its after-dark options. **$$**

NIGHTLIFE AND ENTERTAINMENT

Aswan is the capital of Nubian music, but the best venues to listen to it come and go. For tourist-friendly performances, stick to the Nile-side floating restaurants such as the Aswan Moon *(see opposite)* or the cultural shows offered by Nubian island-based restaurants. For something more authentic, you'll need to ask the Nubian music sellers in the souq for advice on where to go and when.

The Nubia Museum *(see p.162)* offers occasional demonstrations of Nubian music and dance, although renovations are currently curtailing the performance schedule, so it's best to check before you go.

Abu Simbel sound and light show

Sound and Light Show

The sound and light show at Philae is one of the most highly recommended in Egypt (although you need to appreciate kitsch to share the view). English-language shows are held every evening. For further details, contact the tourist office in Aswan or go to www. soundandlight.com.eg

SPORTS AND ACTIVITIES

While Aswan offers an ideal Nile-side setting, there are few sporting facilities on offer to the casual tourist. Most of the larger resorts have a swimming pool on site; some may even have a small gym. Joggers can be found enjoying the Corniche during the early morning hours before the sun gets too hot, and bicycle rentals can be negotiated through most hotels. However, there is no natural bicycle tour route to take, as distances between sites are long and the landscape is not very inspiring.

Sofitel Old Cataract Hotel in Aswan

TOURS

As the major departure point for cruises and *felucca* trips up the Nile, much focus is placed on boat trips by the copious tour operators based in Aswan. Tours tend to be strictly of the boat or coach variety, with some visitors choosing to make the most of their time by flying to Abu Simbel to see the famous temples. There are a number of tour operator offices that can be found along the Corniche, near the cruise ports. Travelling with one of these operators does cost – as much as three times what you would pay if you book through your hotel or by negotiating directly with a taxi driver.

Getting on a camel is not easy

The tourist office, at Meadan Al Mahatta (tel: 097-231 2811) near the train station, is a good place to find out going rates for both tours and *felucca* trips.

Boat trips

Aswan is the main location in Egypt from which to arrange extended cruises and *felucca* trips up the Nile. Short jaunts by *felucca* from Aswan can be arranged taking in the sites of the West Bank or onwards to Seheyl Island. Longer trips can be done on *dahabiyyah*, *felucca* or by cruise ship south to Lake Nasser or north to Luxor. For details on how to arrange a trip, see *Nile Cruising on p.xx*.

Day trips

There are a number of popular itineraries departing from Aswan on a daily basis. The most frequently offered day tours (in order of popularity) are:

Abu Simbel

By air or coach, a day trip to Abu Simbel is a must for many travellers visiting Aswan. Tours by air depart in the morning and return in the early afternoon. While this cuts down on the journey time, it is much more expensive and time on the site can be as little as two hours – less if the flights are delayed. The cost per person starts from E£1,200.

Coach tours are much cheaper, but you are looking at a 3–4-hour trip each way.

Additionally, you can only visit Abu Simbel as part of the security convoy system, meaning visitors are limited to strict departure times (twice a day between 3–4am and 11am from Aswan, returning about 90 minutes after arrival in Abu Simbel). Cost per person starts from E£300.

Philae

Easily done in an afternoon, a visit to this island-based temple can be combined with the Unfinished Obelisk and Aswan High Dam.

The West Bank

The Tombs of the Nobles and Aga Khan's Mausoleum are usually visited as part of a *felucca* trip. You can either visit it as part of a tour through an operator or by dealing direct with the *felucciyah* (boat captain).

Daraw Camel Market

Sunday and Tuesday mornings are the best times to head to Daraw to see trading at this busy camel market north of Aswan (see p.156).

Recommended tour operators which can book any of the above activities include:

ATB Egypt
Al Semad
Tel: 012-328 1212
www.atbholidays.com
One of the largest tour operators in the Middle East, with an office in Aswan. Its particular strength is in arranging Lake Nasser cruises and longer-stay itineraries. This is also a good option for gay and lesbian travellers as the operator is a member of the International Gay and Lesbian Travel Association (IGLTA).

Glory of Nubia
No address – contact by phone or website
Tel: 010-193 5639

www.welcome2Aswan.com
Luxury *felucca* offering day trips to Seheyl Island or around the cataracts. They can also take you as far as Luxor. Make sure you book in advance of your arrival in Aswan.

Thomas Cook
Shari' An Nil
Tel: 097-230 4011
www.thomascook.com.eg
The most well-established tour operator in town, offering a wide range of day-trip and extended-stay tour options, including cruises up the Nile. Clients tend to have deep pockets, as the commissions certainly add up. Prices can be as much as three times what you would pay if you booked direct – but the time-saving and professionalism have their advantages.

FESTIVALS AND EVENTS

Aswan's strong sense of community means that small events seem to pop up all the time. All of the major religious dates on the Islamic calendar are celebrated – and the laid-back nature of the city means that it is often the best place in Egypt to visit if you are looking to mix with the locals during major holiday periods. One of the most beautiful events occurs in Abu Simbel when sunlight washes over the interior of the Temple of Rameses II. This natural phenomenon actually occurs a day later than intended following the move of the temple from its original location *(see p.170 for details).*

January/February
International Sculpture Symposium
International stone sculptors come together to demonstrate techniques and display superb art pieces at the Basma Hotel, Shari 'Abtal At Tahrir, Aswan.

February and October
Ascension of Rameses II
The Temple of Rameses II at Abu Simbel faces east, and twice a year the dawn sunlight is aligned to light the entire length of the temple entrance corridor, illuminating three of the four statues at the end of the corridor (not that of Ptah, god of darkness). This commemorates the date of Rameses II's ascension to the throne (22 February)

and birthday (22 October). Celebrations continue outside with music, dancing and market stalls catering to the crowds.

Abu Simbel

Alexandria and the Delta

Like a vintage gown, Alexandria has been glamorous, lost its allure and is now back in fashion. The beaches are being spruced up, a new airport is welcoming visitors and underwater discoveries are revealing past glories. Use the city as a base to explore the Delta, Egypt's agricultural heartland, and the engineering wonder of the Suez Canal.

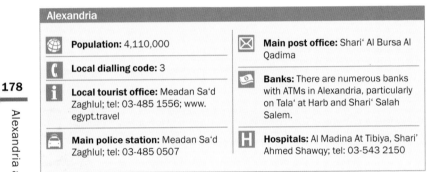

Alexandria

Population: 4,110,000

Local dialling code: 3

Local tourist office: Meadan Sa'd Zaghlul; tel: 03-485 1556; www.egypt.travel

Main police station: Meadan Sa'd Zaghlul; tel: 03-485 0507

Main post office: Shari' Al Bursa Al Qadima

Banks: There are numerous banks with ATMs in Alexandria, particularly on Tala' at Harb and Shari' Salah Salem.

Hospitals: Al Madina At Tibiya, Shari' Ahmed Shawqy; tel: 03-543 2150

The spotlight of power shone brightly in the south during the early years of the Egyptian empire. But the invasion of Alexander the Great and demand for a new centre that could link the rich Nile Valley with the Mediterranean meant a shift in focus away from the traditional power centre of Thebes. In 331BC, Alexandria was built over the city of Rhacotis and the fortunes of the north blossomed.

Hellenistic influences transformed Alexandria into a centre of learning and trade, quickly making the city one of the richest on the planet both financially and intellectually. Recent underwater excavations are revealing much about Alexandria's former magnificence, and plans to create an underwater museum off the coast within the next 10 years will one day bring a new dimension to the city's cultural scene.

Surrounding Alexandria, the Delta region is the centre of farming and manufacturing for the nation – a relatively recent development thanks to the construction of the Aswan Dam *(see p.163)*. Until the dam was completed in 1970, the Delta was subject to cycles of drought and flooding that made the region challenging to build on and live in. To the east lies Egypt's largest source of revenue, the Suez Canal. Nationalised by the Egyptians in 1956, the canal is now one of the world's most important shipping lanes. Little visited by tourists, it is a marvel of 19th-century engineering.

Alexandria

Founded by Alexander the Great, **Alexandria** ❶ was once the jewel of the Mediterranean and home to the Ptolemaic Pharaohs, including Cleopatra. Today, the crumbling homes and seaside Corniche merely whisper at the city's great triumphs, but a revival of sorts is on the horizon. The construction of a collection of luxury properties and new airport means that Alexandria is finally returning to its position as Egypt's grande dame of the sea.

The city stretches along the shore from east to west for about 48km (30 miles) but is only 3km (2 miles) wide, so wherever you are you are never far from the sound of surf or the smell

The Corniche, Alexandria

of fresh fish. The sea lends a sense of freedom to Alexandria, which is refreshing after the heat and dust of the Nile Valley.

The Corniche

Popular with families and couples out for a stroll, the **Corniche** runs along the Mediterranean shore from Fort of Qayetbay as far as Montazah. Numerous restaurants and cafés, haunts of

Getting a good view of the city

the now-gone expat communities, line the boardwalk serving fresh fish and leisurely coffees from their atmospheric establishments. A walk along the Corniche is especially beautiful at sunset or on a hot day when the sea breezes are refreshingly cool.

Citadel of Qayetbay

At the western edge of the Eastern Harbour, where the Corniche begins, stands the **Citadel of the Mamluk Sultan Qal'at Qayetbay** (Eastern Harbour; daily 9am–4pm; charge).

Sitting on the site of one of the wonders of the Ancient World, the Pharos Lighthouse, the fort is of little historical interest but offers wonderful views of the bay and city centre. The best time to see the fort is just before dusk, when the warm reds and oranges of an Alexandrian sunset turn the sandstone building the colour of rich honey.

Meadan Sa'd Zaghlul

Head along the Corniche to reach the centre of the city, **Meadan Sa'd**

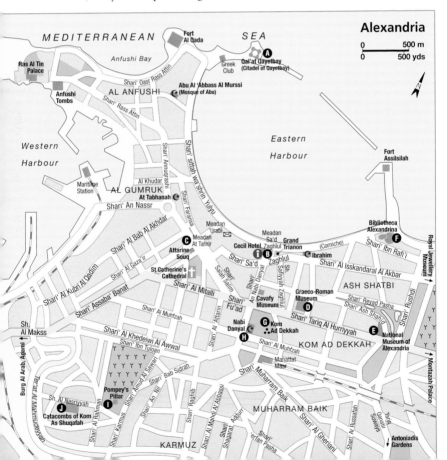

Zaghlul . This square on the seafront is the unofficial heart of Alexandria, often clogged with traffic during the rush hours. On the square's west side is the historic **Cecil Hotel** (16 Meadan Sa'd Zaghlul; tel: 3-487 7173), once home to Alexandria's glittering expat community, including Noel Coward, Somerset Maugham and Winston Churchill, and now a symbol of the city's former glamour.

Nearby is the **Grand Trianon** (Meadan Sa'd Zaghul; daily 7am–midnight; patisserie closes at 8pm), a jewel of Art Nouveau style housing a popular café, patisserie and restaurant.

In the 1920s, this is where Europeans conducted business, gossiped and dined – now they've been replaced by upwardly mobile Egyptians.

Meadan At Tahrir ** (Liberation Square) was laid out by Muhammad Ali in 1830, and his impressive equestrian statue stands at the centre. This was the heart of the European quarter during colonial times. The city's labyrinthine **Attarine Souq lies at the southwestern end of the square.

A city of museums
Alexandria's recent revival owes much to the city's investment in culture.

Alexandria Transport

 Airports: Borg Al Arab Airport (tel: 03-459 1483) is 60 km (37½ miles) west of the city centre. To and from the airport: the official airport bus takes passengers to the city centre, dropping off in front of the Cecil Hotel. The journey takes one hour and costs E£6 plus E£1 for each bag. Alternatively, public bus 475 can take passengers directly to the train station. Taxis cost between E£100 and E£150, depending on which hotel you are going to and how strong your bargaining skills are. Journey time is about 45 minutes.

 Buses: A double-decker bus travels the length of the Corniche between Ras Alt Tin and Montazah outside the Sheraton every 15 to 30 minutes, depending on the time of day. There is no set schedule, nor are there formally marked stops. Instead, head to a major junction and flag the bus down. Rides cost E£3 regardless of how far you travel.
Microbuses: Do as the locals do and flag a microbus. Hail one by putting your hand out when you see one approaching and then yell out your destination. Most journeys cost about E£1.

Taxis: Taxis can be hailed on the street in Alexandria. There are no meters, so it is best to negotiate your fare before you get inside the car. Taxis are your best bet if you wish to explore the Delta while using Alexandria as a base. A day rental will cost between E£150–E£300 depending on distance and your negotiating skills.

Car hire: Renting a car is not recommended in Alexandria, as driving can be chaotic. Parking is even more of a challenge, with few spaces available for the ever-growing number of cars on city streets. If you do decide to rent a car, check its condition thoroughly before you sign the rental agreement, as rental agencies in Egypt are notorious for trying to charge travellers for every dent or scrape.
Avis; Cecil Hotel, Meadan Sa'd Zaghlul; tel: 03-485 7400.

From Meadan Sa'd Zaghlul, it's a short walk southeast to reach the **Graeco-Roman Museum**  (closed for restoration at time of publication). As home to one of the world's greatest collections of Graeco-Roman art, the museum will be a must-see stop when it reopens in 2012.

Until the museum returns to the tourist trail, the **National Museum of Alexandria** ❸ (110 Tariq Al Hurriyyah; daily 9am–4.30pm; charge) remains the prime centre for understanding the great significance of the city through its artefacts. Housed in a beautifully restored Italianate villa, the museum is laid out chronologically over three floors; the basement is devoted to the Pharaonic period, the ground floor to the Graeco-Roman period (where many of the Graeco-Roman Museum's collection can be found until it reopens, including sculptures found in the Eastern

Harbour) and the top floor to Coptic, Muslim and modern Alexandria.

Bibliotheca Alexandrina

Less a museum and more a cultural centre and icon of the city, the **Bibliotheca Alexandrina** ❻ (www.bibalex.org; Sun–Thur, Sat 11am–7pm, Fri–Sat 3–7pm; charge 🅼) opened to great fanfare in 2002. Inspired by the Great Library of Alexandria, the Bibliotheca has the capacity to house up to 8 million books and 50,000 rare manuscripts.

Points of interest include the world's largest reading room, which can hold up to 2,000 people, a concert hall, planetarium and small antiquities museum, containing many historic items found in and around Alexandria.

A permanent exhibition called 'Impressions of Alexandria' traces the history of the city through maps,

The strking architecture of the Bibliotheca Alexandrina

Fort of Qayetbay and Alexandria harbour

drawings and early photographs. There's also a Manuscripts Museum, with a copy of the only papyrus text to survive from the ancient library, and an interactive history 'experience' called Culturama, which takes visitors on a walk through Egypt's past.

Kom Ad Dekkah

Since 1959, archaeologists have been excavating a collection of Muslim tombs dating from the 9th–11th centuries, located along the southwest of Tariq Al Hurriyyah near the train station. Near here is the site of **Kom Ad Dekkah** Ⓖ ('Pile of Rubble'; daily 8.30am–4.30pm; charge), home to Roman-era baths, houses, assembly halls and the site where early Christian mobs burnt objects plundered from Roman temples. The main attraction is the small 2nd-century theatre, the only Roman theatre in Egypt, with marble seating and well-preserved mosaic flooring.

Coffee and Past Glories

The independence movement of the 1950s did much to erase European influence from the streets of Alexandria, but the traditional café and pastry culture remains firmly entrenched in the local way of life. These are not typical Egyptian cafés, wtih sheeshas and football on the television. Rather, many of these cafés feature pastries and coffee so strong, a first-timer could be kept awake for weeks.

Many still have their early 20th-century decor and, although they have all seen better days, their shabbiness merely adds to the atmosphere. The most interesting cafés can be found on or near Meadan Sa'd Zaghlul, including:

- Athineos (21 Meadan Sa'd Zaghlul; tel: 03-482 8131)
- Trianon (56 Meadan Sa'd Zaghlul; no phone)
- Delices (46 Shari' Sa'd Zaghlul; no phone)

A short walk up Shari' Al Nabi Danyal will bring you to the **Nabi Danyal Mosque Ⓗ**, on the left side of the street with an entrance set back. Mistakenly believed to lie over the tomb of the prophet Daniel, it is actually the burial place of Sheikh Danyal Al Maridi, who died in 1407. It is also falsely believed to be the site of the Soma, where Alexander is buried.

Roman-era ruins

The **Serapeum**, once a temple of great importance that housed over 700,000 manuscripts given to Cleopatra by Mark Antony, lies on top of the former citadel of Rhacotis, the original settlement from which Alexandria developed. Little remains from the period bar a few tunnels and pillars.

The principal remaining attraction is a solitary 30m (98ft) high pillar of pink Aswan granite known as

Pompey's Pillar Ⓘ (daily 8.30am–4.30pm; charge). It actually has nothing to do with Pompey: according to an inscription on its base, it was dedicated to the Emperor Diocletian in 291.

The Catacombs

A short walk south of Pompey's Pillar are the **Catacombs of Kom As Shuqafah Ⓙ** (daily 8.30am–4.30pm; charge). Come out of the enclosure of Pompey's Pillar, turn right up a crowded street and at the top you will come to a small crossroads. Just beyond it is the entrance to the catacombs, cut out of the rock to a depth of about 35m (115ft). Immediately inside the entrance are four very fine sarcophagi of purplish granite. They date from around the 2nd century AD, a time when the old religions began to

Catacombs of Kom As Shuqafah

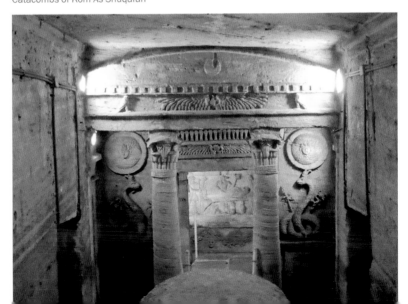

from the stifling heat and politics of Cairo. While the palace is off-limits, the exterior is beautiful, and the lush gardens, planted with pine trees and palms, are a pleasant spot for a picnic. There's also a sandy cove with a semi-private beach (charge) here, a great family-friendly destination if you need a place to cool off.

Al 'Alamean

West of Alexandria, 105km (65 miles) along the shore road on the Mediterranean coast, is **Al 'Alamean** ❷, the location of the first major battle won, in 1942, by the Allies against the Axis forces during World War II. Al 'Alamean is a poignant reminder of a dark period in global politics. More than 80,000 soldiers were killed or wounded here and in the subsequent battles for control of North Africa. The thousands of graves in the cemeteries near the town are a bleak reminder of the losses.

The cemeteries and War Museum

The historic site is made up of three cemeteries, a war monument and a museum. Of the three main war cemeteries in Al 'Alamean, the Commonwealth cemetery is the first one you come to. It is on your left as you enter the town from the east. A walk around the simple tombstones, each of which carries an inscription, cannot fail to move. In the centre of town is the **War Museum** (daily 9am–4pm; charge), housing memorabilia, uniforms and pictorial material of each country involved in the battle,

185

Alexandria and the Delta

fade and merge with one another, as demonstrated in the curious blend of classical and Egyptian designs. The distinctive Alexandrian blend of Egyptian, Greek and Roman motifs is exemplified by the gods Anubis and Sobek dressed as Roman legionaries.

Montazah Gardens

If you need to escape the bustle of the city centre, do as the locals do and head eastwards along the Corniche to the **Montazah Gardens** (daily dawn to dusk, charge M). In the middle of the gardens is the Montazah Palace, a summer residence built by the Khedive Ismail as a place of refuge away

⭐ TOUR OF ALEXANDRIA

Atmospheric and relaxed, Alexandria is a breath of fresh air (literally) after Cairo, and boasts attractions ranging from Roman ruins and catacombs to medieval forts, old-world cafés and fabulous fish restaurants.

Giving a tangible idea of the city's prestigious past – Alexander the Great's city, Cleopatra's capital, the site of the Pharos (one of the Seven Wonders of the Ancient World), and the Great Library – is the **National Museum of Alexandria** (110 Tariq Al Hurriyyah; daily 9am–4.30pm; charge). Carefully selected exhibits are well arranged in a former pasha's palace.

Due to reopen in 2012 is the **Graeco-Roman Museum** (5 Al Mathaf Ar Romani; tel: 03-486 5829). With over 41,000 artefacts, it's one of the world's largest collections.

About 6.5km (4 miles) east lies the **Royal Jewellery Museum** (27 Shari' Ahmed Yehia Pasha; tel: 03-582 8348; daily 9am–4pm; charge), containing an eye-popping collection of gold and glittering jewels that once belonged to the Farouks, Egypt's last royals.

Nearby, the 2nd-century AD site of **Kom Ad Dekkah** contains Egypt's last surviving Roman theatre (tel: 03-486 5106; daily 8.30am–4.30pm; closed Fri 11.30am–1.30pm; charge). Other ruins include a Roman bath and the Villa of the Birds (separate charge), with floor mosaics dating to Hadrian (AD117–36).

The 2nd-century AD **Pompey's Pillar** (Shari' Amud Al Sawari, Karmouz; tel: 03-484 5800; daily 8.30am–4.30pm; charge) towers 62.8m (206ft) above the remains of Rhacotis, Alexandria's first settlement. It once formed part of the Serapeum, which was one of the Roman empire's most important religious and intellectual centres.

Roman theatre

Tips

- Distance: 5km (3 miles)
- Time: a full day
- Trains depart Cairo regularly from 6am (returning until around 10pm) taking 2–3 hours. Book tickets in advance at Rameses Station, Cairo. To do this in a day, take one of the earliest and fastest trains.
- Try to read Lawrence Durrell's *Alexandria Quartet* or C.P. Cavafy's *Collected Poems* to get the feel of the city.

Not far from here, the 2nd-century AD Roman **Catacombs of Kom As Shuqafah** (tel: 03-484 5800; daily 8.30am–4.30pm; charge) constitue the largest Roman burial site in Egypt.

Lying at the western end of the Corniche is the renovated, Mamluk **Citadel of Qayetbay** (tel: 03-486 5106; daily 9am–4pm; charge). It occupies the site of Alexandria's famous Pharos (ancient lighthouse).

The return to town along the Corniche makes a lovely stroll or calèche (carriage) ride past the fishing harbour, dilapidated colonial houses, and the **Mosque of Abu Al 'Abbas Al Murssi**

(daily 7am–dusk; free). Built in 1943, it's dedicated to the patron saint of sailors and fishermen. About 1km (2/3 mile) further lies the Monument of the Unknown Soldier on Meadan Urabi and, on Meadan Sa'd Zaghlul, the once-grand Cecil Hotel immortalised in Lawrence Durrell's *Alexandria Quartet*, where Winston Churchill is said to have planned World War II.

At the Corniche's eastern end is Alexandria's new library, the **Bibliotheca Alexandrina** (www.bibalex. org; Sun–Thur 11am–7pm, Fri–Sat 3–7pm; charge) inaugurated in 2002, an icon of 21st-century architecture.

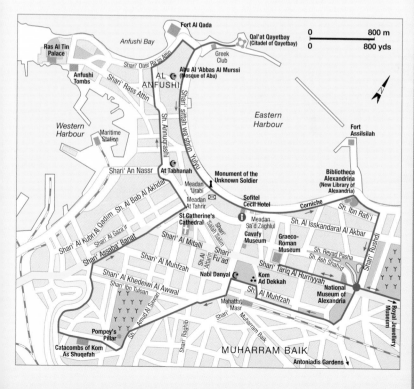

with clear explanations about each phase of the campaign. Outside are tanks and hardware. Beyond stands the stone monument to Germany's fallen soldiers, in a beautiful setting that overlooks the sea. Further down the coast is the Italian memorial, reminiscent of a railway station in a provincial Italian city.

The Delta

After the noise of Cairo, the River Nile is ready for the peace of the sea. In its hurry to get there it splits, first in two, then into the myriad canals and streams of the Delta. This is the most densely populated region of Egypt, so named by the Greeks for its similarity on the map to their triangular capital letter D.

Around 160km (100 miles) wide at its Mediterranean base and about the same length, the flat, rich Nile Delta contains more than half of Egypt's agricultural land and much of its industry. More than 16 million Egyptians live in its thousands of villages, cultivating extensive mango and citrus orchards, cotton, wheat and vegetables for the population. Roads, railways, bridges and canals crisscross the land. To the east and west, the once impenetrable desert is giving way to mammoth land reclamation projects.

A Delta tour

The Delta was once part of the sea. Millennia of Nile alluvia washing down from Ethiopia created first swamps, then exceptionally fertile farmland. During the annual flood, river water turned the Delta into a vast lake. Consequently the Ancient

The Delta

0   20 km
0   20 miles

Damietta Mosque

Egyptian inhabitants built their towns on hills and hummocks, which appeared like islands when the inundation was at its full height.

This area of Egypt is largely workaday, with few major sites on the 'must-see' tourist map. This is largely due to the constant flooding that affected the region until the completion of the Aswan High Dam. Temples built here were constructed of mud-brick, and the regular flooding washed the structures away during the rainy season.

Unsurprisingly, the people of the Delta are known chiefly for their industriousness, in contrast to the laid-back image of the Upper Egyptians. Despite its proximity to Cairo and Alexandria and a relatively prosperous economic base, patches of the Delta do not display much of this prosperity, as can be seen from the vintage taxis that chug along its byways.

Tanta and Damietta

The largest city of the Delta is **Tanta** ❸, a ramshackle place that marks the halfway point between Cairo and Alexandria. Every October its half-million inhabitants are swollen to four times their number during the Islamic saint's day of Ahmed Al Bedawi, a 13th-century mystic who founded Egypt's biggest Sufi brotherhood. This ancient, perhaps even pre-Islamic, *mawlid*, the biggest of the Egyptian calendar, is celebrated with the enthusiastic use of megaphones, strobe lights and riot police. By day, pilgrims flood to the grandiose tomb and mosque of the saint, which is ringed by the kind of commercial enterprises that usually surround an important tomb or pilgrimage centre – from circumcision booths to stalls selling nougat, dates, whistles and party hats. By night increasingly rowdy revellers throng the streets.

Other towns hold smaller festivals for their local saints, but these days Delta cities are better known for their industries. **Talkha** is dominated by its mammoth fertiliser plant; **Kafr Addawwar** and **Al Mahallah Al Kubra** are centres of the cotton industry.

Further north on the coast is **Damietta** ❹, an ancient seaport which once rivalled Alexandria in the Middle Ages and is now the centre of Egypt's furniture industry, making the Rococo furniture styles favoured by the Egyptian upper middle classes.

Ancient sites of the Delta

The town of **Zaqaziq**, heavily polluted by the fumes from a soap factory, is the nearest town to the ancient site of **Bubastis** (daily 8.30am–4pm; charge), a thriving cult centre for the cat-goddess Bastet. Some 157km (97 miles) northeast of Zaqaziq is one of the oldest known sites in Egypt, the city of **Tanis** ❺, was the capital of the 21st Dynasty. On the site there are further impressive remains of a large temple devoted to Amun, and royal tombs, many of which were discovered with their treasures virtually intact.

Finally, **Rosetta** ❻ is where the famous stone that provided the key to deciphering hieroglyphs was found (*see opposite*). It still has charm; its neat, narrow lanes lined with brick

A gold royal funerary mask from Tanis, now in the Egyptian Museum in Cairo

The Rosetta Stone

About the size of a typical gravestone, the Rosetta Stone was discovered in the Delta village of Rashid (Rosetta) by Frenchman Pierre Bouchard, who described it as 'a stone of very fine granite, black, with a close grain, and very hard... with three distinct inscriptions separated in three parallel bands'.

Two of the bands were in the meaningless scripts to be seen on monuments all along the Nile. No one had been able to understand the hieroglyphs since the 4th century, but the last of the parallel bands was in readable Greek.

Various scholars contributed to the translation, however, French academic Champollion was responsible for the conclusive decipherment giving meaning to the hieroglyphs.

The Rosetta Stone, in the British Museum

houses, characteristic of the Delta, run down to a waterfront crammed with fishing vessels and boatyards.

Suez Canal

At first glance it is a simple waterway carved between two seas. Yet the Suez Canal is both a 19th-century wonder of engineering and Egypt's second-greatest source of revenue after tourism, linking the ports of the Indian Ocean with the Mediterranean and Atlantic beyond.

Port Said

Port Said ❼ (Boar Sa'id) sits on an artificial landfill jutting into the Mediterranean and is named after the Khedive of Egypt, Said Basha. From here convoys of ships depart every morning at 1am

and 7am, passing the green domes of the Suez Canal Authority building to begin the journey to the Red Sea.

Once the major point of entry for tourists stepping off the great Peninsular and Orient (P & O) passenger lines, Port Said is now the Hong Kong of Egypt, where Cairo consumers flock for duty-free goods.

Al Isma'ileyyah

Situated on Lake Timsah halfway between Port Said and Suez, **Al Isma'ileyyah** ❽ (Ismailia) is the queen of the canal cities. With its tree-shaded avenues and colonial-style houses, it retains a certain gentility from the 1950s, when British officers escaped the hardships of their desert postings to relax here at the French

Ships in the Suez Canal

making the pilgrimage to Mecca (*hajj*) from North Africa and Turkey.

Suez is best observed from the Sinai side of the canal, where scores of ships can be seen lining up in the Gulf ready to make the northward passage. It is an amazing sight. The modern canal is 192km (119 miles) long and has a minimum width of 60m (197ft), with no locks. Today about 10 percent of the world's shipping uses it, earning Egypt over US$3 billion per year in revenue.

The Suez Canal

The idea of a canal linking the Nile to the Red Sea was sparked centuries before the actual construction of the Suez Canal. Despite this, construction on the Suez Canal didn't begin until 1859.

It took 10 years, 25,000 labourers and a budget of almost £25 million to finish the 160km (100-mile) channel, transforming international trade and shipping upon its completion in November 1869.

British control of the canal was a symbol of European colonialism that reached a head in 1954 when the independence movement led by Nasser forced British troops out of the canal zone. Two years later, Egypt nationalised the canal, resulting in a Franco-British-Israeli invasion as it struggled to maintain control over the lucrative waterway. Intervention from the US put a stop to the crisis, eventually giving Egypt full control over what is today its second-largest source of foreign currency.

and Greek clubs. It is said to be the cleanest city in Egypt.

There are few places in the world where you can watch giant tankers and container ships glide past at 15km (9 miles) per hour so close and so quietly. The ships take between 11 and 16 hours to pass through, so you are almost certain to see a line of them at around midday.

The Port of Suez

Suez ❾ (Asswayss), the canal's southern terminus, was Egypt's major Red Sea port for hundreds of years and is an important transit point for Muslims

ACCOMMODATION

Until recently, there wasn't much to choose from when it came to booking a hotel in Alexandria. Many of the hotels rode on past glories, requiring extensive renovations, or simply lacked character. That all changed with the opening of the Four Seasons. Suddenly, Alexandria became a popular sun-break destination with a hotel of sufficient class to attract serious money. Outside Alexandria, options are more limited. Your best bet is to base yourself in Alexandria or Cairo and explore the region from there.

Alexandria

Acropole
27 Shari' Al Ghorfa Al Togariyya
Tel: 03-480 5980
No stars and rather run-down, but the rooms in this atmospheric, clean, Greek-owned pension enjoy the same views as the much more expensive Cecil Hotel. **$**

Hotel Crillon
5th Floor, 164 Shari' 26th of July
Tel: 03-480 0330
A true throwback to the years of expats and intrigue. The place has seen better days, but the location on the Corniche and delightful atmosphere make it a good choice. **$$**

El-Salamlek Palace Hotel
Montazah Palace Gardens
Tel: 03-547 7999
www.sangiovanni.com
If you think this former royal guesthouse has an air of the Alps about it, you wouldn't be wrong. The property was built for the Austrian-educated Khedive (and more specifically his Austrian mistress). **$$$$$**

Four Seasons
399 Shari' Al Gaish, San Stefano
Tel: 03-581 8000
www.fourseasons.com
Opened in 2007, this hotel still looks brand new. A private beach was constructed just for guests, including exclusive cabañas and a yacht marina for those who want to sail right on in. **$$$$$**

Nile Excelsior
16 Shari' Al Bursa Al Qadima
Tel: 03-480 0799
Very central hotel with rather grimy public spaces. Don't let that put you off, as the bedrooms are clean and comfortable. **$$–$$$**

Nobel Hotel
152 Shari' Al Gaish
Tel: 03-546 4845
Tidy rooms with private baths. The tiny balconies provide excellent views. Pay a surcharge for air conditioning if you need it. **$$**

Sofitel Alexandria Cecil Hotel
16 Meadan Sa'd Zaghlul
Tel: 03-487 7173
www.sofitel.com
The Cecil is haunted by the ghosts of Noel Coward, Somerset Maugham and Lawrence Durrell, who immortalised it in *The Alexandria Quartet*. The glamour has long gone, but the charm of the place, and views over the bay, still pull in the romantics. **$$$$**

Union Hotel
164 Shari' 26th of July, Al Ramy Station
Tel: 03-480 7312
The cost of rooms varies depending on how good your view is – but if you book well enough in advance, you should get a good view at reasonable cost. **$$$**

RESTAURANTS

When it comes to dining, Alexandria offers a few more options than most other Egyptian cities. Thanks to its Mediterranean location and history as an expat haven, there are a number of well-regarded Greek and Italian eateries mixed in with the usual grill spots and *fu'ul* stands. Also unlike the rest of the nation, seafood is the preferred item of choice on menus, with most restaurants serving fish caught that very day.

Abu Ashraf
28 Shari' Safar Basha, Bahari
Tel: 03-481 6597
A 24-hour fish restaurant, very simple but with excellent fresh fish and seafood straight from the market. **$$**

Al Farouk
Al Salamlek Hotel, Montazah
Tel: 03-481 6597
Enjoy excellent traditional Egyptian cuisine in a regal location. **$$$**

Byblos
399 Shari' Al Gaish, San Stefano
Tel: 03-581 8000
www.fourseasons.com
Phenomenal Lebanese meze in truly palatial surroundings. The food, Mediterranean views and total on your final bill are sure to stun. **$$$$**

Chez Gabi
22 Shari' Al Hurriyyah
Tel: 03-487 4404
Quality Italian cuisine in a typical taverna-style restaurant complete with red-checked tablecloths and candles on the table. **$$**

China House
Sofitel Cecil Hotel, 16 Meadan Sa'd Zaghlul
Tel: 03-487 7173, ext 782
Alexandria's only Chinese restaurant, with great views over the Eastern Harbour. **$$**

Elite
43 Shari' Safia Zaghlul
Tel: 03-486 3592
Vast menu of Greek and Egyptian dishes and windows with a view on the world. **$**

Muhammad Ahmed
17 Shari' Shaqour Basha
Tel: 03-487 3576
By far the best *fu'ul* and *ta'amiyah* in town. No alcohol. **$**

Plats d'Or
16 Meadan Sa'd Zaghlul
Tel: 03-487 7173
www.sofitel.com
Fine dining French-style in the former headquarters of the expat community. Locals find it delivers more on atmosphere than on flavour. **$$$$**

Samakmak
42 Qasr Ras At Tin, Anfushi
Tel: 03-481 1560
One of the best fish restaurants in town. Choose from the display and then discuss how you want it cooked. **$$**

Tikka Grill
Al Kashafa Al Baharia Club, 26 Corniche
Tel: 03-480 5119
Excellent fish kebabs and meat dishes. Good views over the bay. **$$**

Trianon
52 Meadan Sa'd Zaghlul
Tel: 03-482 0986
Elegant wood-panelled restaurant with Mediterranean-Levantine food and occasionally live music. The next-door patisserie does a large, good-value breakfast. **$$**

NIGHTLIFE

Thanks partly to its large expat community and also to its location, Alexandria has a happening bar and café scene. Those looking to dance might be hard-pressed to find a decent venue – what 'nightclubs' there are usually only have a dance floor the size of a postage stamp. Still, evenings out can be a lot of fun. Enjoying drinks on the terrace at sunset is a popular pastime, especially along the waterfront. The rest of the Delta is early to bed and options are extremely limited once the sun sets.

Cap d'Or

Alexandria
Bars
Cap d'Or
4 Shari' Adib, off Meadan Sa'd Zaghlul
Tel: 03-487 5177
Difficult to find, but it attracts a loyal crowd of locals and expats who come to chat over a beer and vintage French pop music.

Spitfire Bar
7 Shari' Al Bursa Al Qadima
Tel: 03-480 6503

Smoky and fun rock-and-roll bar with walls decorated with interesting memorabilia. Attracts a mixed crowd of local diehards, expats and a few American sailors if the fleet is in town.

Nightclubs
Athinelos
21 Meadan Sa'd Zaghlul
Tel: 03-487 7173
Old-fashioned patisserie, nightclub and pleasant restaurant serving Levantine and Mediterranean fare.

ENTERTAINMENT

Alexandria's past as an expat centre means that it tends to embrace Western entertainments more readily than other locations in Egypt. It is common to find the latest Hollywood hits in the local cinemas, although you should check in advance to see if they are subtitled and not dubbed. Touring performers often visit Alexandria. The wonderful Bibliotheca acts as the cultural hub of the city, and its staff keep up to date with what's happening around town.

Cinemas
Green Plaza Mall Cineplex
14th of May Bridge
Tel: 03-420 9155
Six screens of Hollywood hits.

Renaissance City Center
Carrefour City Center Mall, at the beginning of the Cairo Desert Road

Tel: 03-397 0156
Seven screens for Hollywood blockbusters

Library
Bibliotheca Alexandrina
Shari' Al Bahr, Chatby
Tel: 03-483 9999
www.bibalex.org
This is the most important cultural venue in

town and hosts major music festivals, international concerts and plays.

Opera
Alexandria Opera House
22 Tariq Al Hurriyyah
Tel: 03-486 5106

www.cairooperahouse.org/
sayed_darwish.aspx
Built in 1918, this opera house was refurbished in 2000 after being placed on Egypt's Heritage List. Today, it hosts classical and operatic performances by both domestic and international names.

SPORTS AND ACTIVITIES

As Egypt's second-largest city, Alexandria offers a lot of sports both to watch and participate in. Its seaside location makes it an especially good destination to head for if you're a fan of watersports and diving. An underwater museum is in the works and should be open within the next decade.

Diving
The wealth of treasures lying submerged just offshore is waiting to be explored. The most recommended operator for divers is:
Alex Dive
Corniche, Anfushi
Tel: 03-483 2045
www.alexandra-dive.com

Football
Al-Ittihad
Shari' Grinfel, on the way to Misr Train Station
www.ittihad.com
While they've never won a championship, Al Ittihad is one of the most popular teams in the Egyptian Premier League. Touts sell tickets outside the stadium on the day of a match, but your best bet is to contact the club via the website.

Rugby
Alexandria Rugby Union Club
www.alexrugby.com
Rugby is in its infancy in Egypt, but is growing in popularity. Check the website for match locations.

Swimming
If your hotel doesn't have a pool, there are many public beaches along the coast. The most popular stretch lies between the Eastern Harbour and Montazah, but this area is not recommended for tourists as it is often litter-strewn and regularly packed. Try and get out of Alexandria to Al 'Alamean in order to enjoy a more peaceful, cleaner beach. Closer to town, Mamoura Beach is 1km (2/3 mile) east of Montazah and maintains a more subdued air thanks to the small charge they impose on all visitors. If kids are in tow, head instead to Miami Beach [YH], located 2km (1¼ miles) west of Montazah, where you will find an activity centre and collection of water slides.

A diver takes a close look at a huge manta ray

TOURS

There is little reason to book a guided tour in Alexandria and the north, as the number of sights is limited and transportation is easy. Few tour operators offer unique options; instead, negotiate with a taxi driver for trips outside Alexandria into the countryside.

Ann and Medhat Hashem
Street 15, Sidi Bashr, Alexandria
Tel: 012-035 4711
www.muzhela.com

Car services, transfers and trips out of town can be arranged by this English/Egyptian husband and wife team.

FESTIVALS AND EVENTS

Alexandria is the destination in Egypt most influenced by European sensibilities. Festivals and events reflect this, with the film festival acting as a big draw for cinephiles each year. You won't find as many religious *moulids* celebrated as you will in rural parts, but Alexandrians do know how to enjoy themselves when a festival comes along.

Contestant at the Alexandria Song Festival

July
Alexandria Song Festival
www.alexandriasongfestival.org
International competition for singers, song-writers and composers, usually held towards the end of the month.

September
Alexandria Film Festival
http://alexfilmfestival.com
Easily Egypt's most prominent film festival, this celebration of film grows in stature each year. Prizes are awarded to international and Arabic feature films, as well as to best short films and documentaries.

October
Egyptian Naval Day
As headquarters for the Egyptian navy, Alexandria is the centre of the action on this national holiday. The date, 21 October, marks the anniversary of the 1967 sinking of the Israeli warship INS *Eilat*.

November
Alexandria International Marathon
Tel: 03-573 5565
Runners from around the world can choose their distance, ranging from 1km (²/₃ mile) to the full 45km (28 miles). Designed to encourage participation from people of all fitness levels, this is a sociable, entertaining event.

December
Alexandria Biennale
www.alexbiennale.gov.eg
Celebration of local and international artists with focus on works from the Mediterranean region. Held every two years, with the next event scheduled for December 2010/January 2011.

The Sinai

'Egypt's paradise' is how the brochures like to dub the Sinai, the region wedged between Africa and Asia. Most visitors head to one of the many resorts along the coast for a beach holiday with guaranteed sun, but you can also enjoy world-class diving in the Red Sea or head inland to experience traditional Bedouin culture and extreme desert adventures.

Population:
Sharm Al Sheikh 35,000

Local dialling code: 069

Local tourist office: Zoo Street, Sharm Al Sheikh; tel: 069-366 4721; www.egypt.travel.

Main police station: City Council Street, South of Bank Street, Al Hadbah; tel: 069-366 0311.

Main post office: Bank Street, Al Hadbah.

Banks: Banks with international

ATMs are located throughout the region in the major resort areas.

Hospitals: Mount Sinai Clinic (specialises in diving-related medical emergencies and ailments); locations at Mövenpick Hotel and Sofitel Sharm Al Sheikh; tel: 012-218 9889. Sharm Al Sheikh International Hospital; Sharm – Na'ama Bay Road, Sharm Sharm Al Sheikh; tel: 069-366 0893.

Local newspapers/listings magazines: Most major hotels provide glossy guides to the region, especially diving options.

The Sinai (Sina') Peninsula has developed rapidly from the time Israel returned the region to the Egyptian government following the signing of the Camp David Accords in 1978. South Sinai is now Egypt's gleaming tourism beacon, with Sharm Al Sheikh acting as the central gateway to the region. Despite terrorism activity in the area, the local tourism industry is proving resilient, as foreigners are drawn by an intoxicating range of plush five-star resorts at relatively low prices. A lot of this has to do with the huge discounts the

government is giving to hotels and airlines that operate in the region – but the near-guaranteed good weather is also a strong draw.

But for visitors looking beyond sea-and-sand holidays, Sinai's marine and desert environments offer much more. Divers can explore the extraordinary Red Sea reefs, either from a base on the coast or on a liveaboard. Inland are desert adventures, close-up encounters with traditional Bedouin culture and treks up Mount Sinai to see the sunrise over St Catherine's Monastery.

Sharm Al Sheikh and South Sinai

Sharm Al Sheikh ❶ (Sharm Ash Shaikh) started its life as a small fishing village known amongst divers as a secret find. Today, the secret is well and truly out, as the resort town has grown to become Egypt's biggest and fastest-growing holiday destination. While the towns along the Nile focus on their cultural and historical links to draw visitors, Sharm boasts sun, sea and sand at affordable prices – perfect for the sun-starved visitors who flock here every year.

Sharm Al Sheikh

The region of Sharm Al Sheikh covers everything from Sharm Al Mayah, Old Sharm, Ras 'Om Sid and Al Hadbah in the southwest around to Na'ama (Ne'mah) Bay, Coral Bay,

A tea shop in Old Sharm

Shark's Bay and Ras Nasrani, and past the airport to Nabeq in the northeast. Distances between the sections are too far to walk – especially in the heat – but there are plenty of taxis and minibuses running along the main highway, Peace Road (Tariq As Salam), which links all the bays together.

At the western end is the main port of **Sharm Al Mayah**, beyond

Important sign in Dahab

UMBI SHARK'S BAY

برجاء ساعدنا في المحافظة
على الشعاب المرجانية

PLEASE SAVE THE CORAL

БЕРЕГИТЕ КОРАЛЛЫ

Avoiding Visas

Visas are needed by almost every nationality entering Egypt. However, there is one exception to this costly rule. In an effort to promote tourism to the region (and a throwback to the 1978 Camp David Treaty), visas are not required for tourists staying 15 days or less solely on the Sinai Peninsula.

If you know you have no plans to venture off the Sinai, then write 'Sinai only' on the back of your landing card and hand it to the customs officer to avoid paying. There are reports of officials trying to steer tourists into visa-payment queues at Sharm Airport. But, if you stand your ground, you should be allowed to enter without buying a visa.

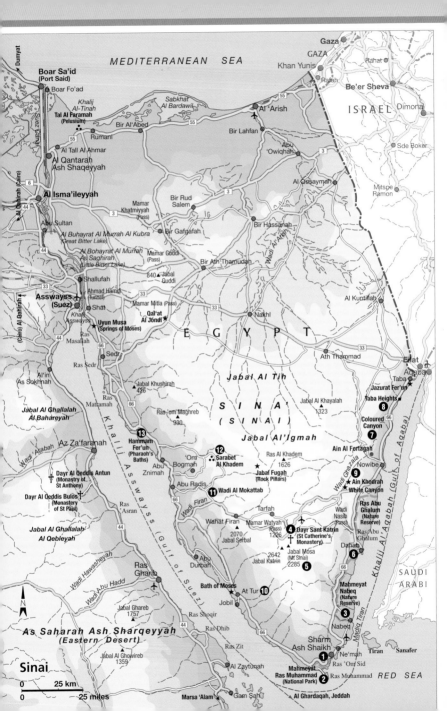

The popular beach at Na'ama Bay

which the road runs west towards Ras Muhammad, Suez and Cairo. Hundreds of dive boats are moored in the harbour, which is also the departure point for the ferry to Hurghadah (Al Ghardaqah). Inland is Old Sharm (Sharm Al Adimah) – as authentic a piece of Egypt as you will see on this part of the Sinai coast. Some modern restaurants and shopping malls have been built, but essentially this is the Old Town, with an unhurried atmosphere.

One of the landmarks of the safe, enclosed bay here is a large tower which gives residents of the Beach Albatros Hotel direct access to the beach. Beyond this is a clifftop walk with wonderful views along the coast leading out of the bay and around the Ras 'Om Sid headland. The small Sadiki café has fine views towards the

Sinai Transport

 Airport: 10km (6 miles) north of Na'ama Bay.

 Buses: The bus station at Sharm Al Sheikh is in Na'ama Bay Road, near the main Mobil petrol station. The main bus company is East Delta Travel Co; tel: 069-366 0660. Also Superjet; tel: 069-366 1622.

 Car hire: Avis; tel: 069-360 2400; www.avis.com; Europcar; tel: 016-554 4313; www.europcar.com
As the Sinai has a large expat community, car rental is becoming

easier. Travelling into the interior can therefore be done independently, with a private car and driver or through a tour operator. Maps can be confusing, so if you do decide to go it alone, make sure you get your route checked out by a hotel concierge or at the tourist office prior to departure, and that you are fully prepared.

 Taxis: Taxi drivers work independently; hail a taxi from the street or have your hotel concierge flag one for you. Negotiate the price for all trips prior to getting in the vehicle.

Al Fanar lighthouse on the headland. The lighthouse itself gives wonderful views east towards Ras Nasrani and distant Tiran Island, and west to the Ras Muhammad headland. Below the lighthouse is the popular El-Fanar bar and restaurant.

The **Ras 'Om Sid** area, with its many hotels and private beaches, runs from the bay lighthouse to an isolated rock known as 'The Tower'. The reefs off this coast are popular for diving and snorkelling due to their easy access. Inland is **Al Hadbah** ('hill'), also with many hotels, resorts and activity centres.

Na'ama Bay

This is Sharm's main tourist centre, with crowded shopping malls, tightly packed restaurants and the busiest bars and nightclubs. The downtown area of Na'ama Bay (Khalij, Ne'mah) has now been pedestrianised, which makes it a little less frenetic.

About 10km (6 miles) further along the coast is **Shark's Bay** (Bayt El 'Ersh), named for the enormous but gentle whale sharks that are frequently seen here. Local Bedouin offer camel rides along the beach, and there are plenty of opportunities to interact with locals. The headland beyond this is **Ras Nasrani**, meaning 'Christian Cape' after the Arabic word for natives of Nazareth (An Nasrah). Peace Road continues right around to the airport and the Nabeq Protectorate beyond.

Diving hotspots

The waters around Sharm Al Sheikh are world-renowned for their coral reefs (see p.31).

Ras Muhammad National Park

At the very southerly tip of Sinai, **Ras Muhammad National Park** ➋ (daily; sunrise–sunset; charge) separates the Gulf of Suez from the Gulf of Aqaba and has exceptionally

Scuba-diving in crystal clear waters

St Catherine's Monastery, parts of which date back to the 6th century

nutrient-rich water flowing in strong currents, attracting fish of all sizes, especially during the summer months. Great shoals of snapper, jack and tuna can be seen, as well as large Napoleon wrasse, moray eels and curtains of barracuda.

To the west of Ras Muhammad lies the wreck of the English freighter *Thistlegorm*. The ship was sunk by German bombers in 1941 and still has much of its cargo intact, including Norton and BSA motorbikes, tanks, army supplies and even railway engines.

Tiran Island

Tiran Island is situated east of Sharm Al Sheikh in the Strait of Tiran. The island belongs to Egypt but is only accessible to the military, because 12km (7 miles) beyond its easterly towering peak is the mainland of Saudi Arabia. The waters around it, however, are popular with divers as the string of reefs are home to

---

Five Best Dive Bars

When it comes to finding good bars, the diving community is always a good resource. Cheap beer and a casual vibe is what they're after, where they can swap stories and compare tips. Here are five of the best in the Sinai:

Na'ama Bay

- Camel Roof Bar, Camel Hotel
  Loved by dive instructors – a great place to start an evening.
- Pirates' Bar, Hilton Fayrouz Village
  Pub-style drinking den with popular happy hour daily from 5.30–7.30pm.

Dahab

- Carm Inn, Masbat
  A slice of Asia, serving Indonesian fare in relaxed surroundings.
- Penguin Restaurant, Mashraba
  More of a backpacker haunt than a divers' establishment during high season.
- Tota Dance Bar, Masbat
  Everyone ends up at Tota's – considered party central in Dahab.

exceptionally beautiful coral and many large fish. Its popularity means there can be as many as 20 boats at each site through the peak season (July–December), so to avoid the crowds, try to arrive early (7am–10am) or later in the day.

Nabeq Protectorate

Preventing any further development north of Nabeq is the 600-sq-km (230-sq-mile) **Nabeq Protectorate** ❸ (sunrise–sunset; charge), which stretches along the coastline for over 40km (25 miles). The park's main entry gate is at Nabeq, and there are some walking trails inside. Several wadis drain the mountains, carrying soil and silt to make the area fertile. Roots of dense mangrove trees dig deep into the saltwater marsh flats, providing valuable protection for newly hatched and developing immature fish.

St Catherine's Monastery

One of the most popular and historically interesting day excursions offered by the tour operators in Sharm Al Sheikh is a coach visit to **St Catherine's Monastery** ❹ (Dayr Sant Katrin; 9am–noon, closed Fri, Sun and Greek Orthodox holidays, but sometimes open 11am–noon; free; visitors must be modestly dressed, with legs and arms covered), tucked below Mount Sinai. The logistics of this day trip are not ideal as the monastery is only open in the mornings, thus requiring a very early start or an overnight stay in the nearby town of St Catherine's. Another option is to visit the monastery on the way down from an overnight climb up Mount Sinai (see p.205).

St Catherine's Monastery is an important biblical site, nestling at the foot of stark mountains. Seemingly protected by giant natural

Watching the sunrise from Mount Sinai

Mount Sinai

Mount Sinai ❺ (known locally as Jabal Mosa or Mount Moses), said to be where Moses received the Ten Commandments from God, is one of the highest peaks in Egypt at 2,285m (7,497ft). For many Christians, Jews and Muslims this is a very spiritual place. You can gain a greater understanding of the site's significance by reading chapters 19 to 40 of Exodus, which describe Moses' experiences on Mount Sinai.

In winter it is possible to visit St Catherine's Monastery in the morning and then climb the mountain in the afternoon, witnessing sunset over the mountain peaks, and then descend in the gloom of early evening. This is a long and physically demanding day, but feasible for adults.

From the monastery there are two main routes to climb the 700m (2,300ft) to the summit, both of which children will find difficult. A flight of over 3,700 steps called the Sekket Sidna Mosa (Path of Moses) winds its way steeply up a narrow ravine from behind the monastery, passing through two main gateways. The other route, which is less steep, continues up the valley past the monastery and winds its way around the side of the mountain. It is called the Sikket Al Basha, named after Pasha Abbas I, who had the track constructed. It is also known as the camel track, as people can ride almost to the top, dismount and climb just a few hundred steps to the summit. A night ascent requires a good

walls of rock, it is believed to mark the spot where God appeared as a burning bush and spoke to Moses, as described in chapter three of Exodus. The first building on the site was a chapel built around AD330 under the orders of Saint Helena, mother of Constantine, the first Christian Roman emperor, to provide shelter for the hermits who lived in caves close to Mount Sinai.

The main structures date from the 6th century, when Emperor Justinian paid for the chapel to be extended (even though he wanted it built on the summit of Mount Sinai). The monastery was named after St Catherine, who was born in Alexandria and martyred in the early 4th century, after her body miraculously appeared on a nearby mountain some 300 years after her death. A **visitor centre** (Sat–Thur; free) further down the valley gives more details about the history of the site.

★ BEDOUIN CULTURE

The great nomads of the desert, the Bedouin, have been travelling throughout the Sinai, Eastern and Western Deserts for centuries. Thanks to their long experience of living in the harsh conditions, they have developed a sophisticated understanding of their environment. When planning a desert tour it's best to take Bedouin advice, as the 'people of the desert' know best when exploring Egypt's last frontier.

It is estimated that there are approximately half a million Bedouin in Egypt – their traditionally nomadic lifestyle makes it difficult to measure their population accurately. They arrived in Egypt from the Arabian Peninsula about 1,000 years ago and belong to 14 distinct tribes, each with its own customs and culture. Arab-speaking and possessing invaluable knowledge of the harsh environment, Bedouin have long been valued as desert guides and traders. However, as modern methods of transport have erased the need for desert caravans, some Bedouin are adapting their skills to the needs of the tourism industry.

Recently, Bedouin handicrafts and beadwork have appeared in the markets of Egypt as tribespeople have sought to capitalise on their unique talents and skills. Bedouin women are well known for their weaving, necklaces and rugs, and their products can

Bedouin man in traditional garb

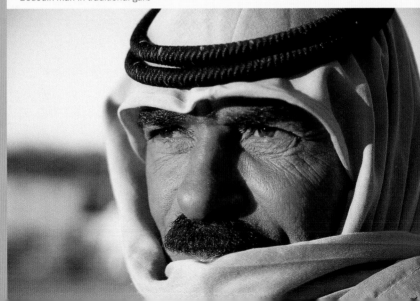

be found in souqs throughout Egypt, with the best for this being Dahab.

The draw of modern life is having an effect on the Bedouin as the government is encouraging these travellers to settle in permanent homes and take jobs. Bedouin can now be found as guides, drivers, in construction and in maintenance roles.

Bedouin father and son

The greatest concentration of Bedouin desert 'experiences' can be found in the Sinai, where Bedouin involvement in the tourism industry is strong. Bedouin women traditionally were restricted to the family home and could never come into contact with men not of their own family, but even this has been changing as they take on child-minding roles in some resorts.

You can experience Bedouin culture by taking a desert tour with a recommended Bedouin operator, such as:

• **Bedouin Safari**, Bahei Ad Dien, 35km (22 miles) west of Siwa near the Libya/Egypt border; www.bedouinsafari.org; tel: +201-030 33896. Join the Abu-Zahra family on a choice of three tours taking in the oases of the Western Desert using new 4x4s.

• **Red Sea Desert Adventures**, Shagrah Village, Marsa 'Alam; www.redseadesertadventures.com; tel: +201-239 93860. This Dutch/Austrian company ensures Bedouin guides lead their wide selection of day trips.

• **Bedouin Safari Dahab**, Al Mashrabah, Dahab; www.bedouin-safari-dahab; tel: +206-936 40317. Bedouin family-owned operation offering trips into the interior and St Catherine's Monastery.

Bedouin woman preparing a meal

flashlight, water and a fleece or jacket for the coldness of sunrise at altitude. There can be snow on the mountain in winter.

At the summit is a small chapel dedicated to the Holy Trinity, rebuilt in 1934 using stones from earlier destroyed churches, dating back to AD532.

Eastern Sinai

East of Sharm Al Sheikh, resort atmospheres change and price tags drop. Backpackers and those looking for more relaxed experiences favour the towns that line this part of the coast. There's a wider range of accommodation options, and activities to suit all tastes and budgets.

Divers, too, often prefer the focus on underwater fun rather than five-star luxury, and many can be seen swapping stories in the bars and dive shops in the region. The area is not quite the hippy centre it once was; tie-dye and Bob Marley tunes now coexist with internet cafés and upmarket restaurants. Bedouin guides saturate the tourism scene in Dahab, offering cultural trips into the desert.

Dahab

Compared to Sharm, **Dahab** ❻ is a sleepy town catering to the back-packer brigade with a good range of well-priced basic properties. Dahab's tourist area is known as **Asilah**, which is located about 4km (2½ miles) north of the town's administrative centre. There is public access all the way along the 3km (1¾ miles) of seafront, which is lined with bars, cafés and restaurants. The excavated ruins at **Tall Al Mashrabah** (Al Mashrabah Hill), located at the southern end of Asilah, were uncovered in 1989 and are said to be the remains of a 1st-century BC Nabataean town, part of a civilisation whose capital was at Petra.

Horses, camels, quad bikes, jeeps and bicycles can all be hired, and a popular excursion is north along the coast into the **Ras Abu Ghalum Protectorate** (sunrise–sunset; free). The protectorate boasts a raised fossilised coral reef and two famous dive sites – the Blue Hole and the Canyon.

Nuweiba

Nuweiba (Nowibe) is a resort that has seen better days. Popular with budget-conscious Eastern European package tourists, its chief function is as the main town for ferry departures to Aqaba (Al'Aqabah). There are two ferries in each direction daily, both leaving in the mid-afternoon.

Stroll along the beach in Dahab

Beach-side picnic spot in Dahab

Coloured Canyon

Between Dahab and Taba, one of the easiest and most popular excursions is to **Coloured Canyon** ❼, a wonderfully eroded small gorge. You will need the assistance of a local guide, and permission is required to pass through the checkpoint on the road up Wadi Watir, which runs directly inland from Nuweiba and eventually leads to Suez and Cairo.

From a local Bedouin café a steep footpath drops for 15 minutes down through brilliant white rocks to the foot of Jabal 'Aradah and into the Coloured Canyon. The canyon slowly narrows and snakes left and right, and the sandy wadi floor is sometimes only wide enough to fit one shoe in front of the other. The canyon hike takes about 30 minutes and the whole trek about an hour, so once you've explored you can go further afield with your tour guide and jeep.

Taba Heights

Taba Heights (Mortafa'at Taba) ❽ is the Eastern Sinai's answer to Al Gouna resort near Hurghadah – a purpose-built tourist community of a few upmarket resorts sharing a coastline, marina, golf course and other facilities. The setting, between the tranquil turquoise waters of the Gulf of Aqaba and the towering red mountains nearby, is certainly spectacular. A few kilometres north of Taba Heights the road swings inland, obscuring the view of the Sun Pool, an unusual natural lake isolated from the sea. The road then rejoins the coast at the beautiful inlet known as the Fjord, one of the best natural harbours in the Gulf of Aqaba for small boats.

Ain Khodrah

Returning to **Ain Al Fortagah**, another track goes due south along Wadi Ghazalah. After 30km (18 miles) of tough 4x4 driving you arrive at **Ain Khodrah** , said to be the place mentioned in both the Bible and Torah as part of the route Moses and his followers took after they left Mount Sinai. The fact that anything grows here seems a miracle, but thanks to a small spring there are extensive palm, olive, lemon and fig trees supporting three Bedouin families. The tribespeople supply visitors with tea and food, and sell locally made handicrafts. Thursday night is the main Bedouin wedding night, and visitors are welcomed if they happen upon one of these traditional tribal celebrations.

There are also two trekking routes from Ain Khodrah – the ancient Moses trail and an interesting walk through the White Canyon that leads back to Wadi Ghazalah. It is possible to see desert foxes, wild goats and gazelles (after which the valley is named), but a local guide must always be taken as it is easy to get hopelessly lost.

Western Sinai

The present Sharm Al Sheikh conurbation is referred to as Sharm I, but northwest of Ras Muhammad National Park is a large empty coastline identified as Sharm II – the next huge area earmarked for future development. Western Sinai's coastline is connected with the oil industry, but the area also has an ancient history dating right back to Pharaonic times.

At Tur

The capital of South Sinai is the modern town of **At Tur** , which initially looks to be of little interest. It

Pharaoh's Island near Taba Heights

originally developed as the port closest to St Catherine's Monastery, which is less than 50km (30 miles) away. Excavations are continuing at the site of the old Raithou Monastery, where food and supplies were stored before being carried up to St Catherine's.

A small road runs north along the coast for 3km (1¾ miles) to a natural spring known as the Bath of Moses (8am–sunset; charge). There are indoor and outdoor pools for taking the sulphurous waters, said to be good for rheumatic treatment and curing skin diseases.

Wadi Firan and Wadi Al Mokattab

Around 66km (41 miles) further along this road, a right turn leads up Wadi Firan, the main modern road from the west coast to St Catherine's. About 22km (13 miles) along this road, a wide valley enters from the north, which has been a major thoroughfare for thousands of years. Known as **Wadi Al Mokattab ⓫** (meaning 'Valley of Writing'), it has many inscriptions made by Bedouin traders and religious pilgrims, and was probably part of the route taken by Moses and his followers. This is the shortest route to St Catherine's and Mount Sinai if travelling from Suez. The wadi is extremely difficult to find, being something of a 'hidden valley', and requires a 4x4 and local guide.

Further east, Wadi Firan opens up into a fine palmery known as the Oasis of Feiran (Wahat Firan), with many date palms along the roadside, shading the local houses. The village of Tarfah is said to be the location of the 'manna from heaven' as described in Exodus chapter 16, manna being a tiny white nourishing deposit produced on tamarisk bushes.

Sarabet Al Khadem Temple

Back on the coastal road is the prosperous modern oil town of Abu Radis, the centre of Western Sinai's oil industry, with many offshore rigs. Just before the port of Abu Znimah is an inland road that accesses new ore mines, but this area also has some of the oldest mines in Egypt.

One of the most remarkable buildings in Sinai is **Sarabet Al Khadem Temple ⓬** (sunrise–sunset; free). This Ancient Egyptian temple, complete with ceremonial entranceway, pylon, courtyard and inner sanctuary, dates from around 2700BC to 1100BC. It seems to have had a double function – it is dedicated to the goddess Hathor, who is referred to here as 'the lady of the turquoise', but also glorifies the power of the Pharaohs who commanded the mining expeditions.

The excursion from Abu Znimah takes at least six hours, and the temple can only be found with a local guide and 4x4. The temple is finally reached after an hour's walk up a small pass

The Sinai

The oasis at Ain Khodrah

Sarabet Al Khadem ruins

called Rod Al Air (meaning 'track of the little donkey') that has been used for thousands of years.

Another three hours of 4x4 driving further east of the temple, in a location about as remote as you can get in the central Sinai, are a strange set of weathered rocks known as the Jabal Fugah rock pillars. A desert safari of several days could link all of these unusual sites, together with Wadi Al Mokattab and St Catherine's.

Northern Gulf of Suez

North of Abu Znimah the coastal road swings inland around Jabal Hammam Fer'un, which rises to almost 500m (1,640ft). At the foot of this mountain, where it drops into the sea, is an outpouring of hot sulphurous water from a natural hot water spring known as **Hammam Fer'un** ⓫ (Pharaoh's Bath).

A small cave overlooking the sea gives access inside the mountain, which soon becomes a natural sauna surrounded by the hot rocks. The humidity increases further inside the final tunnel, which can only be reached on hands and knees. The springs are popular with the local Bedouin who use them to help treat rheumatism, but are too hot for all but the most dedicated sauna-lovers.

Several roads run eastwards from the top of the Gulf of Suez, crossing the central and northern Sinai. The main road, which carries a regular bus service linking Suez with Taba, passes through Nakhl and Ath Thammad, and has always been an important route between the heads of both gulfs. This is the main overland road from Cairo to Mecca, and has been used by millions of pilgrims over the years.

Access from the Sinai to the city of Suez and the rest of Egypt is through the Ahmad Hamdi Tunnel, which is 37m (121ft) below the Suez Canal.

ACCOMMODATION

As Europeans look outside Europe for better value, Sinai resorts are continuing to attract new visitors. If you shop around, you can find accommodation packages at very reasonable prices, especially in the off-season. Stay in Sharm and its surrounds if you like large resorts with plentiful amenities. Further up the coast, the atmosphere tends to be more laid-back until you reach Taba, where there are many more five-star properties like the Hyatt and the Hilton.

Sharm Al Sheikh

Beach Albatros
Ras 'Om Sid
Tel: 069-366 3922
www.pickalbatros.com
One of the best-located hotels in Sharm, high on the clifftop overlooking Sharm Al Maya Bay, giving fabulous views, especially at sunset. A lift gives access directly onto the hotel beach. **$$$$**

Eden Rock
Na'ama Bay Heights
Tel: 069-360 2250
www.edenrockhotel.net
A quiet hotel recently refurbished in an old Viennese boutique style with well-prepared food. No entertainment, but wonderful views across Na'ama Bay from the terraced pool. **$$$**

Four Seasons Sharm
Shark's Bay

Tel: 069-360 3555
www.fourseasons.com
Wonderfully situated on a headland just 10 minutes' transfer to the airport. The five-star classification does not really do justice to the excellent service and facilities at this award-winning hotel. Secluded private beach, swimming pools, wellness, health and spa centres. With the possible exception of the Ritz-Carlton, this is as good as it gets. **$$$$$**

Iberotel Palace
Sharm Al Maya Beach
Tel: 069-366 1111
www.iberotel.com
In a quiet area just 150m/yds from Old Sharm, with its lively area of shops and restaurants. Many of the 243 rooms are located around the tiered pools, which descend down to the beach. Full range of watersports. **$$$$**

Ritz-Carlton
Ras 'Om Sid
Tel: 069-366 1919
www.ritzcarlton.com
All 321 guest rooms at this resort are in low-rise apartments, each with a private terrace and the latest facilities, including internet via the television. Facilities include several top-quality restaurants serving everything from Italian to Lebanese and Japanese cuisine, together with a cigar lounge, two big pools, waterfall, fitness centre and games room. **$$$$$**

The pool at Eden Rock

Sanafir

Na'ama Bay
Tel: 069-360 0197
www.sanafirhotel.com
The Sanafir is the heart and soul of Na'ama Bay, one of its oldest hotels but also the most buzzing at night – many people return again and again for the social life. The characterful rooms have air conditioning, private bathroom/shower and satellite TV. The hotel's large open-air courtyard has a Bedouin tent, a rock swimming pool with waterfall, a diving centre, five restaurants and four bar-discos. **$$$**

Umbi Diving Village

Shark's Bay
Tel: 069-360 0942
www.sharksbay.com
One of the original resorts here, which retains its relaxing atmosphere. Choose a beach cabin, bamboo hut or room in the Bedouin village perched on a small clifftop. **$$**

St Catherine's

Daniela

St Catherine's Village
Tel: 069-347 0379
www.daniela-hotels.com
Spacious stone-built hotel in a spectacular location on high ground with 74 rooms split into small chalets or villas around the site, all with television. The ideal place to stay for a morning visit to St Catherine's Monastery or a night climb up Mount Sinai to see the sunrise. **$$**

Plaza

St Catherine's Village
Tel: 069-347 0289
www.catherineplaza.com
This resort is set like an oasis in the mountainous desert, with 168 rooms in villas, all around a beautiful swimming pool. There's a restaurant, coffee shop and adventure centre for activities in this rugged area. **$$$**

Dahab

Coral Coast

Asilah

The Hyatt Regency at Taba Heights

Tel: 069-364 1195
www.embah.com
Very quiet, relaxing locally run place with popular BSAC-affiliated dive centre and great open-air restaurant set alongside a beautiful beach. Located on the coast north of Dahab, from where desert safaris are expertly led into the tribal interior by Embah Safaris. **$$**

Nesima

Al Mashraba
Tel: 069-364 0320
www.nesima-resort.com
Good hotel and diving centre, inspired by traditional architecture, with lots of domes and a great swimming pool. Childcare is available. **$$$**

Taba Heights

Hyatt Regency

Taba Heights
Tel: 069-358 0234
www.taba.regency.hyatt.com
One of several large luxurious hotel chains in Taba Heights that share a golf course, marina and conference centre. **$$$$$**

Taba

Hilton Taba Resort and Nelson Village

Tel: 069-353 0140
www.hilton.com
Situated right at the border with Israel, this large 400-room hotel dominates the landscape, with fabulous views across the gulf to Jordan and Saudi Arabia. **$$$$$**

RESTAURANTS

Catering to the demands of the large international base of tourists, culinary options in the Sinai are decidedly diverse. Italian, American, Asian and, thankfully, Egyptian foods are all available. Many of the best restaurants are located inside the prime resorts,

however, so you will pay a premium to eat there if you're not a guest. If you are on an all-inclusive holiday, try to leave your hotel for at least one meal to sample the street food options in Sharm's Old Town or market area.

Sharm Al Sheikh

Café Picasso
City Council Street, beside the go-kart track, Al Hadabah
Tel: 010-926 6913
A bit off the beaten track, but there's the choice of eating inside or out, and a great Sunday roast lunch with a free camel ride included. **$**

Da Franco
Ghazala Beach Hotel
Tel: 069-360 0150
On the pedestrianised walkway behind the beach in Na'ama Bay. Genuine Italian specialities, with pizzas straight from the wood-fired clay-brick oven. **$$**

Kanzaman
Al Zhoor Mall, opposite Cataract Hotel, Na'ama Bay
Tel: 012-710 5877
www.kanzamanredsea.com
This place specialises in barbecue and seafood on a street where the competition is fierce. **$$**

Tam Tam
Ghazala Hotel, Na'ama Bay
Tel: 069-360 0150
Excellent Egyptian and Middle Eastern speciality dishes served indoors in a very pleasant first-floor restaurant or outside on the terrace, both overlooking the beach. **$$$**

Tandoori
Camel Hotel, King of Bahrain Street

Tel: 069-360 0700
Authentic Indian cuisine at a great price. Most expats consider that it offers the best Indian food on the peninsula. **$$$**

Zaza Panorama
Above Sharm Museum, Na'ama Bay
Tel: 069-731 2972
Pizzeria and wine bar built into the cliffs on a series of cushioned terraces with stunning views over Na'ama Bay. **$**

Dahab

Al Capone
Beside the bridge, Asilah
Tel: 010-372 2220
Italian cuisine and fish come together at this busy central location along the Corniche walkway. **$$**

Al Capone is in a great setting

Arisha
Coral Coast Hotel, Asilah
Tel: 069-364 1195
Good food from the kitchens of the Coral
Coast Hotel served in the wonderfully
relaxed atmosphere of a thatched beach-
side bar. **$**

Lakhbatita
Al Mashraba
Tel: 069-364 1306
A little of everything is served in this beach-
side eatery, which is decorated with Egyptian
antiques. **$$$**

Nuweiba
Dr Shishkebab
Nuweiba Bazaar
No phone
Located in the centre of the souq, this
Egyptian greasy spoon serves up great
versions of Egyptian favourites, includ-
ing the ever-popular *baba ghanoush* and
humos. **$**

Taba Heights
Hyatt Regency, Intercontinental
Marriott, Sofitel, Three Corners,
Sea Club and Uptown
www.tabaheights.com
Extend your choice of eating by joining the
'Dine Around' programme, which allows you
to eat at any of the seven locations in the
Taba Heights complex regardless of your
hotel of residence. See the website for more
details. **$$$–$$$$**

NIGHTLIFE AND ENTERTAINMENT
The Sinai caters to the party-hard-all-night-long tourist, with world-class
clubs, often hosting big-name international DJs. High culture options are thin
on the ground, with hotels preferring to offer culture shows as part of their
entertainment. Most late-night venues stay open until 2am.

Sharm Al Sheikh
El Fanar
Ras 'Om Sid
Tel: 012-736 7383
www.elfanarsharm.com
Open-air dance party with fantastic views,
drink specials and a happening vibe.

Little Buddha Bar
Na'ama Bay Hotel, Na'ama Bay
Tel: 069-360 1030
www.littlebuddha-sharm.com
Lounge-style establishment with comfy
cushions and chilled-out sounds. The place
to head for once the big clubs close.

Pasha in Na'ama Bay

Hard Rock Café
Downtown Na'ama Bay
Tel: 069-360 2664
www.hardrock.com
You really can't miss the sky dome, huge guitar and pink 1950s car outside this extremely popular night spot. The usual American hamburger-and-chips options are served in this lively and noisy bar.

Pacha
Sanafir Hotel, Na'ama Bay
Tel: 069-360 0197
www.pachasharm.com

Sinai branch of the global super-nightclub. This is the place to be if you want to let your hair down; being young and beautiful is not essential but it helps.

Dahab
Funny Mummy
Al Mashraba
Good-value food at a lively bar-restaurant with great views of the coast from the roof terrace, attracting a faithful clientele. Opposite is the Sphinx Bar, which livens up at night with loud music and free pool tables.

SPORTS AND ACTIVITIES

On sea or on sand, the Sinai Peninsula offers something for everyone. Most people who come here want to go diving and snorkelling, but there are other options if you don't want to get wet; development has brought golf and go-karting, bowling and bird-watching to the area for all to enjoy.

Snorkelling and Diving
The southern tip of the Sinai Peninsula is one of the world's prime dive sites. If you have never dived before there are plenty of training centres, and most also offer an introductory diving session to give you a taster. This involves a half-day of theory and swimming pool work to learn the basic techniques before signing up for a course.
If you don't want to explore the depths then you can snorkel in shallow offshore waters along the Red Sea and Sinai coasts to see excellent tropical marine life. Snorkelling equipment is on sale at the resorts. *For more information and a list of recommended operators, see the Unique Experiences feature on page 30.*

Other Watersports
Every conceivable watersport is available, from windsurfing, kitesurfing and wakeboarding to parasailing, waterskiing and banana rides, which are organised virtually on the spot. Watersport activity centres that provide equipment rental or watersport activity sessions can be found in major hotels and near the beaches of the major resort towns. Sun'n'Fun Sinai, established in 1990, is a specialist in sporting options such as parasailing, waterskiing and pedalo tours. Contact www.sunnfunsinai.com.

Camel- and Horse-Riding
Riding a horse or camel across the desert or through the coastal surf is a great thrill and is not hard to organise. It's best to go early morning or late afternoon to avoid the searing heat. Reputable stables and riding schools are located at some of the larger resort hotels, such as the Sofitel Equestrian Centre, overlooking Na'ama Bay at Sharm Al Sheikh (tel: 069-360 0081) or the Omar Riding Club on the Ring Road in Al Rwaysat (tel: 012-794 7973; http://omararabian.com).

Golf
Golf is popular despite the environmental concerns about its heavy use of a scarce commodity. There is an 18-hole championship course at Jolie Ville Golf, Maritim

Taba golf course

Jolie Ville Resort, Coral Bay, Sharm Al Sheikh (tel: 069-360 0635; email: info@ sgr-maritim-jolieville.com and a 6,500m (7,100yd) 18-hole course, beautifully situated between the Sinai Mountains and the Gulf of Aqaba at Taba Heights (tel: 069-358 0073; download a golf-course factsheet at www.tabaheights.com).

Bird-Watching

Spring and autumn are particularly good times to observe birds migrating between their winter habitats in Africa and summer breeding areas in Europe and Asia. Cranes, storks, flamingos, bee-eaters and falcons can be seen along this natural corridor, as they use the Red Sea coast to navigate their route. Visit www.osme.org for further details.

Go-Karting

One of the area's latest crazes is to hurtle around a track full of twists and turns in a small go-kart. Sharm Al Sheikh has three circuits, of which the largest is the Ghibli Raceway (tel: 069-360 3939; www.ghibliraceway.com), built to professional FIA standards, next to the Hyatt Regency to the east of Na'ama Bay.

Bowling

The MAS Bowling Centre (tel: 069-360 2220) at Na'ama Bay has six bowling lanes and numerous pool tables.

TOURS

Short daily excursions, boat and submarine tours and desert safaris are available in the main tourist centres and will be accompanied by a guide, but it is also possible to arrange guided trips in advance that will follow your own itinerary. Book in advance through a recommended tour operator.

Glass-Bottomed Boat and Submarine Tours

There are several ways to see the wonders of the reef without even getting wet, let alone hiring loads of equipment and becoming a qualified diver. The simplest way is on board a glass-bottomed boat that slowly drifts across the top of the reef, allowing you to see the wonderful coral and fish. Many operators offer these tours from the beaches.

Larger boats go further out to more colourful reefs. Once in place, the viewer climbs down into an underwater section from which you can look horizontally at the reef wall as it slowly passes by. Divers often accompany these boats to feed the fish. Seascope semi-submarine operates at Sharm Al Sheikh (tel: 069-366 1393) and Taba (tel: 069-353 0560; www.seascope-sub-marine.com).

Desert Safaris

Embah Safaris, based in Dahab, run informative jeep safaris led by local Bedouin tribesmen lasting from one to seven days, exploring the hidden history and natural beauty of the Sinai's stunning interior. Red Sea Desert Adventures, based in Shagra Village near Marsa 'Alam, offer safaris into the mountains to visit the ancient inscriptions and sites, lasting from one to several days and using local Bedouin leaders from the Ababda tribe as guides. *For more information on the Bedouin, see p.206.*

Guides and Tours

Reputable tour companies include:

Sharm Al Sheikh
Highway Travel
Office 11, Mall #8, Na'ama Bay
Tel: 012-743 4260
email: sharmelsheikh@highwaytravel.travel

Seti Palm Sharm Beach Resort
Sharm Al Maya
Tel: 069-366 0870

Spring Tours
Mall #8, Na'ama Bay,
Tel: 069-360 0131
email: ssh@springtours.com

Dahab
Embah Safaris
Tel: 069-364 1690
www.embah.com

Camels in Dahar

Marsa 'Alam
Red Sea Desert Adventures
Shagra Village
Tel: 02-3337 1833
www.redseadesertadventures.com

Taba
Sea Star Resort
Tel: 012-743 4258
email: taba@highwaytravel.travel

FESTIVALS AND EVENTS

The Sinai Peninsula celebrates all national holidays along with a couple of special events specific to the region. Most residents of the Sinai have arrived from other parts of Egypt in order to secure employment. As such, national holidays tend to be more subdued than in other locations in the country, as any who get the chance to return home for the day will do so in order to spend time with family and friends.

April

Sinai Liberation Day

This public holiday on 25 April commemorates the day the Sinai was returned to Egypt by Israel following the signing of the Camp David Accords. On 25 April 1982, President Mubarak raised the Egyptian flag over the Sinai. Israel had occupied the peninsula since the 1967 Six Day War. Most locals treat the day as a chance to relax, perhaps watching one of the military displays.

May

South Sinai Camel Festival

www.exploresinai.com

A month-long celebration of the camel in Sharm Al Sheikh, with camel racing the main event. Over 250 camels from 17 different Egyptian tribes take part, so this event takes over the town for the month. Even though camels may look slow they are in fact incredibly fast, and can run up to 65 km/h (40 mph) in short bursts.

Red Sea Coast

The Red Sea coast established its reputation as a holiday destination about three decades ago, when divers flocked here to access the reefs teeming with marine life lying just offshore. Fast-forward to the present day and the area is now filled with resorts, ranging from bargain fleapits to five-star fantasies. For guaranteed sun and plenty of watersports, the Red Sea coast offers good value for money.

Population: Hurghadah 40,000

Local dialling code: 065

Local tourist office: Resort Strip, tel: 065-344 4420; www.egypt.travel.

Main police station: Shari' At Tahrir, Ad Dahr; tel: 065-344 4774.

Main post office: Shari' An Nasr, Ad Dahr.

Banks: Banks with ATMs are located throughout the region, especially near major resorts.

Hospitals: As Safa Hospital, Shari' An Nasr, Ad Dahr; tel: 065-354 6965. As Salam Hospital, Corniche; tel: 065-354 8785.

Local newspapers/listings magazines: None in English.

About half a century ago, the stretch of the Red Sea coast between Al Gunah and Al Qasir was populated by little more than a few fishermen and their families. Today, this is the most popular resort destination in the country for international visitors, and more hotels and resorts have been constructed here in the last few years than anywhere else in the country.

Sunbathing and diving are the main attractions here, but if you want a change from the beach and the water, head inland to the sites of the Eastern Desert. Here, amid the silent expanse of the vast desert, are two of Christianity's oldest monasteries, and traces of Pharaonic and Roman settlements. You can hire a tour guide and explore wadis, tribal cultures and ancient rock art.

Hurghadah and Al Gunah

The largest tourist centre on Egypt's Red Sea coast is Hurghadah, known locally as Al Ghardaqah. Being just outside the Gulf of Suez, the corals grow well, attracting marvellous marine life. This is the fun centre of Egypt, where you sometimes have to remind yourself that you are in a Muslim country; in fact, in the resort of Al Gunah, further north, frequented by Egypt's rich and famous as well as Europeans on package tours, you may need to remind yourself that you are in Egypt, such is the level of Westernisation in parts.

Hurghadah

A far cry from the fishing village it once was, **Hurghadah** ❶ has become a large, popular and sprawling resort. There seems to be no end to the amount of expansion both to the north and south, and even the government concedes that development has reached critical levels. Most luxury properties are now found outside the traditional city centre, as resort owners move away from the clutter in search of cleaner beaches and clear water.

However, on the positive side, most people come here for the sunshine and the diving, which, despite some damage to the reefs, is still excellent, especially away from the coastline. Hurghadah is also a good option if you want to combine diving with a visit to Luxor and other Nile Valley sites.

Hurghadah can be regarded as three separate suburbs – the old downtown

Coral on the Hurghadah coast

(known as Ad Dahr), the new downtown (now called Saqalah) and the developed strip running south along the coast for over 20km (12 miles), known as New Hurghadah or the Resort Strip.

Ad Dahr

To the north, Ad Dahr is the part of town which feels the most Egyptian, with lively backstreets and a busy, colourful souq. This is where some of the earliest hotels and resorts sprang up, between the Jabal Al Afish hill and the sea, and they still tend to be cheaper than elsewhere.

The main attraction here is the **Red Sea Aquarium** (6 Corniche Street; tel: 065-354 8557; daily 9am–10pm; closed Fri for prayers; charge; 🛗), which gives non-divers a great opportunity to observe the Red Sea's rich marine life, including sharks, turtles and stonefish.

Between Ad Dahr and Saqalah are the remnants of what Hurghadah used to be – a public beach, naval dockyards, fishing harbour and port from where the ferry to Sharm Al Sheikh departs.

Ad Dahr, the old part of Hurghadah

Red Sea Coast

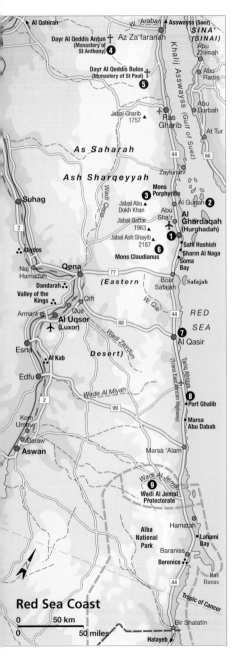

Al Qahirah
W. 'Araba
Asswayss (Suez)
SINA'
(SINAI)
Dayr Al Qeddis Antun
(Monastery of
St Anthony) ④
Az Za'faranah
Abu
Znimah
Dayr Al Qeddis Bulos
(Monastery of St Paul) ⑤
Abu
Radis

Khalij Asswayss (Gulf of Suez)

Jabal Gharib
1757
Ras
Gharib
Abu
Durbah
At Tur

As Saharah
44
66

Ash Sharqeyyah
Zaytunah
Mons
Porphyritis ③
Al Gunah ②

Suhag
Wadi Qena
Jabal Abu
Dokh Khan
Jabal Qattar
1963
Abu
Sha'r
Al
Ghardaqah
(Hurghadah)
2
Jabal Ash Shayib
2187 ①
Abydos
⑥
Mons Claudianus
Sahl Hashish
Sharm Al Naga
Soma
Bay

Qena
Naj
Hamadah
77
(Eastern
Boar
Safajah
Safajah
Dandarah
Valley of the
Kings
Qift
Qus
RED
Armant
Al Uqsor
(Luxor)
88
44
SEA
W. Qai
⑦
Al Qasir
Esna
Wadi Zaydun
Desert)
Al Kab
Edfu
2
Wade Al Miyah
99
⑧
Port Ghalib
Kom
Umbu
Marsa
Abu Dabab
Daraw
Aswan
Marsa 'Alam

Wadi Al Jemal
⑨
Wadi Al Jemal
Protectorate

Alba
National
Park
Hamatah
Lahami
Bay
Baraniss
Berenice
Ras
Banas
44
Tropic of Cancer

Red Sea Coast
0   50 km
0   50 miles
Bir Shalatin
Halayeb

Saqalah

Continuing south, busy Saqalah comes into view, with resorts, shops and restaurants running along its main street, off which lead roads to the beach. Here are the Western fast-food and retail outlets favoured by many of the tourists who visit, and the usual souvenir shops filled with leather items, brasswork, papyrus and the ubiquitous furry camels.

The ambitious Hurghadah Marina Boulevard project, opened in June 2008, was designed to regenerate the central beach area with shops, restaurants and a marina. At night the whole area comes alive with pubs, restaurants, beach bars and nightclubs.

The main Sheraton Road (Shari' Sheraton) rejoins the coast and climbs past the Felfela restaurant to reach the abandoned circular Sheraton Hotel, beyond which are endless upmarket

Fishing boats, Saqalah

The resort of Al Gunah

resorts catering for the modern beach-loving tourist.

Al Gunah

One of the most dramatic tourist developments in the area is **Al Gunah** , about 20km (12 miles) north of Hurghadah, now one of the Red Sea's premier destinations. The vision of an Egyptian entrepreneur, it was planned as a self-contained community served by its own airstrip, where everything would be done at an easy pace and to a high standard. There are several hotels, a brewery, several shopping malls and an open-air amphitheatre; concerts and sporting events are often held here.

A series of natural and man-made lagoons break up the coastline into small islands and peninsulas, while lush gardens and an 18-hole golf course designed to USPGA standards by Fred Couples and Gene Bates have been landscaped out of the barren desert sands.

Hurghadah Transport

 Airport: 5km southwest of Ad Dahr. The best way to get into town is to take a taxi.

 Buses: There is no central bus station. Microbuses run throughout the day from the centre of Ad Dahr to the InterContinental Hotel on the resort strip. Superjet has daily buses to Cairo and Alexandria; tel: 065-354 4722. Upper Egypt Bus Company has daily departures to Cairo, Luxor, Alexandria, Suez and Aswan; tel: 065-354 7582. You'll need to book ahead for long distance trips.

 Ferries: International Fast Ferries (to Sharm Al Sheikh); tel: 065-354 1870 (Thomas Cook). The port is at Meadan Shedwan, Saqala.

 Car hire: Most of the car rental agencies are located on the Sheraton Road in Saqalah. Europcar; tel: 016-661 1025; www.europcar.com.

 Taxis: There are plenty of taxis you can hail on the street. The service taxi station is at Shari' An Nasr in Ad Dahr, where you can book a taxi to take you to most major cities.

Remains of the Roman quarry at Mons Porphyritis

Coastal resorts between Hurghadah and Safaja

This stretch of coast heading south is dotted with resorts offering less crowded alternatives to Hurghadah. **Sahl Hashish** is a self-containted resort similar to Al Gunah. Either side are scores of large resort hotels, each with their own expansive beaches.

Bortsch on the Beach

As Hurghadah offers such value and is within easy flying distance of Eastern Europe, it has become incredibly popular with 'New Europe' holidaymakers, especially from Russia. These tourists are pumping a lot of money into the region, spreading their new-found wealth where it is needed. Another benefit is that you can sample some amazing Eastern European cuisine in one of the resort strip restaurants – it's the best bortsch this side of the Urals.

Makadi Bay is a well-protected natural arc of coastline further south. These new resorts provide an almost continuous string of developments towards Sharm Al Naga, a protected inlet that is also popular with divers and snorkellers.

Further south, near Safaja, is **Soma Bay**, with three top-class resorts and the Gary Player-designed Cascades championship golf course. Deep-sea fishing is good from here, and several new dive centres have opened, offering trips to the Panorama and Abu Qafan sites, which both have impressive reef walls.

Mons Porphyritis

Around 40km (25 miles) northwest of Hurghadah is the site of ancient porphyry quarries. In Pharaonic times, the mountainous Eastern Desert was exploited for gold and other precious metals as well as ornamental stone.

The Romans established permanent quarrying camps in the mountains and particularly valued the purplish-red stone called porphyry found at **Mons Porphyritis** ❸ (Mountain of Porphyry), below Jabal Abu Dokh Khan (meaning 'Father of Smoke'). It was used in columns and to decorate buildings throughout the Roman empire. Camps, workshops and temples were established here, but all that remains today are roughly hewn columns, half-inscribed blocks and a ruined fort; still, it's an atmospheric spot.

The route along the wadi to Mons Porphyritis is a fascinating if slow and bumpy journey, through major land upheavals where geology is laid bare, and takes at least two hours each way from Hurghadah. Access is only by 4x4, and an expert driver and guide are needed to find the correct route through the countless desert tracks.

Welcoming locals

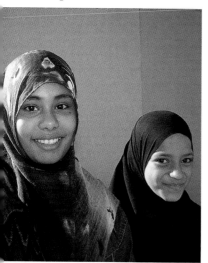

Eastern Desert

Nestled between the Red Sea Mountains and the Nile Valley, the Eastern Desert is an arid, atmospheric region that once contributed great wealth to the ancient empire through its vast mineral resources. Trade routes crisscrossed the desolate region, taking gold and semiprecious stones from the mines.

Day trips with guides – essential in this harsh environment – can be organised from Hurghadah to venture into the Eastern Desert, where as well as the mines you can see early Christianity's oldest monasteries and impressive rock inscriptions.

Monastery of St Anthony

The **Monastery of St Anthony** ❹ (Dayr Al Qeddis Antun; daily 7am–5pm; closed during Lent and Advent;

The Story of St Anthony

St Anthony was born in Upper Egypt in the middle of the 3rd century AD and lived for over 100 years. A great miracle-worker and protective saint, his life was recorded by Athanasius and his temptations became the subject of many works of religious art over the centuries. Halfway through his life he became a hermit, living in a cave high up a cliff face in the Eastern Desert. Early Christian followers escaping persecution settled at the foot of the mountain, forming the first hermitage in Egypt, and the country's largest monastery subsequently developed. Thanks to its remoteness, the community was spared during the arrival of Islam, but it has always suffered from Bedouin raids.

entry and guides free but donations welcome) marks the beginning of the Christian monastic tradition (see p.225). This and St Paul's Monastery are among Coptic Egypt's holiest sites.

The oldest part of the complex is the church built over St Anthony's tomb, which dates from the 6th century and is full of beautiful Coptic wall paintings, most of which date back to the 13th century. There are other small churches looked after by the 70 monks who live here, as well as a bakery, a lush garden and a spring, which allows the monks to cultivate olive and date trees and other crops.

Perched high above the monastery is the original cave where St Anthony lived. The 45-minute climb up 300m (1,000ft) of rock-cut and metal steps is tough in the heat of the day, so take plenty of water.

Monastery of St Paul

The **Monastery of St Paul** ❺ (daily 8am–3pm except Lent and Advent; entry and guides free but donations welcome), known locally as Dayr Al Qeddis Bulos, is another hugely important Christian monastery. Although only about 20km (12 miles) away from St Anthony's across the mountains as the crow flies, the road journey to get there is almost 100km (62 miles) back through Az Za'faranah.

The original church dates from the 5th century. The interior is filled with altars, candles and murals; a white marble sarcophagus sits on the site of St Paul's cave, and is said to contain his body. The monastery now has four churches, a canteen, a central tower and the monks' private quarters, but is altogether smaller and more low-key than St Anthony's.

The Monastery of St Anthony, where the Christian monastic tradition began

The new church at the Monastery of St Paul

Port Safajah and Al Qasir

South of Hurghadah lie 700km (435 miles) of coastline before you reach the border with Sudan. This is still an area of unspoilt coastal villages and harsh mountain landscapes. There is some development around Safajah, but for the most part there are endless sandy beaches and gorgeous turquoise seas, where adventurous divers are always searching for new sites.

Port Safajah

This port (*bur*) developed at the end of the shortest route through the mountains to the River Nile at Qena, and as such could be one of the oldest on the Red Sea. The port is protected by Safaja Island, and in Islamic times it became the main transit point for pilgrimage crossings to Mecca and Medina. Modern Safajah has only recently encouraged tourism, and remains a rather workaday town when compared to other resort communities on the coast.

Mons Claudianus

The quarries at **Mons Claudianus** ❻ (Mountain of Emperor Claudius) were used to obtain a high-quality quartzy diorite granite, which found

Nomads of the Eastern Desert

The Eastern Desert has long been populated by nomadic tribes, including the Ababda; a people who make their living as camel herders and traders along the coastal region. Known widely for their warm welcomes, the Ababda have a tradition of welcoming one and all to their communities. If travelling through the region, try to ensure that a stop at an Ababda village is included on the tour, as it provides not only an invaluable opportunity to understand the Ababda way of life but also a restful break in the day. A typical visit will include copious cups of sweetened coffee roasted on a fire in the village accompanied by the playing of traditional music.

its way all over the Roman empire. Many structures in Rome built under the emperors Nero, Trajan and Hadrian, including the Pantheon, Temple of Venus and Hadrian's Villa, as well as the later public baths of Caracalla, have architectural elements made from this stone. Today the quarry is reached via the main road between Safajah and Qena, but the trip should only be attempted with a 4x4 and a local guide.

Al Qasir

Al Qasir ❼ is a sleepy old town that has somehow largely escaped the tourist industry. The modern harbour is near the town, but a few kilometres to the north is a much more interesting ancient harbour. The old port of Al Qasir, called Al Qasr Al Qadim, had been a thriving port since Pharaonic times, when it was known as Thagho.

Despite being the best natural harbour in the northern Red Sea, there have always been problems supplying fresh water to Al Qasir. During the early 16th century the harbour appears to have irreversibly silted up. At the same time, the discovery of the sea route around Africa meant that vessels bypassed the Red Sea completely. The town expanded further south at this time, building the **Ottoman Fort** (daily 9am–5pm; charge) in 1571. Since the construction of the Suez Canal, Al Qasir has lost most of its trade to Safaja, but some of its former glory can be seen between the fort and the modern seafront with its wonderful Ottoman Red Sea houses.

Marsa 'Alam and the Far South

Sometimes the further you go out of your way, the better the experience. Marsa 'Alam and the far south is

The pleasant town of Al Qasir

just such an example. Still relatively unspoilt compared to the resorts further up the coast, it's the perfect place for those wanting pristine pleasure. Novice divers and snorkellers benefit from having the best reef sites lying just a few metres from the beach. As the region is underdeveloped, accommodation is limited, and it may cost a little more in expense and time to reach, but the rewards certainly outweigh the inconvenience.

Port Ghalib

Between Al Qasir and Marsa 'Alam, a fairly nondescript town, sits the resort of **Port Ghalib** ❽, a large new development set to rival Al Gunah near Hurghadah. Strategically located just outside the airport, 50km (30 miles) north of Marsa 'Alam, Port Ghalib is a huge, self-contained complex that will ultimately have several resorts run by top-class hotel companies, a marina, golf course, shops and restaurants. Presently in its infancy, it has a couple of places to stay and a virtually empty marina with coffee shops and cafés.

Other more rustic beaches include **Marsa Abu Dabab**, 32km (20 miles) to the north of Marsa 'Alam, which has for many years had a resident dugong (an endangered sea cow).

Wadi Al Jemal and the Alba National Park

Wadi Al Jemal Protectorate ❾, 54km (33 miles) south of Marsa 'Alam, is an ambitious project similar to the Nabaq Protectorate near Sharm Al Sheikh. The marine coast and inland areas here have been protected since 2003, but can be used by

Clownfish in Marsa 'Alam

the local Ababda tribe under strict conditions. Sustainable trades, such as producing leather products for tourists, are encouraged. Offshore are mangrove swamps and Wadi Al Jemal Island, an important breeding site and haven for migrating birds, a nesting site for turtles and a habitat for dugongs.

The protectorate is linked to the Alba National Park, a remote mountainous region with wild ostrich, Dorcas gazelle and Barbary sheep.

Hamatah and Lahami Bay

Just north of the Ras Banas Peninsula, Hamatah is a somewhat windswept community popular with kite- and windsurfers and for dive boats going to remote dive sites. The most southerly resort in Egypt is Lahami Bay, just south of here, with an entire lagoon to itself, extensive 'house' reef diving and a fleet of dive boats for the more distant reefs.

★ RAMADAN

The ninth month of the Islamic calendar, Ramadan is a period for reflection and spirituality during which Muslims fast from sunrise to sunset. Many tourists stay away from Egypt during this time, fearing it will have a negative impact on their visit – but with a few itinerary adjustments, a trip during Ramadan can be incredibly rewarding. Time a holiday with the celebration that ends the month, Eid Al Fitr, and join in the feasts and parties.

The holiest month of the Islamic calendar, Ramadan, one of the five pillars of Islam, is believed to have been the period when the prophet Muhammad had the first verses of the Qur'an revealed to him. At this time Muslims fast during daylight hours. While it can't be argued that Egypt slows down during Ramadan, it doesn't stop completely. Businesses remain open, albeit with shorter opening hours, and major tourist sites tend to close from 2pm onwards. Restaurants that aren't located in tourist-class hotels or resorts will shut completely until sunset, and alcohol will be unavailable in almost all corners of the country (except in tourist hotels).

However, there are benefits to travelling during Ramadan, especially for families. Package prices are invariably cheaper, and holiday costs can be a fraction of what they would normally be at any other time of year.

Ramadan

Eid Al Fitr festival celebrates the end of Ramadan

Harira Ramadan soup

To enjoy Ramadan, the best thing to do is adjust itineraries to ensure that most of your sightseeing is done in the morning. Don't try to cram a lot of strenuous activity in, and avoid going out at noon when the heat can be overwhelming, as being seen drinking in public (even water) is culturally insensitive. Return to the hotel for lunch and then relax until sunset when the party really begins.

As soon as sun has set, Egyptian Muslims enjoy the meal of *iftar* (breaking the fast). Tradition dictates that strangers should be welcomed into the home during Ramadan, so don't be surprised if you receive an invitation to join a family. If you're lucky enough to be asked, be sure to go as it is an unforgettable experience featuring countless delicious dishes only served during this month, such as *kunafa* (a sweet pastry with cinnamon and mixed nuts) or *katayef* (a sweet stuffed pancake filled with either nuts or sweet cheese).

The celebration to end the month, Eid Al Fitr, lasts for three days and sees the population dress in their finest clothes as they greet friends and strangers. It is also customary for children to be given treats such as chocolate or baklava, and markets come alive with food sellers and social activity.

As the Islamic calendar is lunar, dates change every year. Ramadan dates for the next few years are:

1–29 August 2011
20 July–18 August 2012
9 July–7 August 2013

Festival lanterns

ACCOMMODATION

Package holiday companies pack out the hotels along the coast, so you will often get a better deal if you book through an operator instead of going direct. Families and those who like Western comforts should stick close to Hurghadah.

Further south, prices tend to be lower and properties are a bit more basic, although this is rapidly changing as developers see the opportunities provided by the 'untouched' beaches in these parts.

Accommodation Price Categories

Prices are for one night's accommodation in a standard double room in low season.

$ = below E£200
$$ = E£200–E£450
$$$ = E£450–E£750
$$$$ = E£750–E£1,250
$$$$$ = over E£1,250

Hurghadah

4 Seasons
Just off Shari' Sa'id Al Korayem, Ad Dahr
Tel: 065-354 5456
Don't confuse this hotel with the luxury hotel of the same name. Hurghadah's 4 Seasons is a simple, budget property with a nice rootop patio. Guests have use of the pool at the nearby Geisum Village. **$**

Happy Land Hotel
Shari' Shaykh Sebak Ad Dahr
Tel: 065-354 7373
The rooms are pretty drab and the noise from the markets can be annoying, but you can't beat this hotel if you have an early ferry journey to the Sinai as the port is located almost next door. **$**

The Sheraton Miramar at Al Gunah

Oberoi Sahl Hasheesh
17 km (10½ miles) south of Hurghadah, Resort Strip
Tel: 065-344 0777
www.oberoihotels.com
If money is no object, then book into this 140-room, suites-only resort where you will be attentively cared for. The beautifully appointed rooms feature elegant decor with elements of traditional Islamic design. **$$$$$**

Sea Garden
Saqalah, between Meadan Al 'Arusah and the sea
Tel: 065-344 7492
www.seagarden.com.eg
This relatively new hotel offers clean, comfortable rooms at fair prices. Far from the sea, but the on-site swimming pool compensates. **$$$**

Sofitel Hurghadah Red Sea
Resort Strip, Hurghadah
Tel: 065-346 4641
www.sofitel.com
Classy resort boasting a large beach, kids' club and plenty of on-site courts and tracks for sporting enthusiasts and keep-fit aficionados. **$$$$$**

Triton Empire
Hospital and Shari' Sa'id Al Korayem, Ad Dahr
Tel: 065-354 9200
www.threecorners.com
Good-value hotel set in two buildings within the Ad Dahr suburb about 500m/yds from

the sea, but with access to a beach club for guests. Two swimming pools at the hotel and two at the beach. 🚹 **$$**

Al Gunah
Captain's Inn
Abu Tig Marina
Tel: 065-358 0052
www.elgouna.com
Intimate, boutique hotel with a central, marina location. Amenities are limited, but guests can use the swimming pool at the Ocean View Hotel nearby. **$$$**

Mövenpick
Al Gunah, 20km (12 mile) north of Hurghadah
Tel: 065-354 4501
www.moevenpick-elgouna.com
Huge resort hotel with plenty of amenities for the entire family. Enjoy the four swimming pools, the lagoons or the large stretch of beach. 🚹 **$$$$**

Sheraton Miramar
Al Gunah, 20km (12 mile) north of Hurghadah
Tel: 065-354 5606
www.starwoodhotels.com
This fairytale hotel blends Nubian and oriental styles with the surroundings of the Red Sea. Facilities include a handful of pools, diving centre, waterskiing school, eight restaurants and a shopping arcade. 🚹 **$$$$**

Port Safajah
Al Remal
In front of Safaja Port
Tel: 065-325 7316
www.remalhotel.com
Ideally situated for catching a ferry from the port, but in quite a busy area with port traffic. Provides a free shuttle bus to its large private beach, five minutes away. **$$**

Nemo Dive Club and Hotel
Magles Al Madina, Corniche Street
Tel: 065-325 6777
www.nemodive.com
This good-value 30-room Belgian/Dutch-managed hotel is 3km (2 miles) north of the

Mövenpick Resort

main centre and specialises in catering for divers keen to explore the area. **$$**

Al Qasir
El Qaseir Hotel
Corniche Street
Tel: 065-333 2301
There are just six rooms in this 19th-century converted Ottoman merchant's house overlooking the sea. Unique along the entire coastline, but bathrooms are shared and there is no air conditioning. **$**

Mövenpick Resort
Sirena Beach, El Qadim Bay
Tel: 065-333 2100
www.moevenpick-quseir.com
Beautifully designed resort with 250 domed rooms built and decorated in traditional style. **$$$$$**

Marsa 'Alam
Red Sea Diving Safari
Marsa Shagrah, 20km (12 miles) north of Marsa 'Alam
Tel: 02-337 1833
www.redsea-divingsafari.com
For those who would like to get away from the sprawl in Hurghadah, this is ideal: a collection of three eco-diving 'villages' that give friendly, personalised service. **$$–$$$**

RESTAURANTS

International and local specialities pepper the menus of the Red Sea coast. Branches of many of the big-name Western fast-food and restaurant chains can be found, specifically in Hurghadah. Fresh fish and seafood come highly recommended – often caught just hours before winding up on your plate. Many hotels are all-inclusive and favour buffet-style dining.

Hurghadah

Café del Mar
Sea Tower building, beside Meadan Al 'Arusah, Saqalah
tel: 010-071 6770
A simple, no-nonsense café with generous portions of fresh food. **$–$$**

Felfela
Shari' Sheraton, Saqalah
tel: 065-344 2411
Branch of the popular Cairo chain, serving good-value tasty Egyptian food. 🍴 **$**

El Joker
Meadan Saqalah
tel: 065-354 3146
Popular fish restaurant in the centre of Saqalah on the roundabout, serving fresh fish by weight. No alcohol. **$$–$$$**

Hard Rock Café
Nawarra Centre, Shari' Al Kora
tel: 065-346 5170
International chain known for its American and TexMex menu items. 🍴 **$$$**

Portofino
Shari' Sa'id Al Korayem, Ad Dahr
tel: 065-354 6250
Italy meets Egypt at this expat favourite that serves both delicious *baba ghanoush* and authentic wood-fired pizzas. **$$–$$$**

Al Gunah

El Ferdos
Corniche (opposite police station)
tel: 018-332 4884

Sheraton Miramar

Great for local grilled fish or seafood caught that day. No alcohol. **$**

Orient 1001
Sheraton Miramar
tel: 065-354 5606, ext 110
Good Lebanese dishes and Egyptian seafood in a wonderful oriental setting located on its own island. Live shows every Sunday and Thursday. **$$$**

Al Qasir

Restaurant Marianne
Shari' Port Sa'id
tel: 065-333 4386
Great seafood place serving the freshest fish around. Hours can be erratic. **$$**

Marsa 'Alam

All of the hotels in Marsa 'Alam currently operate on an all-inclusive basis. As such, there are no recommended restaurants.

NIGHTLIFE AND ENTERTAINMENT

If you're looking to party into the night, then Hurghadah is the place to be. Outside the town, nightlife is relatively subdued and drinking tends to happen in-resort after the diving day is done. While the resorts offer plenty of entertainment options, most of the shows are far from authentic. In fact, many of the floorshows are Eastern European in flavour to cater to the large Russian tourist contingent. Belly-dancing shows are often put on in the major hotels, but quality is inferior to what you find in Cairo. Performance schedules vary, so it is best to head to the major resorts such as the Mövenpick in Hurghadah or Sheraton Miramar to see what's planned for the week.

Hurghadah

Black Out

Ali Baba Palace, Resort Strip
tel: 065-344 7442

The most hedonistic disco in town, with weekly foam parties. Drunkeness is frowned upon by the locals, but that doesn't stop the party animals in this crowd, who sometimes get too boisterous.

Chill

Shari' Sheraton
tel: 012-382 0694

A relaxed beach bar with good music, which really swings on weekend nights, with lively beach parties.

Ministry of Sound

Hurghadah City Marina
tel: 065-738 2442
www.ministryofsoundegypt.com

Red Sea branch of the British super-club, very popular with the young and energetic. International DJs frequently appear.

Al Gunah

Le Tabasco

Kafr Al Gunah
Tel: 065-354 5516

This is the trendiest place in Al Gunah, impressively laid out over two floors and three terraces. A great place to come late at night.

SPORTS AND ACTIVITIES

There are literally hundreds of diving and snorkelling centres in all the resort towns along the Red Sea Coast. Watersports are big business, and the battle for your pound is fierce. Cheaper is not necessarily better as what you save in your wallet, you usually give up in terms of equipment and quality. *For more information on diving and snorkelling, see page 30.*

If you prefer your fun to be on solid ground, there are plenty of land-based alternatives in the Eastern Desert. Hiking, cycling and championship golf are available for landlubbers.

Red Sea angel fish

Cycling

Basic bicycles can be rented from most hotels in the area. Quality varies and models are usually quite simple.

Diving and Snorkelling

Week-long PADI certification lessons, day trips and liveaboard holidays can all be arranged along the coast. Prices tend to be more competitive here than in Sharm Al Sheikh due to the volume of operators. *Details on the diving experience along the Red Sea coast can be found on page 33.*

Hurghadah

Aquanaut Red Sea
Corniche, Ad Dahr
tel: 065-354 9891
www.aquanaut.net
Well-respected operator with a strong focus on safety. They may not be the cheapest, but the instructors are well trained and care about your overall experience.

Emperor Divers
Hilton Hurghadah, Resort Strip
tel: 065-344 4854
www.emperordivers.com
Respected dive operator with high safety standards.

Menaville Divers
Resort Strip, Safajah
tel: 065-326 0060
Safaga tends to be quieter, but this dive centre is at the heart of the local action.

Al Qasir

Rocky Valley Divers
Al Qasir
tel: 065-333 5247
www.rockyvalleydiverscamp.com
Budget-friendly dive camp with excellent safety standards.

Marsa 'Alam

Red Sea Diving Safari
Marsa Shagrah, near Marsa 'Alam
tel: 02-337 9942
www.redsea-divingsafari.com

The best operator in the far south of the country, with strict environmental standards to protect the fragile reefs.

Golf

Championship golf courses are available throughout the region. Options include:
The Cascades Golf & Country Club
Soma Bay
tel: 065-354 2333
Gary Player-designed course that is consistently rated the best in the region.

The Steigenberger Golf Resort
Al Gunah
tel: 065-358 140
Eighteen-hole golf course surrounded by the Al Gunah lagoon.

Hiking

Red Sea Desert Adventures
Marsa Shagrah, near Marsa 'Alam
tel: 012-399 3860
www.redseadesertadventures.com
Contact Red Sea Desert Safaris for advice regarding hikes between the Monasteries of St Paul and St Anthony.

Watersports

Almost all of the large resorts along the coast have an in-house activity centre available to both guests and non-guests. Non-guests may need to pay a day charge to access the facilities, but this is usually waived if an activity is booked. Activities include sailing, jet-skiing, wind- and kite-surfing, parasailing, kayaking and more.

Windsurfing is popular too

TOURS

The sea meets the Eastern Desert along the Red Sea coast, meaning that travellers can enjoy both land- and sea-based day trips and extended tours. Choose diving, snorkelling and submarine experiences or head inland to explore the mountainous interior on a desert adventure. The sites of Luxor and Cairo are also within reach as long as you don't mind a long journey. Minimum numbers are usually required for all tours, so it is best to book in advance.

Day Trips

Day trips to long-distance destinations don't happen every day, so it is best to let your concierge or hotel receptionist do the negotiating on your behalf. Day-long jeep safaris in the Eastern Desert start from E£200 per person, while excursions to Cairo and Luxor start at around E£300 per person for budget trips involving long transfer times – 7 hours to Cairo or 4 hours to Luxor by coach. Double that cost to add a bit of luxury and comfort.

Desert Safaris

Red Sea Desert Adventures
Marsa Shagrah, near Marsa 'Alam
tel: 012-399 3860
www.redseadesertadventures.com
Explore the Eastern Desert with this European-managed company. Bedouin guides are employed for most tours. Choose from camel, foot or 4x4 safaris.

Memphis Tours

Corniche, in front of Orabia Village, Hurghadah
tel: 065-355 2010
www.memphistours.com
Jeep tour specialist offering adventurous itineraries into the interior.

Submarine Tours

Sindbad Submarine
Sindbad Beach Resort
tel: 065-344 4688
www.sindbad-group.com
Enjoy the spectacular sea life without having to negotiate snorkels, fins or tanks.

FESTIVALS AND EVENTS

The Red Sea coast was not very populated until the arrival of the tourism industry. Most locals originally come from other points in Egypt and only live in the region due to the draw of tourism-related employment. As such, Egyptians will try to get home to see family during the main national festivals, so events like Eid Al Fitr are quiet along the coast.

February

International Fishing Competition
www.egaf.org
International fishing competition in Al Gunah and Hurghadah run by the Egyptian Angling Federation.

Egypt International Festival
Elite sporting event in Hurghadah held over 12 days, with a triathlon, half-marathon and off-road race run between the sea and the mountains.

March

Egypt Yoga Festival
www.egyptyogafestival.net
Leading yoga teachers come to Hurghadah to teach and offer workshops and demos.

July

Red Sea Open Amateur Golf Championships
www.somabay.com
Amateur golf tournament in Soma Bay that brings entrants from around the globe.

The Oases and the Fayyum

Five isolated oases dot the barren landscape of the Western Desert. Siwah is in the northwest of the country, its lush gardens standing against a backdrop of eroded sandstone hills and a sea of sand dunes. The other four oases are strung out in a loop parallel to the Nile, and provide a fascinating change of scene for the more advenurous.

Siwah Town

Population: 23,000

Local dialling code: 046

Local tourist office: tel: 046-460 1338; www.egypt.travel.

Police station: tel: 046-460 2047.

Main post office: Behind the Arous Al Waha Hotel.

Banks: Banque du Caire, located next to the tourist police station, where the ATM works intermittently.

Hospitals: Shari' Sadat; tel: 046-460 0459.

Local newspapers/listings magazines: There are no English-language publications specific to the region.

From the Nile, the Sahara stretches 5,000km (3,000 miles) westward, to the Atlantic. The world's greatest expanse of desert is broken only by dots of green, where human habitation has survived the spread of sands. Contrary to popular imagination, oases generally lie in rocky lands where wind and time have scratched out vast depressions whose depths allow natural underground aquifers to reach the surface.

In Egypt's Western Desert a single aquifer flows north from Sudan, running in an arc of five oases roughly parallel to the Nile. Prehistoric remains show that man has been exploiting nature's gift since at least 5000BC. Under the Pharaohs the four Nileward oases – Al Khargah, Al Dakhlah, Al Farafrah and Al Bahareyyah – formed a useful line of defence against Libyan tribes.

These days the desert and the oases are popular with wealthy Cairenes and expats who happily exchange the city's noise and pollution for a weekend of peace and quiet in the desert.

Siwah Oasis

The most mysterious of Egypt's oases, **Siwah ❶** was long off-limits to tourists thanks to troubles along the Libyan border, to which it is adjacent.

At present, not even a visitor's permit is needed, and foreigners can venture freely to the oasis. Daily buses now ply the asphalted 300km (190 miles) between Siwah and Marsa Matruh on the Mediterranean coast.

Siwah Town

The oasis' main population centre is in **Siwah Town**, dominated by the remains of the ancient hilltop settlement known as Shali Fort, a tight collection of ruined mud-brick houses, to which the Siwis moved from the fortress of Aghurmi in the early 20th century. Bicycles, for rent in Siwah Town, are the best way of getting to the main sites in the oasis.

On the rock of Aghurmi, 4 km (2½ miles) from the centre, sit the remains of the temple of Jupiter-Amun, home of the famous oracle

Dunes in the Western Desert

that confirmed Alexander the Great in his status as a god.

Another major historical site is **Jabal Al Mawta** (Mountain of the Dead; Mon–Thur 8am–2pm, Fri 7am–noon; no official charge, but baksheesh is expected), less than 1km (²/₃ mile) north of Siwah Town, where tombs have been cut out of the rock of a conical ridge. Paintings cover some of the walls, especially in the tomb of Si-Amun, but much was destroyed when the tombs were used as shelters during the Italian air raids of World War II.

Among the orchards, palm and olive groves lie numerous springs,

Remains of Shali Fort

The Oases and the Fayyum

Crafts in Siwah

Siwah boasts a long tradition of craft-making and artistry. Unfortunately, most of the best pieces are quickly snapped up, leaving visitors left with poor-quality souvenirs. Craft-making is experiencing a bit of a revival though, and the Government Handicrafts Shop opposite the mosque in Siwah Town is a good place to see top-quality items and get an idea of local prices. Note that the shop is not open on Fridays or Saturdays.

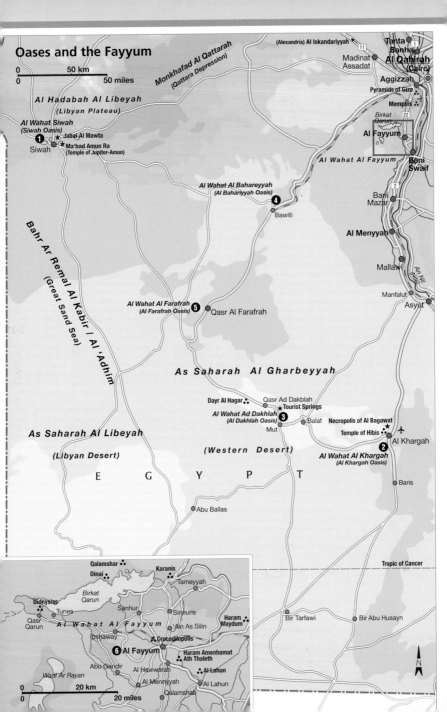

Oases and the Fayyum

0 ——— 50 km
0 ——— 50 miles

Al Hadabah Al Libeyah
(Libyan Plateau)

Monkhafad Al Qattarah
(Qattara Depression)

(Alexandria) Al Iskandariyyah

Tanta
Benha
Al Qahirah
(Cairo)

Madinat
Assadat

Aggizzah

Pyramids of Giza

Memphis

Al Wahat Siwah
(Siwah Oasis)
❶ ★ Jabal Al Mawta
★ Ma'bad Amun Ra
Siwah (Temple of Jupiter-Amun)

*Birkat
Qarun*
Al Fayyum

Al Wahat Al Fayyum

Beni
Swaif

Al Wahat Al Bahareyyah
(Al Bahariyyah Oasis)
❹
Bawiti

Bani
Mazar

Al Menyyah

Bahr Ar Remal Al Kabir / Al 'Adhim
(Great Sand Sea)

Mallawi

Manfalut

Asyut

Al Wahat Al Farafrah
(Al Farafrah Oasis)
❺
Qasr Al Farafrah

As Saharah Al Gharbeyyah

Dayr Al Hagar ∴
Qasr Ad Dakblah
★ Tourist Springs

Al Wahat Ad Dakhlah
(Al Dakhlah Oasis)
❸
Mut
Balat

Necropolis of Al Bagawat ∴
Temple of Hibis ★
❷ Al Khargah

As Saharah Al Libeyah
(Libyan Desert)

E   G   Y   P   T

Al Wahat Al Khargah
(Al Khargah Oasis)

(Western Desert)

Baris

∴ Abu Ballas

Tropic of Cancer

Bir Tarfawi

Bir Abu Husayn

Qalamshar ∴
Dinai ∴
Karanis ∴
Tameyyah

Birkat
Qarun

Dionysias ∴
Tunes ●
Sanhur
Sinnuris

Qasr
Qarun

Al Wahat Al Fayyum
Ain As Silin

Haram
Maydum ∴

Ishaway
Crocodilopolis

❻ Al Fayyum
Haram Amenhamat
Ath Thaleth ∴

Abu Gandir

∴ Al Lahun

Al Hawwarah
Al Mennyyah
Al Lahun

Qalamshah

0 ——— 20 km
0 ——— 20 miles

Wadi Ar Rayan

N

such as the 'in Al Gubah, the ancient **Well of the Sun**, whose waters were said to have purifying properties. Indeed, the water is so plentiful that large salty lakes have formed and drainage is a major problem.

Other Oases

The remaining oases of the Western Desert can't boast the same spectacular natural beauty as Siwah but offer their own delights in the form of mineral-rich springs spouting geothermally heated water. Tourist baths allow visitors the opportunity to experience the bliss – an unmissable option when you can commune with the stars in the quiet of the desert.

Al Khargah Oasis

Al Khargah (The Outer) is the largest and most developed of Egypt's oases, by virtue of its proximity to the Nile and because it is the seat of the New Valley Governorate. However, the concrete and modernity is probably not what you expect from an oasis. Five kilometres (3 miles) north of Asyut, a paved road leads past industrial complexes up into the desert. Two hundred kilometres (120 miles) of barren gravel later, the road suddenly

Temple of Hibis, near Al Khargah

The Oases and the Fayyum

descends a magnificent cliff into the Al Khargah Depression, which extends southwards, narrowing at its extremity, for 100km (60 miles). Descending from the plateau on the left-hand side are the remains of the old railway track that once linked the area to the Nile Valley.

About 2 km (1¼ miles) northeast of the town, not far from the main road, lies a cluster of monuments. Chief amongst them is the **Temple of Hibis** (daily 8am–4pm; charge), important

---

Siwah Transport

 Buses: The bus station is opposite the tourist police station in Siwah Town. Three daily buses leave for Alexandria via Marsa Matruh. Microbuses depart from the square outside King Fuad Mosque for trips to Marsa Matruh on the Mediterranean coast.

 Car hire: Due to the vast distances and challenging terrain, car rental is not recommended for tourists visiting the Oases and the Fayyum.

 Taxis: Taxis can be hailed on the street. To travel beyond the oases, you'll need a 4X4.

as one of the few remnants of Persian rule. Made of local sandstone, it was mainly built under Darius I, but the colonnade was not completed until the reign of Nectanebo II in the 4th century BC, and other additions date from the Ptolemaic period.

At the edge of cultivation to the north of the temple lies the Christian necropolis of **Al Bagawat** (daily 8am–4pm; charge), a huge area of mud-brick domes and vaults, some of which date back to the 3rd–7th century AD and therefore are one of the earliest Christian cemeteries in the world. It is worth engaging the services of one of the guardians (tip expected) to show you the highlights of the site.

Al Dakhlah Oasis

Al Dakhlah ❸ (The Inner) conforms much better to the image of a classic oasis, with palm groves, orchards and fields flourishing in the desert. It has a population of 80,000 and produces wheat, mangoes, oranges, olives and

dates. The New Valley Project, an ambitious scheme to bring water from Lake Nasser to irrigate the Western Desert, has more than doubled its size in recent years, but Al Dakhlah retains more of its original laid-back charm than Al Khargah, to which it is connected by a 190km (120-mile) road and daily buses.

The first important village in the depression is **Balat**. In the 13th century it was the terminus of a direct caravan route from Asyut in the Nile Valley, and a hive of mud-brick dwellings testifies to medieval prosperity. Using only mud and straw, builders attained a sophistication in architecture that combines utility, beauty and harmony with natural surroundings.

Al Dakhlah's current capital is at **Mut**, some 35km (22 miles) further west. The town contains most of Al Dakhlah's hotels, and, as well as the ruins of the Old Town, there are several small antiquities worth visiting which a local guide can show you. Just

Early Christian tombs at Al Bagawat

Spectacular rock formations in the White Desert

outside Mut, to the northwest, are the so-called **Tourist Springs**, with a pool (charge) and a rest house.

Al Bahareyyah

Al Bahareyyah ❹ is reached from Cairo by an excellent road that leads westwards off the Al Fayyum desert road behind the Giza Pyramids. About 330 rather dull kilometres (205 miles) later is a new settlement around Egypt's only iron mines. Not far beyond the mines, the road descends into the Al Bahareyyah Depression. Here, near the town of **Bawiti**, archaeologists have revealed an ancient Egyptian cemetery, thought to be the largest ever uncovered.

Bawiti sits atop a rock outcrop overlooking gardens that spread for several kilometres along the base of this cliff. The view from the cliffs at the spring called Ain Bishmu is stunning.

Al Farafrah

From Al Baharreyyah, a well-travelled road goes southeast, through 185km

---

Crocodile Worship

- The largest Graeco-Roman temple at Karanis was built in the 1st century BC to honour two local crocodile gods. The great Nile crocodiles were worshipped and sanctified in ancient times, with the main crocodile-god, Sobek, considered one of the most important to worshippers. He is seen as a human figure with crocodile head on countless temple carvings. Upon their deaths, both young and adult crocodiles were mummified.

- Since the building of the Aswan High Dam they have survived only in Lake Nasser. Today their numbers are increasing, and adults can grow up to 7m (22ft) in length.

(115 miles) of some of Egypt's most spectacular scenery, including the White Desert, to the oasis of **Al Farafrah 5**. Compared with the other oases, Al Farafrah has a fairly small area of land under cultivation, but it has the greatest potential for land reclamation, with more than 100 natural springs.

Al Fayyum

Sprouting from the west bank of the Nile, **Al Fayyum 6**, 100km (62 miles) southwest of Cairo, is Egypt's largest oasis, although strictly speaking it is not an oasis at all, as it is fed not by springs but by the Bahr Yusef, an ancient Nile canal. An excellent road across the desert connects Al Fayyum to Cairo, two hours away.

Exploring Al Fayyum

Approaching from Cairo, the first place of interest is to the left of the main road at a point that overlooks the fertile oasis. At the ancient site known as **Karanis** (daily 8am–5pm; charge) a cult of crocodile worship existed. Dating from the Ptolemaic period, it has extensive ruins of a temple dedicated to the crocodile-headed god Sobek, a temple to Serapis and a later Roman temple to Jupiter-Amun. On the outskirts of Al Fayyum is **Hawara**, the site of the remains of a Middle Kingdom pyramid of Amenemhat III.

Lake Qarun is a popular weekend retreat for Cairenes, offering vast open spaces and water activities. There are several pleasant lakeside restaurants serving fresh grilled fish, and opportunities to take a local fishing boat onto the lake. The main town is now known as Madinat Al Fayyum, but was previously ancient **Crocodilopolis**, where the reptiles were revered.

The mudbrick core of the pyramid of Amenemhat III at Hawara

ACCOMMODATION

There is great disparity in the accommodation choices in the Oases and Fayyum. Properties tend to be either simple and functional or 'lap of luxury' chic, with very little in between. Due to the remoteness of the Oases, prices are high in order to cover the cost of providing food, drink and amenities.

Siwah

Adrére Amellal
Sidi Ja'far
Tel: 012-2736 7879
www.adrereamellal.net
This 40-room desert retreat is set in its own oasis. Built in mud-brick mixed with salt crystals, the architecture is dramatic and the landscape stunning. Rates include all meals, drinks and desert excursions. **$$$$$**

Desert Rose
Siwah Town
Tel: 012-440 8164
One of the best-value options in Siwah – the Desert Rose boasts its own natural pool and a beautiful roof terrace overlooking the dunes. All rooms have shared bathrooms. **$$$**

Shali Lodge
Shari' As Sebuqah
Tel: 012-460 1299

Close to the main square, yet quiet. The location in a palm grove and traditional architecture give it an elegance other mid-price hotels in Siwah lack. **$$–$$$**

Bawiti

Desert Safari Home
2km (1¼ miles) from town, call for pickup
Tel: 012-731 3908
Free wireless internet, bike rental and city pickups make up for the slightly musty rooms in this friendly budget property. **$$**

Fayyum

Helnan Auberge
Qarun Lake, Al Fayyum
Tel: 084-698 1200
www.helnan.com
Converted former hunting lodge of King Farouk, built in 1937 on the banks of Qarun Lake in the Fayyum oasis. Seventy rooms set around swimming pool with gardens, as seen in old Egyptian movies. **$$$$$**

Simple elegance at Shali Lodge, Siwah

RESTAURANTS

What you get in remoteness and solitude, you have to give up in food quality. Options tend to be limited to traditional dishes or familiar Western favourites such as pizza and pasta. Stick to what the locals know how to make and you'll enjoy simple, filling food that may lack flair but is tasty.

Siwah

Abduh's
Central Market Square
Tel: 012-460 1243
This is the oldest restaurant in town, with consistently good, simple food. There's a large menu of traditional and Western options available. If you're looking for someone in town, then chances are you'll find them here. **$–$$**

Al Babinshal
Near Shali Fortress
Tel: 012-460 1499
A popular choice with couples as the setting is very romantic, with great views of Siwah. The food isn't as good as the panorama, but it's tasty enough to warrant the trip. **$$**

Bawiti

Popular
Just off main road in centre of town
No phone
Simple food served with a smile. Alcohol also available. **$**

Siwah café with sheeshas

Fayyum

Due to travel restrictions placed on foreign tourists for security reasons, visitors are advised to stick to eating in hotel-based restaurants. The central market is also a good place to stock up on local produce. Alcohol is difficult to find anywhere in the region.

NIGHTLIFE AND ENTERTAINMENT

Due to the security restrictions for foreign travellers in the Fayyum, visitors are required to return to their hotels early in the evening and cannot go out unless accompanied. As such, entertainment and nightlife in this region is non-existent. In Siwah, options aren't much better. Some of the higher-end resorts and hotels may provide folklore shows or native music performances, but there are no set times or locations, and visitors will have to simply ask locals or hotel staff for information upon arrival.

SPORTS AND ACTIVITIES

Some of the higher-end properties may offer swimming pools, and some pools are fed directly by water from the oases. But the best sporting activity in the area is taking a dip in the hot springs. There are several near the towns of Mut and Bawiti. Although the rust-coloured water may not look very inviting – and may stain your clothes – it is both hot and very relaxing. Women should wear a long baggy T-shirt over their swimsuit.

Cycling

Bicycles are a popular method for getting around Siwah if you want to 'hot spring hop' and can be rented from every hotel in town.

Hot Springs

Bir Al Gebel

Take the signposted turnoff 20km (12 miles) north of Mut

The best-situated and busiest of the local hot springs. Try to visit at night, when the crowds go down. 🛏️

Bir Al Gadid

West of the Bedouin Camp, Mut

The newest spring to be dug in the area, and very popular with locals and visitors.

Bir Ar Ramlah

3km (2 miles) north of Bawiti

Very hot spring. Location close to passing traffic means women should stay covered when taking a dip.

Cleopatra's Bath

Past the temple of 'Om Ubayd, Siwah

The most popular bathing spot for locals and tourists alike. No changing facilities, but you can use rooms at the Tanta Waa café nearby (for a small charge).

TOURS

You can take a tour into the desert by camel or 4x4 or take a day trip to the hot springs and oases. Competition to arrange tours is fierce. Your hotel will have a preferred operator, or you can try the tourist office in Siwah. *For recommended operators and a full description of desert tour options, see pp.38–43.*

FESTIVALS AND EVENTS

Harvest time is an excuse for celebration in this region. A bad harvest could mean hunger, illness and death, so traditionally good harvests are worth cheering. Join in the fun during the late summer and early autumn.

August/September

Mouled At Tagmigra

The date of this festival, which takes place at the tomb shrine of Sidi Suleiman behind King Fuad Mosque in Siwah, depends on the success of the corn harvest. Devotional acts are performed outside the tomb to thank Allah.

October

Seyahah Festival

This is the biggest celebration in the region, held during full moon in October, when thousands of locals gather to celebrate the date harvest. You can see Sufis practising their whirling dance without too many tourists.

PRACTICAL ADVICE

Accommodation

On the Red Sea coast and Sinai, there is a good range of accommodation as considerable investment has been pumped into these regions in the past decade. Peak season occurs during the school holiday periods of Christmas, Easter and the summer, so it is essential to book ahead at these times.

In Luxor and Aswan, tourism numbers are creeping up again after a marked decline following the terrorist threats of the 1990s. Discounts are available in these cities throughout the year.

Cairo and Alexandria are busy year-round due to business travel needs. On summer weekends, Alexandria can sell out, as Cairenes flock to the coast to get away from the heat.

HOTELS

Egyptian hotels run the gamut from fleapit to Pharaoh's glory and everything in between. The introduction of the Four Seasons chain to Alexandria and Cairo has done much to spark up some much-needed competition. Prior to the arrival of the luxury chain, international hotel groups would arrive in Egypt, build a new five-star and then run it into the ground, filling every room with package tourists and investing very little in its upkeep.

While the hotels faded in quality, they still retained their five-star status due to the amenities they offered (and the name). This means that a five-star hotel built recently could vary hugely from one built 20 years ago.

In Cairo, renovations have now become a must – and the closure of the Nile Hilton for refurbishment is a sign that the big hotel players are finally paying attention. You'll find that if you book a five-star in the

The outdoor pool at the luxurious Nile Hilton Luxor

capital, you'll get the level of service and amenities you expect.

In Luxor and Aswan, a number of excellent five-star hotels have been built in the last few years. But visitors should still be wary when booking what is sold as a luxury room in either location.

If you arrive in any city without a reservation, head for the tourist office, which in most cities is located near the train station. There is no 'one-stop-shop' accommodation booking service in Egypt, but the tourist office provides useful impartial advice.

Beware of high fees charged by tour operators; it's better to book your rooms in advance on the internet. Online prices are often much lower than those you will be quoted on the phone or in person.

BUDGET ACCOMMODATION

The difference between the cost of budget accommodation and three-star hotels is diminishing rapidly, mainly due to the volume of hotels on the cheaper end of the scale. You can get a clean, comfortable, spacious room in a decent hotel with a balcony or view for as little as US$30 per night. In off-peak season, it can be even less.

Hostels are available in Cairo, but prices vary little between multi-bed dorms and mid-price hotels that offer private bathrooms, your own room and that extra privacy. Often the price difference can be as little as US$5–10 per night. Pay the difference if you can, especially during the summer months when air conditioning is vital.

Outside Cairo, hostels are less prevalent as independent backpacker

New hotel in Dahab

travel has been so restricted until recently. Cheap rooms are also difficult to come by in the Sinai along the coast. Dahab is the resort to head for if funds are limited. Sharm Al Sheikh is priced at Western levels and should be avoided unless you are visiting during the off-season.

Be wary of hotel scams from taxi drivers when you arrive in any city by air or rail. There have been stories of travellers giving the name of their hotel to the driver only to be told the property 'just burnt down', or 'is closed'. Ignore what they say and insist on going there to see for yourself. If you get a room from the hotel they are offering, the chances are you'll end up at an inferior property which will cost you more money.

OTHER ACCOMMODATION

Egypt is only just beginning to embrace the trend for boutique-style

Feluccas on the River Nile

accommodation. Bed and breakfasts and homestay experiences remain limited for now as the government tries to prop up the major hotel groups on which the lucrative travel industry demands. Smaller-scale accommodation options are more likely the further away from an urban centre you go. Abu Simbel, the west bank of Luxor, the Oases and Western Desert offer more intimate accommodation choices, often combined with the opportunity to mix with the locals as part of a greater cultural experience. You will have to pay for the privilege though, as prices tend to be about US$20–50 more than the national average to include these additional personal touches.

Cruise ships and *feluccas* offer another accommodation choice for those exploring the Nile. Experiences can be booked in advance through a tour operator or directly through the ship captain or manager upon arrival in the country. Prices depend on the quality of the ship you are booking.

Basic-level ships can offer great value for as little as US$20 per night. *Feluccas* are even less at just E£100 per trip depending on the number of passengers. For five-star cruises and private *dahabiyyahs*, you are looking at spending a lot more. *More information on taking a cruise, including tips on how to book your trip, see pp.22–9.*

CAMPING

Camping is not advised in Egypt and in many cases is illegal. Travellers undertaking a Bedouin experience tour, desert adventure or a guided trek or climb may camp as part of their tour, but independent camping is not permitted by the authorities unless accompanied by Egyptian police or security forces.

You will need to file your travel plans with the police and secure a member of the force to accompany you if you decide to undertake a trip – but the volume of paperwork and baksheesh required will probably make you think twice.

Transport

GETTING TO EGYPT

Egypt is served by international airports at Alexandria, Cairo, Aswan, Luxor, Hurghadah, Taba, Marsa 'Alam and Sharm Al Sheikh.

Cairo International Airport (tel: 02-2265 5000; www.cairo-airport.com), 20km (12 miles) to the north of the city, is now a first-class facility with links to many cities worldwide.

Alexandria Airport is 7km (4 miles) from the city centre and is served by a range of Middle Eastern scheduled carriers. However, in 2011 it will cease operations, and all services will be transferred to Borg El Arab Airport located 40km (25 miles) south of the city.

Luxor Airport (www.luxor-airport.com), 6km (3½ miles) east of the city, now has direct flights from many European cities via Egyptair and several charter companies.

Just 5km (3 miles) southwest of Ad Dahr is Hurghadah Airport, serviced

Egypt's national carrier

by easyJet, Austrian Airlines and a number of Eastern European budget carriers, while Sharm Al Sheikh Airport receives charter and scheduled flights from all over Europe, including British Airways and easyJet. Marsa 'Alam and Taba International Airports are mainly for charter flights.

Other airports in Egypt are at Asyut, Aswan, Abu Simbel, Al 'rish, St Catherine's and Al Khargah Oasis.

Flight time to Egypt from the UK is approximately four hours. From the US, it's a 10-hour journey between New York and the Egyptian capital.

By air

British Airways (www.ba.com) Non-stop flights to Cairo and Sharm Al Sheikh available from London.
BMI (www.flybmi.com) Non-stop flights to Cairo from London Heathrow.
Delta (www.delta.com) Non-stop flights available from New York JFK Airport to Cairo.
easyJet (www.easyjet.com) Non-stop flights available to Hurghadah and Sharm Al Sheikh from London Gatwick and London Luton.
Egyptair (www.egyptair.com.eg) Non-stop flights available from New York JFK and London Heathrow to Cairo with onward connections to all domestic airports.

By sea
From Sudan
There is a weekly ferry from Wadi Halfa up Lake Nasser to Aswan. A

ferry leaves Aswan every Monday at 3pm and arrives the following morning in Wadi Halfa, returning on Wednesday. Tickets are available in 1st or 2nd class from the Nile Navigation Company in Aswan (tel: 097-203 3348; in the office located next to the Marhaba Hotel). Visas must be presented prior to purchasing a ticket in either direction.

All arrangements to enter Sudan, including visas, must be made in Cairo. Be aware that it can take the Sudanese embassy (3 Ibrahim Street, Garden City; tel: 02-2794 9661) up to a month to issue a visa.

Cruise ships

Egypt features highly on cruise ship itineraries. Most ships dock on the Mediterranean coast and then transport passengers to the major sights of Egypt for a full itinerary of museum-hopping and Pyramid-exploring.

By road

All private vehicles entering Egypt must have a *triptyque* or *carnet de passage en douane* from an automobile club in the country of registration or pay customs duty, which can be as high as 250 percent.

Emergency *triptyques* are available at the port of entry via the Automobile and Touring Club of Egypt. This permits a car to enter Egypt for three months with one extension. The extension is available from the Automobile and Touring Club of Egypt, Qasr An Nil, Cairo. All persons travelling in the vehicle must have a valid passport, and drivers must have an international driver's licence.

Cruise ships in Aswan

GETTING AROUND EGYPT

For long distances, flights offer the best way to get around. Unfortunately, Egyptair's near-monopoly means that prices can be expensive. Overnight train journeys can be effective, particularly along the Nile Valley, but you will need to book well in advance to secure a seat. Between Cairo and Alexandria or the Sinai, coach travel is the most common choice, with regular departures throughout the day.

Domestic flights

Egyptair (www.egyptair.com.eg) is the largest domestic carrier and has a near-monopoly on internal routes. Many popular routes (Cairo–Aswan, Aswan–Abu Simbel) fill up well in advance and it is advised to book ahead during peak seasons.

Ferries

There is a thrice-weekly service between Sharm Al Sheikh and Hurghadah operated by Red Sea Ferries. Bookings can only be done on arrival in either port or by contacting a third-party operator, who will add a hefty charge. The trip costs E£250 per person, one-way and take 1½–2 hours.

By rail

The Egyptian State Railway services the entire Nile Valley down to Aswan, the Red Sea cities of Suez and Port Said, the Delta and northern coastal cities of Alexandria (two stops) and Marsa Mutrah. There are at least half a dozen through trains a day on major routes, but train travel for foreigners is restricted – check at stations.

There are two main types of train: air-conditioned (tourist class), and non-air-conditioned (third class or local trains), which are best avoided.

Of the air-conditioned trains there are a number of options, including Espani (Spanish) trains, so called as that is where they were renovated, French trains and Turbini, refer-ring to the type of engine used. The privately owned Wagon-Lits train company runs three fast turbo-trains a day from Cairo to Alexandria (2½ hours). Booking should be done in advance at Rameses Station, Cairo or at Alexandria Station. Wagon-Lits also operate sleeper trains between Cairo and Luxor (10 hours) and Aswan (15 hours).

An English-speaking tourist office attendant can be reached 24 hours a day by calling 02-2579 0767. Bring passports for everyone travelling.

By bus

Air-conditioned buses link most parts of Egypt to Cairo and Alexandria. Seats may be reserved up to two days in advance. There is also a fleet of cheaper non-air-conditioned buses, with very frequent departures.

Tickets for air-conditioned buses must always be booked in advance.

The fastest buses to Alexandria (3 hours) are operated by the Superjet and West & Middle Delta companies. The principal carrier to Aswan and Luxor is Upper Egypt Travel. One bus departs each day to complete the run to Aswan, departing early evening and arriving early the next morning.

Air-conditioned Superjets to Luxor and Aswan are not recommended, as the services involve overnight travel

If you plan on travelling by train, avoid the third class or local trains

Traditional transport is still common in the countryside

with non-stop loud videos.

The East Delta Co. covers the Canal Zone and most of the Delta. Most buses leave from the Turgoman Bus Station (Mo'af Turgoman), in Bulaq, 1km (2/3 mile) northwest of Rameses Station near the crossing of Shari' 26th of July and Galaa. Services for the Sinai can still also be picked up from the old Sinai Terminal in Abbaseya.

Cycling

Cycling in Egypt is possible in some locations and outright dangerous in others. Luxor's west bank offers the most obvious opportunities, with its wealth of sights linked closely together along relatively flat plains. Rental is available through your hotel concierge.

Don't even think about cycling around Cairo unless you crave an early death.

Driving

Driving is not advisable in Egypt for many reasons. Not only does the nation have one of the highest traffic mortality rates in the world, but infrastructure is poor and driving standards range from non-existent to thoroughly aggressive. The best alternative is to hire a driver and a car together, thus freeing yourself to enjoy the scenery.

Rental agencies in Cairo

Avis
Entrance 1, Sadat Academy Street, Ma'adi
Tel: 02-2527 5400
www.avis.com
Budget
22 Al Mathaf Al Zerai Street, Dokki

Distances from Cairo

NORTH	
to Alexandria	225km/140 miles
to Damietta	190km/115 miles
to the Barrages	25km/15 miles
SOUTH	
to Al Minya	235km/150 miles
to Asyut	360km/225 miles
to Luxor	665km/415 miles
to Esna	720km/450 miles
to Kom Ombo	835km/520 miles
to Aswan	880km/550 miles
EAST	
to Port Said	220km/137 miles
to Isma'illiyyah	140klm/87 miless
WEST	
to Al Fayyum	105km/65 miiles
to Al Bahareyyah Oasis	315km/200 miles
to Farafrah Oasis	420km/260 miles
to Ad Dakhlah Oasis	690km/415 miles
to Al Khargah Oasis	585km/365 miles

Tel: 02-2539 1501
www.budget.com
Outside Cairo, most rental agencies
are located at the regional airport.

Driving conditions

The roads that go from Cairo to
Upper Egypt are the longest, most
congested and most dangerous in
Egypt. Most traffic moving south from
Cairo must travel a route along the
western shore of the Nile.

Road signs are similar to those used
throughout Europe. Driving is on
the right-hand side of the road. Speed
limits are posted on major highways
and are enforced by radar.

It is not advisable to drive at night;
vehicles stop dead on the road and
turn out their lights; unlit donkey
carts move at a snail's pace and are
usually not seen until it is too late;
and long-distance taxis and over-
loaded trucks travel too fast, often
without lights.

Driving in Egypt is not recommended; it's far
better to hire a car with driver

There are petrol stations throughout the country, with those operated
by Mobil, Esso and Shell offering
full service with mini-markets on the
premises. Fuel, inexpensive and sold
by the litre, is available in 90 octane
(*tisaʻiin*), referred to as super, or 80
(*tamaniin*), regular. Super is the better
fuel for most purposes.

Accessibility

Few public or other buildings provide
special facilities for the disabled in
Egypt, but things are slowly changing.
Before going, visit www.egyptforall.
com, an excellent website dedicated to
disabled travellers in Egypt.

Most airports in Egypt are now
equipped with ramps and lifts. Many
five-star hotels have rooms equipped
for the disabled, but smaller hotels
usually don't. Some hotels which are
not specifically equipped for disabled
guests might still be a good option.
The Mövenpick in Giza (02-3377
2555) and the Maritim Jolie Ville in
Luxor (09-5227 4855) are built on
ground level, and the doorways are
large enough to allow wheelchairs to
pass through.

The Egyptian Museum in Cairo
is now furnished with ramps and
elevators. The Giza Plateau is accessible by bus from which tourists can
view the Pyramids and the Sphinx.
The Citadel and Khan Al Khalili are
accessible by wheelchair, as are the
High Dam, the granite quarries, and
the Abu Simbel and Edfu temples
in Aswan. In Luxor, disabled tourists
can enjoy visits to Karnak Temple,
the Hatshepsut Temple and the
Valley of the Kings.

Transport

Health and Safety

HEALTH AND MEDICAL CARE

Evidence of yellow fever and cholera immunisation may be required from people who have been in an infected area up to six days prior to arrival. No other inoculations are officially required, but it is always good to be up to date with polio, tetanus and cholera. Good medical assistance is expensive in Egypt, making travel insurance a must for all visitors.

HOSPITALS

There are good hospitals in Cairo and Alexandria, but they require a cash deposit to cover the cost of treatment. Comprehensive travel insurance that covers repatriation costs is essential. Main hospitals are listed below:
Anglo-American Hospital Zohoreya next to the Cairo Tower, Zamalik
Tel: 02-2735 6162
Assalam International Hospital
Corniche An Nil, Madi
Tel: 02-2524 0250
Cairo Medical Centre
4 Shari' Abou Obeida Al Bahr, Heliopolis
Tel: 02-2258 1003

NATURAL HAZARDS

The Egyptian sun is incredibly strong and can cause sunburn and sunstroke on even the cloudiest of days. Avoid getting burnt by keeping out of the sun during peak midday hours when the sun is at its strongest, wear a sunhat and sunglasses when you are out and about, and slather yourself with a high-factor sunscreen. Even if a sunscreen says it is waterproof, re-apply more lotion after you emerge from the sea or swimming pool.

Mosquitoes can be a pain, but cases of malaria are few. Avoid being bitten by using an insect repellent, having an anti-mosquito coil in your room and sleeping under a net when one is provided. Also resist wearing any scents, as mosquitoes are said to be attracted to heavy colognes and perfumes.

Rabies is a problem in Egypt, so steer clear of touching any dogs or pets, and go immediately to a doctor if bitten by an animal of any sort. In the event of emergency, consult your tour operator or embassy for immediate assistance.

Bilharzia (schistosomiasis), a tropical disease caused by parasitic worms, is common in the Nile region; avoid swimming in the river, especially where the current is slow.

Wear sun protection when on a camel trek

Delivery of freshly baked bread

FOOD AND DRINK

Tap water isn't safe to drink anywhere in Egypt. Instead, be sure to use only bottled water and instruct waiters that you do not want ice in your drinks. To avoid stomach upsets, ensure that your food has been cooked through and is piping hot, and avoid salads. Try to stick to eating fruits with a peel that you can remove or that you can wash yourself.

CRIME

Egypt has been troubled in the last decades by right-wing extremists and radical Islamic terrorists, and has also suffered from terrorist violence. In 1997, two attacks specifically targeting tourists – one outside the Egyptian

Emergency Contacts

In an emergency, consult your tour representative if you are travelling with an operator or your hotel concierge or check-in clerk when staying at a hotel. Most emergency contacts do not speak English in Egypt, so you will need someone who can do basic translation to assist. Contact your embassy if you need further help.

Ambulance: 123
Fire service: 125
Police: 122
Tourist police: 126

EMBASSIES AND CONSULATES
Embassies in Egypt
Australia
World Trade Center
11th floor, 1191 Shari' An Nil
Bulak; tel: 02-2575 0444
Canada
26 Shari' Kamel Al Shenawy,
Garden City; tel: 02-2791 8700
Ireland
7th floor, 3 Shari' Abu Al Feda,
Zamalik; tel: 02-2735 8264
New Zealand
Level 8, North Tower, Nile City Towers,
2005c Shari' An Nil, Ramlet Beaulac,
Cairo; tel: 02-2461 6000
South Africa
55 Road 18, 6th Floor,
Madi; tel: 02-2359 4365
UK
7 Shari' Ahmed Ragheb,
Garden City; tel: 02-2794 6000;
http://ukinegypt.fco.gov.uk/en
US
8 Shari' Kamal Salah Addin,
Garden City; tel: 02-2797 3300;
http://cairo.usembassy.gov/

Health and Safety

Armed police guard tourist sights

Museum in Cairo and another at Hatshepsut's Temple, Luxor – significantly raised the overall death toll. In 2004, 34 people died when a bomb exploded in a hotel in Taba, northern Sinai, while a bomb in summer of 2005 killed over 80 people in Sharm Al Sheikh. The most recent notable attack occurred in Khan Al Khalili in February 2009, which resulted in 24 wounded and the death of a French teenager. A heavy military response from the government designed to protect tourists and deter further terrorist activities cannot guarantee security and many feel may exacerbate the situation. However, tourists are statistically safer in Egypt than in many American cities; in fact Egyptian drivers present a greater threat to you than terrorists.

In terms of everyday security, common caution is advised. As Egypt's economic reforms have created great hardship, the incidence of petty thefts has increased, although you are still more likely to have a lost wallet returned intact than in many countries.

Social restrictions on women in Egypt can make foreign women seem particularly enticing to young Egyptian men, so women should exercise caution and be sensitive to cultural and social mores. If you do experience serious difficulties, you should report them immediately to the nearest tourist police post or police station. Egyptian police are usually found wearing an all-black uniform, while tourist police are clad in white.

If travelling in the Sinai (especially Dahab), you may be offered hashish or other drugs during your stay. You'll also probably smell it on the beaches and in the city late at night. Don't think this means it is legal; it is not, and if you are caught in possession you will be given a hefty fine or even a jail sentence.

Money and Budgeting

CURRENCY

The currency in Egypt is the Egyptian pound (E£, also abbreviated to EGP or LE), divided into 100 piastres (pt). Check the most recent exchange rates on www.xe.com. US dollars are occasionally accepted by some retailers and hotels.

A limit of carrying any more than E£5,000 is imposed on all travellers entering the country.

CASH AND CARDS

The cheapest and easiest way to get currency is through one of the numerous ATMs in the many banks and hotels. Credit cards are accepted in hotels and larger stores, but it's advisable to contact your credit card company before you go to tell them the dates of your trip. Most stallholders in the souqs prefer cash. Keep smaller denomination notes where possible, as people rarely have change, especially taxi drivers, and you'll need them for baksheesh.

Tipping

Tipping or baksheesh is common in Egypt for even the smallest of services. Often the tip is given to help supplement a woefully small salary, and is relied upon to make ends meet. Porters, maids and toilet attendants should be given E£1–2, as should other people who help you, like security guards who point something out to you and attendants at a mosque who look after your shoes. Waiters and bar staff can be given anything from 5–10 percent – it's best to pay

the bill separately and leave the tip in cash for the waiter.

Tax

There is no formal tax on goods in Egypt. However, upmarket restaurants add a 25% tax to the final bill, while four- and five-star accommodation include a large government tax in their quoted rates.

BUDGETING FOR YOUR TRIP

Egypt is generally much cheaper than the West, with accommodation, food and shopping all costing significantly less than back home. Flights from the UK can be very affordable now that low-cost carriers have included Hurghadah and Sharm Al Sheikh on their list of destinations.

During the low season, flights to Cairo can cost as little as £290 return including taxes for a non-stop economy-class ticket from London with either British Airways or BMI. Business-class fares from London start from around £900 return non-stop. In high season, fares are about

Tea on a cruise

£50–75 higher for both economy and business-class tickets.

From the US, prices start from $870 return for a flight with connections rising to $1,300 for a non-stop flight with Delta or Egyptair. In high season, fares double to at least $2,500 per person return in economy. Business-class fares stay level at around $5,000 per person throughout the year.

For a budget, backpacker-style holiday you will need to set aside £300/US$460 per person per week including accommodation, touring and meals. From the UK, a standard family holiday for four will cost around £1,700 to a package holiday location per week during low season or £3,600 per week during high season excluding meals and attractions. From America, a family trip runs to at least $5,000 during low season. A luxury, no-expense-spared break starts from £1,000/$1.600 per person per week.

Money-Saving Tips

- If you're a student, get an ISIC card as you can get as much as 50% off the cost of museum admissions with it.
- Avoid booking tours through tour operators as prices can be as much as double what you would pay an independent taxi driver or cruise ship manager directly.
- Note that Luxor, Aswan and Hurghadah offer the best value while the Sinai, the Red Sea resorts of Marsa Alam and El Gouna, and Cairo, veer towards the higher end of the scale.

Budgeting Costs

Top-class/boutique hotel: E£900–2,250 for a double room
Standard-class hotel: E£200–400 for a double
Bed and breakfast: E£175–350 for a double
Youth hostel: E£100–150 per person

Breakfast: E£20–30
Lunch in a café: E£30–40
Coffee/tea in a café: E£10–20
Main course, budget restaurant: E£3–25
Main course, moderate restaurant: E£25–50
Main course, expensive restaurant: E£50–150
Bottle of wine in a restaurant: E£100–200
Beer in a pub: E£25–35

Domestic flight: E£800–1,000 (Cairo–Luxor, one-way)
Intercity coach ticket: E£40–60 (Cairo–Sharm Al Sheikh, one-way)
Intercity train ticket: E£350–500 (Cairo–Luxor, one-way)
10-minute taxi ride: E£10–20
Airport shuttle bus: E£25–45 from Cairo Airport to various points in the city
Short bus ride: E£1

Museum admission: E£60 (Egyptian Museum)
Day trip to Gaza, Memphis and Saqqarah from Cairo: E£200–250 plus entry fees
Theatre/concert ticket: E£250–350 (belly dancing show, including meal)
Shopping item: E£10 (small plaster Sphinx or Pyramid)
Nightclub entry: E£25–50

Responsible Travel

GETTING THERE

While it was once possible to travel overland from Europe to Egypt, travel restrictions through Israel make the trip challenging now. Additionally, the ferries from Greece no longer run frequently, making air travel the only viable way to reach the country.

There are a number of reputable carbon-offset companies which can try to make your flight carbon-neutral. Two of the more notable firms are: Climate Care (www.jpmorganclimate care.com) and Carbon Neutral Calculator (www.carbonneutral.com).

ECOTOURISM

The Red Sea Sustainable Tourism initiative aims to control development along the fragile coast. The organisation works together with local communities to ensure new developments adhere to strict sustainable building codes, and funds programmes to train locals to use sustainable methods when dealing with the region's natural resources. This is beginning to have some success, as previously unchecked building is finally slowing down after years of non-stop growth.

ETHICAL TOURISM

While cultural tours are high on the list for many travellers, most of the money usually goes into the pockets of the (often foreign-based) tour operator and not to local communities. You can do your bit to ensure that local spending finances local projects and people by booking your experiences in the country rather than in advance of your arrival.

If a Bedouin experience is what you're after, head to Dahab, where numerous independent guides can take you into the Sinai – often to their home village for a personalised adventure. In Aswan, go to Seheyl Island or the village of Siou on Elephantine, where local guides can teach you more about Nubian traditions.

THINGS TO AVOID

Large tracts of coral reef are now permanently damaged, as fly-by-night tour operators ignore warnings and anchor in protected regions. Novice divers are often not given enough advance training and end up standing on or touching coral. Do not do this, as it can take years to recover.

Photography is forbidden in tombs and most museums, and throughout the Valley of the Kings. Pay attention to signs or you may have your camera confiscated or you may be fined.

Photography is limited at many sights

Family Holidays

PRACTICALITIES

Egyptians love children and will generally dote on small kids given half a chance, so having children with you can be a great ice-breaker with the locals.

However, child-safety awareness is minimal to non-existent. Seat belts and child seats are rare in the back of most cars and taxis. If you're renting a car, remember to specify you want them, and bring your own child seats with you. Most *feluccas* and other boat operators do not supply children's life jackets. Keep a close eye on your offspring at ancient sites, as restoration and building works may not be protected by barriers, and hazards are often unmarked.

Nappies (diapers), baby food and formula milk are available in bigger supermarkets and pharmacies, although if you are going off the beaten track you may want to bring your own supplies.

Nappy-changing facilities, like all public rest facilities in Egypt, are almost non-existent. Pushchairs can be rented, but only through four- and five-star international-standard properties, especially in the coastal resort towns along the Red Sea and on the Sinai Peninsula.

ACCOMMODATION

Child-friendly accommodation is easy to find in the more modern resort destinations along the coast, but can be more challenging along the Nile Valley. Facilities on the Red Sea coast and in the Sinai will be far-reaching, with babysitting services, kids' clubs,

Sharm Al Sheikh is a very child-friendly resort

child-friendly swimming pools, cots and booster seats available on demand. Along the Nile Valley and on the Mediterranean coast, these facilities will only be available in better-class properties.

FOOD AND DRINK

Kids love Egyptian cuisine – as long as you can get them to try it. Initially children may be put off by the exotic smells, ingredients and textures, but often come around once they've given it a try.

Koshari, a mixture of macaroni, lentils, fried garlic and tomato sauce, is both the favoured dish of the people and a regular favourite with kids. Meze items like hummous with pitta bread and *kofte* (spiced minced lamb) are also popular. When all else fails, there are plenty of Egyptian pizza (*fiteer*) and pasta places to try in the tourist centres. And of course if you are staying in a tourist centre, Western options will be available.

Restaurants welcome all ages, but you probably won't find a specific kids' menu unless you stick to international restaurants in the resort towns.

ATTRACTIONS AND ACTIVITIES

There are plenty of sights to keep children happy in Egypt. They love exploring temples and pyramids, pretending they are Indiana Jones – just bear in mind they will tire easily, especially in the heat, so plan your itinerary carefully. Trying to pack in too much temple-hopping and trekking around ruins will be lead to tantrums, and not just theirs.

Children usually find camels entertaining

The beaches of the Red Sea and Sinai offer plenty of water-based fun, and many of the larger resorts have extensive kids' play areas. Short boat trips are always popular, though children will probably get bored on longer cruises. Green spaces are a rarity in Egypt, but some of the better ones to take kids to when they want to run around include Kitchener's Island in Aswan, Montazah Gardens in Alexandria and Al Azhar park in Cairo.

For budding Egyptologists, try the children's museum in the basement of Cairo's Egyptian Museum, which is filled with Lego models of the historic sights. The mummies in the main museum and in the Mummification Museum may be a little too gruesome for sensitive souls. When all else fails, there are always horse, donkey and camel rides. Seeing the Pyramids by camel is exciting, allowing children to experience thousands of years of history from the back of a one-humped beast.

Family Holidays

History

A BRIEF HISTORY

Egypt's Nile Valley has supported human life for tens of thousands of years. By 4000BC, the early Egyptians had become farmers of wheat and barley, and a unique civilisation with its own distinctive styles of art and architecture had emerged along the banks of the Nile. The invention of paper-making from papyrus, along with a highly complex system of writing, enabled early Egyptians to keep detailed records at a time when developing cultures in Mesopotamia had to resort to clay tablets for communication.

Ancient Egypt's complicated annals are filled with massive communal building projects and great individuals that can be traced through many millennia. Archaeologists are still debating the exact chronology of certain Egyptian dynasties, but there is general agreement that Egyptian history can be divided into distinct periods, each with a specific name. The Pre-Dynastic and Early Dynastic periods are followed by the Old, Middle, and New Kingdoms with Intermediate periods in between. These are followed by the Late, Macedonian and Ptolemaic periods until Egypt was absorbed into the Roman empire in the late 1st century BC.

PRE- AND EARLY DYNASTIC PERIODS (5000–2780BC)

For many years Egypt was not one kingdom but two: Upper Egypt in the south and Lower Egypt in the north.

Around 3170BC, King Narmer of Upper Egypt conquered Lower Egypt. The crowns of later pharaohs are the combined crowns of both Upper and Lower Egypt (the cobra and the vulture), and bear the symbols of both kingdoms. The capital was established at Memphis in Lower Egypt (near present-day Cairo), and the 1st Dynasty was founded. He is also generally thought to have instituted the cult of Ptah, the creator god.

THE OLD KINGDOM

The Old Kingdom was established around 2780BC and lasted more than five centuries. It heralded the first great phase of development in

Slate pallette depicting Narmer, who conquered Lower Egypt, unifying the country

science and architecture, hieroglyphs were developed, and the first building phase took place.

Rulers looked for ways to prove their might both in life and in death. King Djoser of the 4th Dynasty was the first to attempt to build a large funerary monument to hold his mortal remains and protect the riches buried with him for his next life. The result is the Step Pyramid at Saqqarah.

Other rulers followed suit, perfecting the design, and in 2526BC the Great Pyramid at Giza was built for Khufu (Cheops). Shortly before this, between 2575 and 2550BC, King Khafra (Chephren) had the Sphinx erected in his honour at Giza. It was at about this time that the first mummifications began. Khufu's son Redjedef made a major change, introducing the solar deity Ra, or Re, into the Egyptian religion. Worship of Ra became one of the most important facets of Egyptian culture over the next 3,000 years.

Between 2140 and 2040BC rival power bases arose in Heliopolis in Lower Egypt and Thebes (modern Luxor) in Upper Egypt, and a split occurred between the kingdoms. Archaeologists call this the First Intermediate period. The Karnak Temple at Thebes was begun around 2134BC, marking the city's rise to prominence.

THE MIDDLE KINGDOM

The Middle Kingdom, 2040–1640BC, began when the Theban rulers of the 11th Dynasty attempted to extend their control and Egypt was reunified under Mentuhotep II. His successors built a power base at Thebes, and

A funerary stela showing a harpist playing for the god Ra

started a cultural renaissance with wide-reaching effects on Egyptian art and archaeology. This was a time when Egypt began to expand its borders, particularly in the south into Nubia.

In terms of worship, the local Theban god Amun became intertwined with Ra, creating the deity Amun-Ra. Thebes held onto power until the 12th Dynasty, when its first king, Amenemhet I, who reigned between 1980–1951BC, established a new capital near Memphis. However, he continued to pay homage to the Theban god Amun, thereby ensuring that the cult of Amun was observed throughout the kingdom.

The riches of Egypt were coveted by rival peoples, and around 1600BC the Hyksos invaded Lower Egypt (the Delta) from Syria and the desert east of Jordan, and surged southwards,

Entrance to Tutankhamun's tomb in the Valley of the Kings

splitting the kingdom in two once again, thereby starting the Second Intermediate period.

THE NEW KINGDOM

The rule of the Hyksos lasted less than 100 years. They were driven out of Lower Egypt by Ahmose I, who founded the 18th Dynasty, ruling over a united Egypt from the capital of Thebes. The Pharaohs of the 18th Dynasty instigated many reforms. They reorganised the army and consolidated power in the hands of family members at the expense of feudal leaders. Egypt reached its artistic and cultural zenith, and many renowned Pharaohs reigned during the New Kingdom (1550–1070BC). The Valley of the Kings was chosen as a new burial ground for the Pharaohs when Thutmoses I (1504–1492BC) was entombed in a narrow valley across the river from the temple at Karnak.

Throughout the 1400s BC temples and tombs at Karnak and Luxor were greatly expanded, and several huge building projects took place on the west bank of the Nile. However, in 1356–1339BC a new Pharaoh, Amenhotep IV, decided to leave Thebes and, with his wife Nefertiti, created a new capital in the north: Akhetaten (modern Tell al-Amarnah). He introduced a cult of the 'one true god', Aten, and changed his own name to Akhenaten ('He who pleases Aten'). This sudden and radical change caused chaos, and Egypt lost its international influence until Akhenaten's successor – his son, Tutankhamun – reinvested the priests of Amun-Ra and his fellow divinities in Thebes.

Tutankhamun died without an heir, heralding the demise of the 18th Dynasty. A general, who became Rameses I, founded the start of the 19th Dynasty. His successor, Sety I (1291–1279BC), won back many of the lands lost during the Akhenaten years.

The long rule of Rameses II (1279–1212BC) came as a great finale to the New Kingdom era. Over an impressive 60 years he supervised magnificent building projects at Luxor and Karnak, and commissioned the temple of Abu Simbel.

Rameses III tried to follow in the footsteps of Rameses II by building a vast mortuary complex at Madinat Habu, but power was already slipping from royal hands into those of the priests known as the servants of Amun-Ra. In 1070BC the country was split again, by foreign invaders. The Assyrians dominated Egypt from 715BC and began to develop links with the expanding Roman empire.

THE PTOLEMAIC PERIOD

In 332BC Alexander the Great conquered Egypt and appointed as governor his Macedonian general, Cleomenes of Naucratis, who was of Greek origin. After Alexander's death in 323BC, power passed to another of Alexander's generals, known as Ptolemy I. The new city of Alexandria, on the Mediterranean coast, became his headquarters as well as the cultural capital of the Hellenistic world, and Thebes finally lost its influence.

The Ptolemaic era came to an end with its best-known ruler, Queen Cleopatra VII. During her lifetime (69–30BC), the queen tried to link her land to Rome, notably through her liaison with Julius Caesar, with whom she had a son, Caesarion. However, destiny turned against Cleopatra with the assassination of Caesar and defeat of Mark Antony in the Battle of Actium; she committed suicide in Alexandria in 30BC. Egypt was reduced to being a province of the Roman empire, ruled at first from Rome, then from Constantinople.

THE ARAB EMPIRE

The first significant wave of Muslim Arab expansion swept over Egypt in AD630, less than 10 years after the death of the Prophet Muhammad. Egypt became one of the most influential Arab caliphates, particularly from the second half of the 9th century, when it was ruled by the powerful Fatimid Dynasty. They established their capital at Al Qahira ('the Victorious'), which is more familiarly known to Westerners as Cairo.

Over the next two centuries, Cairo became a centre of culture and learning unsurpassed in the Islamic world. The Al Azhar University and mosque were founded during this period. The Fatimid empire was crushed by Salah Addin in 1169. Flush with victories in the Holy Land over the Crusaders, Salah Addin established his own dynasty, the Ayyubids, and created a citadel to protect Cairo. But his control was weak, and his power was usurped by the Mamluks, his guard of Turkish slaves, whose dynasty lasted from 1251–1517.

History

Fatimid period manuscript illustration

OTTOMAN RULE

The Mamluks in their turn were overthrown by Ottoman Turks, but little changed on a day-to-day basis. The Turks effectively left control to a local governor, or pasha, who ran the country as he pleased with Mamluk help. As a result Egypt suffered, especially when the Ottoman empire went into decline in the 18th century.

As Ottoman control weakened, Egypt became a pawn in a larger game. In 1798 a young Napoleon Bonaparte, eager to curtail growing British power, invaded Egypt and after a short and decisive battle claimed the country for France. He set about forming a ruling body, and sent scholars and artists out into the countryside to explore and record its ancient treasures – thus sparking the great interest in Egyptology among scholars in France and the rest of Western Europe.

Napoleon's stay in Egypt was short-lived, however. The British fleet was after him and inflicted a devastating defeat on the French navy at the battle of Abu Qir later the same year.

Meanwhile an Ottoman force had been dispatched from Istanbul to counter the French. They were led by Muhammad Ali, a brilliant intellectual who, in the aftermath of the French withdrawal, asked to be appointed Pasha of Egypt. The Ottoman Sultan agreed to his request. Installed in Cairo, in 1811, Muhammad organised a grand banquet and invited all the notable Mamluks to attend. Once assembled, he had them all massacred. The assassination of their leaders marked the sudden end

Mamluk Ottoman imperial guard.

of the Mamluks' influence in Egypt.

Fascinated by European military strategy, Muhammad Ali set about modernising the army and navy. Attempts were also made to bring agriculture and commerce up to date, and cotton was introduced as a commercial crop. New building projects in Cairo expanded the city's boundaries.

Istanbul eventually granted Egypt autonomy and conferred hereditary status on the role of Pasha of Egypt. The title was subsequently upgraded to Khedive ('king' in Persian, the equivalent of viceroy).

Yet Muhammad Ali's successors lacked their ancestor's talents, and their power was eroded by corruption and irresponsibility. The creation of the Suez Canal, hailed as a marvel of engineering when it opened in 1869, was overseen by Khedive Ismail. The enterprise was financed by unscrupulous bankers, and when the Khedive became overburdened by debt, he had to allow European 'advisers' to control key institutions. The British soon had a tight grip on Egyptian politics and commerce.

THE 20TH CENTURY

During World War I, Egypt occupied a strategic position for Britain, being close to the Ottoman enemy. In addition, the Suez Canal facilitated access to British dominions in India, the Far East, Australia and New Zealand. When the Ottoman empire crumbled in the war's aftermath, Egypt declared itself independent, but control of the country remained in London. The Nationalist Party eventually gained a majority in the 1920s and became a prominent force in the next few decades.

World War II reaffirmed Egypt's strategic importance, and North Africa became an important field of battle. Axis forces were closing in on Cairo but Allied soldiers stopped them at Al 'Alamean in 1942. Egypt remained in British hands for the rest of the war.

The 1947 UN partition of British Mandate Palestine into an Arab and a Jewish state infuriated the Arab world, which went to war to prevent implementation of the resolution. The nascent state of Israel won an unexpected victory over Egypt in 1948, and three decades of hostilities began.

King Farouk, who had come to the throne in 1936, was seen as a luxury-loving playboy. When he attempted to wrestle control of the Suez Canal from the British, he suffered an embarrassing defeat. In July

The battle of Al 'Alamean in World War II

President Mubarak *(left)* meets Israeli Prime Minister Ariel Sharon in 1982

1952 a group of high-ranking military officers led by Colonel Gamal Abdel Nasser overthrew Farouk and nationalised the Suez Canal. Nasser was to rule for 17 years and, with Soviet aid, Egypt carried out a huge modernisation programme. One key building project was the Aswan High Dam, which provides hydroelectricity and prevents flooding.

Anwar Sadat succeeded Nasser, who died in 1970. Less charismatic and more moderate than his predecessor, he too became embroiled in wars with Israel; these weakened the country and left Sinai in Israeli hands. Part of Sinai was regained in the 1973 war and, in the war's aftermath, Sadat launched a diplomatic initiative for which he received a Nobel Peace Prize. In 1979 Egypt negotiated a peace treaty with Israel, despite opposition in the Arab world. Sinai was returned to Egypt, but internally opposition to Sadat's efforts continued. Sadat was assassinated in 1981.

CURRENT AFFAIRS

President Hosni Mubarak has since worked to secure a place for Egypt at the international negotiation table, hosting a succession of Arab-Israeli peace talks. His pragmatic approach has earned him some admirers, but also a lot of enemies among Egyptian extremists who have repeatedly tried to destabilise his regime.

In the 1990s and early 2000s terrorists attacked at several tourist sights, bringing tourism almost to a halt, but the industry has now mostly recovered. The same can't be said of Egypt's economy, as the country faces a huge economic crisis, with a weak Egyptian pound and high unemployment.

Activists of all political persuasions are currently campaigning to prevent Mubarak's son, Gamal, from inheriting power. With the president's health deteriorating, there is much speculation about the direction Egypt will take in the post-Mubarak years.

Historical Landmarks

PRE-DYNASTIC PERIOD (UNTIL 2780BC)
Unification of Egypt under one ruler. Memphis founded as capital. Rulers buried at Saqqarah. Hieroglyphs appear.

OLD KINGDOM (2780–2040BC)
3rd–4th Dynasties. Pyramids built at Saqqarah and Giza.

MIDDLE KINGDOM (2040–1640BC)
11th–12th Dynasties. Expansion of Egyptian empire. New warfare techniques employed. Ended with invasion of Hyksos.

NEW KINGDOM (1550–1070BC)
18th–20th Dynasties. Age of the great Pharaohs, including Akhenaten, Tutankhamun and Rameses II; a period of huge expansion of the empire, and, internally, of peace and prosperity. Construction of temples at Luxor and Abu Simbel.

LATE PERIOD (1070–332BC)
21st–30th Dynasties. Libyan, Nubian, Assyrian, Persian and Greek invasions. Decline and civil war.

PTOLEMAIC PERIOD (332–30BC)
Alexander the Great invades Egypt. Reigns of Ptolemy I–XVI and, lastly, Cleopatra.

ROMANO-BYZANTINE PERIOD (30BC–AD642)
Rule from Rome. Spread of Christianity from AD251 onwards. From AD324 rule from Constantinople (Byzantium).

ARAB EMPIRE (642–1517)
Dynasties of the Umayyads, Abbasids, Fatimids and Ayyubids. From 1250, reign of the Mamluks.

OTTOMAN PERIOD (1517–1914)
Turkish government from Istanbul. French occupation 1798–1805. Muhammad Ali comes to power in 1811. Suez Canal opened in 1869. British occupation in 1882.

PROTECTORATE/MONARCHY (1914–52)
British Protectorate. Monarchy established 1922. King Farouk deposed in July Revolution, 1952.

REPUBLIC (1953–70)
Gamal Abdel Nasser becomes president. Suez Canal nationalised. Israel invades Sinai. The Six-Day War.

1972
Aswan High Dam completed.

1979
Peace treaty with Israel. Egypt banished from the Arab League.

1981
President Sadat assassinated. Hosni Mubarak succeeds him.

1989
Israel returns Sinai. Egypt rejoins the Arab League.

1997
Massacre of tourists at Luxor. Work begins on the Toshka Canal.

2005
President Mubarak introduces selective multi-party elections but still wins a landslide victory, with his term extended to 2011.

2009
US President Obama gives a historic speech in Cairo to the entire Muslim world, confirming Egypt's important position in the region.

2010
The Rafah border crossing is the scene for numerous skirmishes between Egyptian border police and Palestinian black-marketeers, who were using the extensive tunnels to smuggle goods. In football, Egypt become the first team to win the Africa Cup of Nations three times in a row.

History

Culture

REGIONAL DIFFERENCES

While Egypt isn't a multicultural melting pot, even casual visitors will notice differences as they travel through the country. Regional loyalties persist strongly. Each major town and province has its acknowledged characteristic, from Alexandria in the north to Aswan in the south. Alexandrians are known chiefly for their toughness and willingness to fight, but also for their cosmopolitan outlook and business acumen. The farmers of Lower Egypt and the Delta are regarded as hardworking, thrifty and serious.

Cairenes, like New Yorkers or cockneys, are seen as slick, fast-talking and immoral. Simply being from the capital allows them to sneer at less sophisticated compatriots, a Cairene habit that their country cousins dislike. The Saidi people of Upper Egypt are considered to be simple-minded and impulsive and will even joke about these traits themselves. On the positive side, Saidis are noted for their generosity, their courage, virility and sense of honour.

The dark-skinned Nubians of the far south and Sudan, an ancient people with their own languages, are considered to be the most gentle and peaceful of Egyptians. Long isolated by the cataracts that made the Nile above Aswan impassable, Nubian life, relaxed and carefree, had a unique charm (see also pp. 50–55).

The modern trend of rural flight to the cities is having an effect on these

Nubian man at Aswan souq

traditional personality differences as people from villages across the country come together to live in urban neighbourhoods and take on more urban habits; however, people still tend to return to their native regions when looking for a spouse.

ISLAM AND POPULAR PIETY

Any visitor to Egypt will be struck by the piety of its people. Humility is inherent in the very word Islam, the religion of nine-tenths of Egyptians. While many Egyptians do not go to the mosque or pray five times a day, the majority believe in a supreme deity and the imminence of the Day of Judgement. The dawn-to-dusk fast during Ramadan is officially observed by the entire country, a sign of the pervasiveness of Islam. And many Egyptian tastes, habits and preferences refer directly back to the Qur'an.

The Coptic Christians, too, conscious of being members of one of the earliest Christian sects, maintain a degree of devoutness that often bewilders Westerners. Copts ('Egyptian Christians') can trace their religion back to the days of Ancient Egypt, making their faith one of the oldest in the country. Historically, both Copts and Muslims have got along relatively peacefully, but a recent increase in extremism has resulted in an inflation in the number of skirmishes between the two cultures throughout the nation.

LANGUAGE

Egyptian Arabic is the common language of the nation, although for some it is not their first language. Bedouins speak a dialect of Arabic similar to Egyptian Arabic, but with certain differences in pronounciation and vocabulary. For example, in the Bedouin Arabic spoken in the Western Desert, the 'q' sound is said as a much harder 'g'.

Nubians also have their distinct language, related more to the native tongues of Sudan, Kenya and northern Tanzania than to traditional Arabic. English is commonly spoken by those who work in tourist resort areas and in market souqs, but may not be understood in more rural locations or by those who don't deal with tourists on a daily basis.

WOMEN IN SOCIETY

Before the famous Egyptian feminist Hoda Shaarawi deliberately removed her veil in 1922, veils were worn in public by all respectable middle- and upper-class women, Muslim, Jewish, or Christian. Women of all classes and religions stayed at home and

raised families, staying firmly in their world as housewives, mothers, sisters and aunts. Nowadays in Egypt the full veil or niqab, leaving just the eyes uncovered, is worn only by rural conservatives, Bedouin women and by younger middle-class urban women. The issue of the niqab is complicated, as younger women take up the veil for many reasons – mainly to show modesty and piety and to discourage male advances in public, but also as a fashion accessory or as a political statement that goes hand in hand with anti-Western feelings.

From the 1930s onwards, Egyptian women began to enter into businesses and professions. By 1965, thanks in part to social changes effected in the course of the July Revolution, Egypt had a far higher proportion of professional women workers than in the US or in any European country outside

Reading the Qur'an outside Al Azhar Mosque, Cairo

Many women choose to wear a headscarf

Scandinavia. Many Egyptian women still work, and public areas are no longer the sole preserve of men. However, Egyptian women still do not have equality with Egyptian men, either in law or by custom. Women tend to have more freedom in Alexandria and Cairo, reflecting the cosmopolitan outlook of both cities.

SEXUAL ATTITUDES AND MARRIAGE

Attitudes to sex are framed by the belief that no man or woman can be trusted when it comes to the pleasures of the flesh. It is believed that men – and women – cannot resist the temptations of sex and must be watched at all times for signs of heightened desire. This is true in both the Islamic culture as it is amongst the Coptic Christian population.

Marriage is deemed an absolute prerequisite for sex, as well as for full adulthood and respectability. Among women, whose freedom is still very much limited by rigid social norms, finding and keeping the right husband is the major focus of life. Since the 1920s substantial progress towards equality of the sexes has been made, but it is still the rule for a girl to remain in the care of her father until the day she is passed into the care of her husband.

FILIAL PIETY

Respect for parents and elders is so strongly ingrained that it is uncommon for even a male child to leave home before marriage. Things are gradually changing in Cairo and other major urban centres, but few urban males can afford to marry much before the age of 30. Despite Islam's flexibility on the subject – easy divorce and polygamy are both sanctioned – marriage is regarded as a binding agreement, made more absolute by economics. For this reason, couples are expected to work out every detail of their future life together before signing the contract.

THE DIGITAL AGE

While the possession of a television used to be the sign of how wealthy a person was in Egypt, today it is the computer that is most desired by the privileged few. Unlike TV, however, the computer can only be used by people with a minimum literacy level – already removing a significant proportion of the population from benefiting from one.

Internet cafés are now widespread in urban areas and are overtaking the traditional coffee houses as a place for young people of all classes to enjoy – the lack of home computers means that young urbanites along the Nile rely on these centres to play video games, chat with mates or swap news.

There are currently a number of programmes in operation across Africa to provide computer access to all, and Egypt is taking part in many of the projects. It remains to be seen what the long-term impact will be.

EGYPTIAN LITERATURE

Nobel Prize-winner Naguib Mahfouz (1911–2006) and Taha Hussein (1889–1973) were the grand old men of Egyptian letters. Other central figures in the development of modern Egyptian literature are Tawfiq al Hakim (*The Prison of Life*), who defined Egyptian autobiographical writing (1898–1987), and the Alexandrian-Greek poet C.P. Cavafy (1863–1933) (*Collected Poems*), whose explorations of sexuality, memory and history have a universal appeal. They and their contemporaries created a tradition of modern storytelling, rich in folklore and heavy in allegory (a necessity given the censorship laws).

Post-independence writers have taken different routes, with many writers challenging societal norms in their work. The biggest recent hit was *The Yacoubian Building* (2002) by Alaa Al Aswany, which became the biggest-selling Arabic novel of all time. This *roman à clef* follows the fictional relationships between the inhabitants of a downtown office-cum-apartment block and was controversial for its portrayal of homosexual and transvestite characters.

CAIRO, CINEMA CITY

In 1927, Aziza Amir released the first Egyptian-made film, *Laila*. Much of Egypt's claim to cultural supremacy in the Arab world has been due to the phenomenal success of the film industry, which developed in the mid-20th century and peaked in the 1960s, when a new film was released almost every day. Subjects ranged from historical epics to back-alley melodramas, and one of the most popular film forms was the musical, whose plots were often copied from Hollywood.

Rising costs, a failure to control video piracy and the spread of satellite television have seen film production dwindle over the past 15 years, though the opening of a 'Hollywood on the Nile' with up-to-date film and TV production facilities 15km (9 miles) southwest of Cairo is a sign of renewed confidence in the industry, if only for Egyptian-produced films and programmes. In the late 1970s, the

Internet cafés are common in cities

Egyptian government imposed hefty taxes on foreign productions, driving most of Hollywood away to the financially friendlier climes of Tunisia and Morocco. While films such as *Death on the Nile* and *The Spy Who Loved Me* showcased Egypt in all its finery, modern films have to rely on CGI wizardry to bring the Pyramids to the silver screen.

THE SOUND OF MUSIC

Evidence of Egypt's domination of the Arab cultural scene in the 1960s is provided by the music of the Egyptian singer Umm Kalthoum. When she performed a new song, the entire nation came to a standstill, and many Arab leaders attended her funeral in 1975. Her contemporaries, including Muhammad Abdel Wahab, Abdel Halim Hafez and Farid Al Atrash, still have a large audience among the older generation. But, with over half of the 82 million population aged under 25, the biggest slice of Egypt's music market is taken by modern musicians.

Among the latest sounds to be heard is *shaabi* (people) music, mixing protest lyrics with a strong back beat. In contrast, *al-jeel* (the generation) music is a fusion of Western and Egyptian rhythms (also known as Mediterranean music). Muhammad Foad and Hisham Abbas are two names to listen out for, but Amr Diab is the most popular.

Nubian music is very popular in the West as its sound is more accessible, redolent of African warmth and rhythm. Big names include Ali Hassan Kuban, Hamza Ad Din, Sayyed Gayer and Ahmed Monieb.

Amr Diab, who is known as the father of Mediterranean music

THE VISUAL ARTS

Because the Prophet Muhammad denounced 'image-makers', visual art in Egypt cannot claim an ancient tradition. However, contacts with Western culture in the 19th century stimulated a debate, with the pro-independence nationalists being keen to promote a recognisable Egyptian style. Little advance was made until the early 20th century, when the mufti of Egypt suggested the Prophet's comment should be seen in context, having been made in an age of idolatry, and Prince Yusuf Kamal founded the School of Fine Arts in Cairo.

The contemporary art scene is now blossoming, with the opening of the Town House Gallery in Cairo and numerous others. There are a number of festivals, particularly in Cairo, that are celebrating Egypt's contemporary and experimental arts scenes. *Check the Festivals and Events details for Cairo on p.97 for further information.*

BELLY DANCING

As recently as 20 years ago, belly dancing was celebrated as an art form in Egypt, with its stars becoming some of the richest performers in the country. Those glory days are no longer, as the religious conservatism of the recent past has attacked practitioners and branded them as immoral and against the values of Islam.

Today, some of the best-known stars have given up their costumes in favour of traditional acting roles. You can still find performers plying their trade in dinner shows and cabaret bars in Cairo. Many of the five-star hotels offer a belly-dancing spectacular at a greatly inflated price. Dinner-cruise boats also often feature a floorshow with a belly-dancing act. *For more information on this ancient art, see page 86.*

For more information on this ancient art, see page 86.

SUFI SPINNING

Showing off the body isn't the only form of dance expression in Egypt. Also found in Sudan, Sufi dancers

Sufi spinning by the whirling dervishes

(also known as whirling dervishes) are followers of a religious order founded in Turkey that incorporates physically active meditation into its rituals. Dancers abandon their sense of self while listening to music and enter a form of trance while they focus on Allah, spinning faster and faster as the ritual progresses.

While you will find dancing inspired by Sufism in many tourist shows, the one guaranteed location to find the real thing is in the Dervish Theatre at Wikala Al Ghoury *(see p. 80)*, where free performances are offered on Wednesday and Saturday evenings. Travelling Sufi dancers can also be found at public celebrations in villages up and down the Nile.

Food and Drink

Egyptians love their food and drink and are passionate about where they go when eating out, or showcasing their hospitality when celebrating at home with family and friends. Even the poorest of communities consider it impolite not to share meals, and the idea of eating alone is simply too foreign for a local to consider. Locals sometimes find it so uncomfortable to see a person dining on their own that they will go out of their way either to seat you with another solo traveller or to group you in with a collection of locals of the same sex.

THE EGYPTIAN EATING EXPERIENCE

In the Middle Ages, Egyptian cuisine enjoyed a high reputation all over the Islamic empire, but not many now travel to Egypt in search of a culinary experience. Those looking for the best of Middle Eastern cuisine will undoubtedly choose countries like Lebanon or Turkey. Nevertheless, Egyptians consider dining a true pleasure and will endlessly discuss the delight of the dishes served, simple as they may be.

If you are staying in Egypt for an extended period and make friends during your stay, you may be invited to dine at home, especially around holiday periods. This is a great opportunity, as Egyptian home-cooked meals often feature dishes based on recipes handed down generation to generation with flavours you won't find anywhere else.

EGYPTIAN CUISINE

Diners in Egypt value freshness and flavour and expect their food to be bursting with both. As such, imported fruits and vegetables are rarely highlighted on any menus. Until recently, restaurants usually served only the more common Egyptian dishes such as kebabs, meze and perhaps stuffed pigeon or *meloukhia* (a thick soup made of a deep-green leaf, similar to spinach). Over the past few years, trendy restaurants in Cairo and establishments like Sofra in Luxor *(see p. 148)* have rediscovered how delicious traditional Egyptian dishes can be and are making good-

A selection of dishes at the Hilton Luxor

quality Egyptian meals chic again. This does, however, remain the exception rather than the norm.

A POOR MAN'S TABLE

There is a distinct lack of fine dining opportunities in Egypt due to the small number of people who can support dining out on a regular basis. The majority of today's *fellaheen* (peasants) are far too poor to make the most of gastronomic opportunities. As in other Arab countries, their diet consists mainly of locally grown vegetables, lentils and beans, with meat at weekends or on special occasions. With the huge influx of people from the countryside to towns and cities, this vegetable-based peasant cuisine has become common, and most middle-class families will now elaborate on these basic recipes,

Bedouin bread

adding more expensive ingredients when they can afford them. Even in Cairo's most upmarket quarters, colourful carts can be found on street corners early in the morning, where

Food and Drink

Middle Eastern food

Egyptians, like the Turks and Greeks, enjoy eating meze whilst chatting around a table with family and friends. Meze are hors d'oeuvres, salads and dips, served as a starter with drinks or, in larger portions, as a meal. An endless variety of dishes, hot and cold, are brought to the table and eaten with the fingers or scooped up in pieces of flatbread. Some of the most common dishes are:

- *baba ghanoush is tahinah* mixed with garlic and roasted aubergine (eggplant)
- *fu'ul mesdames* is a stew of fava beans, Egypt's national dish, served with egg, meat, yoghurt or cheese
- *hummous*, a paste of chickpeas, garlic, *tahinah* and lemon topped with parsley,

and sometimes served topped with tiny bits of fried lamb, is nothing like the shop-bought varieties found in the UK
- *kibbah* is a fried ball of cracked wheat stuffed with ground beef
- *kibda* is fried chopped calf's or lamb's liver
- *kofta is* minced meat with added herbs and spices
- *salata baladi* is chopped lettuce, tomato and cucumber with lots of parsley and lemon
- *tahinah is* a sesame paste mixed with water, oil and lemon juice, served as a dip or a sauce
- *ta'amiyah* are deep-fried fava-bean balls
- *torshi* are pickled vegetables
- *waraa eynab* are stuffed vine leaves

Bedouin restaurant in the desert serving simple but tasty food

they serve steaming *fu'ul* (fava beans) for breakfast.

DINING OUT

Despite the lack of a regular dining-out culture, Egyptian restaurants do exist and the best are often packed out until the wee hours. A typical Egyptian eatery usually falls into one of two categories. Either it caters to tourists and will feature a menu filled with items familiar to Western eyes such as kebabs, pizza and pasta, or it will be a 'spit-and sawdust' affair that dishes up quick, cheap versions of Egyptian favourites. While the tourist-friendly establishments can be found in all the major tourist destinations and are much more salubrious, the meals they dish up are usually pale versions of the real thing. For authenticity, head to the streetside stalls and hole-in-the-wall restaurants for a taste of the real Egypt.

Koshari is the most popular quick pick-me-up, loved by children and adults alike. This dish is a combination of macaroni, lentils, chickpeas, fried crispy garlic and spiced tomato sauce. *Koshari* restaurants can be found everywhere there is high traffic, including near train stations and in the souqs. *Koshari* establishments will only offer two options to customers: small or large. Enjoy it with a soft drink or glass of fresh juice and then be on your way – turnover at the tables is always high. Everyone has their favourite *koshari* restaurant, and will often go well out of their way to eat there.

Meal Times

While the usual rule of three set meals per day apply, Egyptians don't restrict themselves to just that. Every social opportunity, whether a quick chat with friends or a lengthy business meeting, will be accompanied by food. Meal times tend to be later than what you might find back home, with the traditionally large midday meal occurring as late as 3–4pm. Many businesses will shut for the midday meal in order to give owners and staff the chance to go home to their families. Dinner can therefore be pushed back as late as 9pm. Small bites will be enjoyed throughout the day to keep locals going until the next dining experience.

- Breakfast: Between 8 and 10am
- Midday snack: Noon
- Midday meal: Between 3 and 4pm
- Early evening snack: Between 6 and 7pm
- Dinner: Between 9 and 10pm

Other national favourites include *fu'ul* (a stew of fava beans served with egg, meat, yoghurt or white cheese), which is considered the national dish of the country and *ta'amiya* (deep-fried fava-bean balls).

FOREIGN FLAVOURS

Foreign cuisine restaurants are a rare find in Egypt, usually restricted to the tourist resorts of the Sinai and Red Sea coast or to the major urban centres of Cairo and Alexandria. The Sinai boasts many 'chain' restaurants familiar to Western eyes, while the Red Sea coastal properties offer a number of Eastern European themed eateries, built to cater to the large numbers of tourists who arrive each year from the former Communist bloc.

Cairo and (to a limited extent) Alexandria offer international five-star fare, but they are limited to the dining establishments found in the luxury hotels of both cities. Italian and Asian cuisines are the most commonly found foreign flavours.

Shawarma rotisserie

CELEBRATIONS

Meat has always been considered a food for the rich and aristocratic. Poorer Egyptians rely on a diet of wheat, beans and lentils, and there is only one day in the year when they are sure to get a taste of meat: Eid Al Kehir, the 10th day of the last month of the Muslim calendar. In commemoration of Abraham's aborted sacrifice of his son Ismail, rural families who can afford it will sacrifice a sheep or a lamb. The animal, which should be fat and young, is ritually slaughtered and roasted whole on a spit and usually some of its meat is distributed to the poor, according to the tenets of Islam. Sheep are also slaughtered to mark other important occasions such as death, birth or marriage.

Ramadan, the month of fasting from sunrise to sunset, is another occasion when more meat is consumed than usual. Families visit each other in the evenings and celebrate the end of another day of fasting with a rich display of foods and sweets.

Many Egyptian recipes won't stipulate what sort of meat is to be used, as traditionally there was only sheep or lamb, and occasionally camel, goat or gazelle. Islam prohibits pork, but beef and veal are now widely available in Egypt. Meat is usually grilled as kebab or *kofta* (minced lamb), or used in a stew. Offal – particularly liver, kidneys and testicles – is considered a delicacy.

SWEET AS HONEY

The traditional end to a meal at home is a bowl of seasonal fruit, but

Food and Drink

Produce will usually be grown locally

Western-style ice cream and crème caramel will also be offered as a dessert in most restaurants. Even though they are not usually eaten as a dessert, there are some delicious Egyptian puddings, including *muhallabia*, a milk cream thickened by cornflour and ground rice, and *roz bi-laban*, a creamy rice pudding, both topped with chopped almonds and pistachio nuts. More elaborate is *'om ali*, a warm, comforting bread pudding with coconut, raisins, nuts and cream. According to some sources, *'om ali* was introduced into Egypt by Miss O'Malley, the Irish mistress of the Khedive Ismail.

Pastries are more likely to be served at parties and special, happy occasions such as weddings and births, than as a dessert. Baklava is the most famous oriental pastry, a filo wrapping stuffed with a mixture of nuts or almonds and covered with an orange-blossom syrup. More common are *basbousa*, a semolina cake of syrup and nuts, and the drier *kunafa*, angel hair filled

with thick cream, ricotta cheese or chopped nuts and syrup. A woman who prides herself on making the best baklava or *kunafa* will often keep her recipe secret and only pass it on to her daughters.

JUICY DRINKS

Egyptians will tell you that 'Once you drink water from the Nile, you will always come back to Egypt.' A nice sentiment, but Nile water is more likely to curse than bless; stick to mineral water or fresh juices. Brightly coloured juice bars with their picturesque pyramids of strawberries and oranges and baskets of mangoes attract thirsty customers. Freshly squeezed *asir* (juice) is excellent and very cheap. The most widely available juice is *asir laymun* (fresh lemon or lime), usually served sweetened unless you say otherwise.

Usually there will also be a choice of *asir burtuqan* (freshly squeezed winter or summer oranges), *moz* (banana), *gazar* (carrot) and *gawafa* (sweet guava). Depending on the season there could also be deep-red *asir ruman* (pomegranate juice), *farawla* (strawberry) and thick *manga* (mango). Some stalls also offer *asab* or *gasab*, the sweet juice pressed out of sugar-cane sticks.

In Aswan you will see dried hibiscus flowers *(karkadeh)* for sale in the souq. They are used to make a red herbal tea, served hot or cold to welcome visitors – and potential customers.

ALCOHOL

According to the Qur'an, Muslims should not drink alcohol and, with religious tensions rising, much of Egypt is becoming dry. But you can usually get alcohol in hotels and Western-style bars and restaurants, except during Ramadan, when no alcohol is served to Egyptians, even if they are Copts. Many bars close for the month; others may ask to see a

Hibiscus tea, a popular herbal infusion

Seasonal Delights

As the bread basket of North Africa, Egypt is home to many farms and farming communities up and down the Nile Valley. Harvest time brings a real buzz of activity to the region, so if you are planning a rural retreat, you may be in for a treat if you visit during the harvest seasons. Here is a list of the main crops and their harvest dates:

- Spring (March–May): wheat, corn, flax, garlic, chickpeas, onions and barley
- Summer (June–Aug): grapes, watermelon, plums, leeks, lettuce, tomatoes and cucumbers
- Autumn (Sept–Nov): dates, pomegranates, olives, figs and cumin
- Winter (Dec–Feb): oranges, radishes, lentils, peas, and coriander

Food and Drink

passport before they serve alcohol to foreigners.

Locally brewed Stella beer is quite enjoyable, while the more expensive Stella Export and Stella Premium are stronger, as is the better Sakkara.

The quality of the local wine used to range from drinkable to downright dangerous, but quality has much improved since the Gianaclis Winery was privatised. Cru des Ptolémées is a white wine made from pinot blanc. Rubis d'Egypte is a rosé, while Omar Khayyam is a deep red made from cabernet sauvignon grapes. Obélisque makes red and white wines from imported grapes. The more expensive Grand Marquis, red and white, is very palatable, and Egypt now has its own 'champagne', Aida. Imported wine is considerably more expensive than the local varieties.

PHRASE BOOK

Phrase Book

Arabic is the official language of Egypt, although the Arabic spoken on the streets differs greatly from the Arabic spoken on TV and radio, which is known as Modern Standard Arabic (the version used below). Converting Arabic into the Roman alphabet is notoriously difficult, and a standard system of transliteration has yet to be established. When you hear Arabic spoken, and see the language written down in a series of beautiful lines and squiggles, it becomes clear why the whole business of transliterating is fraught with pitfalls. There is no single "correct" way of transliterating Arabic, as becomes obvious when you travel round and see several different spellings of the same place name.

Many Egyptians in the tourist industry speak English to some degree, though real ability to use languages other than Arabic is confined to the educated. A few words of Arabic are therefore useful.

PRONUNCIATION

This section is designed to make you familiar with the sounds of Arabic using our simplified phonetic transcription. You'll find the pronunciation of the Arabic letters and sounds explained below, together with their "imitated" equivalents. This system is used throughout this section of the book; simply read the pronunciation as if it were English, noting any special rules below.

Consonants

Letter(s)	Approximate Pronunciation	Symbol	Example	Pronunciation
ب	b as in bat	b	بنت	bint
ت	t as in tin	t	تكييف	tak_yeef_
ث	t as in tin	t	ثلاجة	tall_aa_ja
ج	j as in jam	j	جميل	_jameel_
ح	strong, breathy h	H	صحون	su_Hoon_
خ	h from back of throat as in Scottish loch	kh	خدمة	_khed_ma
د	d as in dad	d	درج	_daraj_
ذ	z as in zebra	z	هذا	_haaza_
ر	r as in rain	r	رجل	_rajul_
ز	z as in zebra	z	زيت	zayt
س	s as in sun	s	سلام	sal_aam_
ش	sh as in shut s	h	شمس	shams
ص	strong, emphatic s	s	صباح	sa_baaH_
ض	strong, emphatic d	d	اضافي	e_daa_fee

ط	strong, emphatic t	t	بطاقة	_bitaaqa_
ظ	strong, emphatic z	z	انتظار	_inti<u>zaar</u>_
ع	as the a in a strongly pronounced apple	'aa	عندي	_'aandee_
غ	a softer form of kh, as in loch, but gently holding the sound	gh	غرفة	_<u>gh</u>urfa_
ف	like f in fan	f	فرن	_furn_
ق	q pronounced from back of throat	q	قريب	_qa<u>reeb</u>_
ك	k as in kite	k	كيف	_kayf_
ل	l as in lip	l	لماذا	_li<u>maaza</u>_
م	m as in man	m	ممسحة	_<u>mim</u>saHa_
ن	n as in never	n	نور	_noor_
ه	h as in hat	h	هنا	_<u>hu</u>na_
و	w as in win	w	وسط	_wast_
ي	y as in yet	y	يمين	_ya<u>meen</u>_
ء	the apostrophe shows a sharp start to the word or syllable and is generally omitted in writing	'	تدفئة	_tadfi'a_

Vowels

Vowels take the form of diacritics when they are short vowels but come attached to a particular consonant when they are long.

Letter(s)	Approximate Pronunciation	Symbol	Example	Pronunciation
Short:				
َ	a as in bat	a	لَمبَة	_lamba_
ُ	u as in put	u	كُل	_kul_
ِ	i as in bit	i	بِنت	_bint_
Long:				
آ	ar as in dark	aa	هناك	_hu<u>naak</u>_
و	oo as in boot	oo	فطُور	_fu<u>toor</u>_
ى	ee as in meet	ee	تكِييف	_tak<u>yeef</u>_
و	o as in home	oh	يوُم	_yohm_
ى	ay as in say	ay	إثنَين	_it<u>nayn</u>_

| How much? | بكم؟ | *kam si'rhu* |

A simplified pronunciation guide follows each Arabic phrase; read it as if it were English, giving the underlined letters a little more stress than the others. Among the English phrases, you will find some words included in square brackets; these are the American English equivalents of British English expressions.

General

0	صفر *sifr*	100	مائة *mi'a*	
1	واحد *waaHid*	500	خمسمائة *khamsmi'a*	
2	اثنان *etnaan*	1,000	ألف *alf*	
3	ثلاثة *talaata*	1,000,000	مليون *milyoon*	
4	أربعة *'arba'a*	Monday	الاثنين *al-etnayn*	
5	خمسة *khamsa*	Tuesday	الثلاثاء *al-tulataa'*	
6	ستة *sitta*	Wednesday	الأربعاء *al-'arba'aa*	
7	سبعة *sab'aa*	Thursday	الخميس *al-khamees*	
8	ثمانية *tamaaniya*	Friday	الجمعة *al-jom'a*	
9	تسعة *tis'aa*	Saturday	السبت *al-sabt*	
10	عشرة *'aashara*	Sunday	الأحد *al-aHd*	

Hello!	السلام عليكم!	*al-salaam 'aalaykum*
How are you?	كيف الحال؟	*kayf al-Haal*
Fine, thanks.	بخير، الحمد لله.	*bi-khayr al-Hamdulillah*
Excuse me!	لو سمحت!	*loh samaHt*
Do you speak English?	تتكلم إنكليزي؟	*tatakallam engleezee*
What's your name?	ما اسمك؟	*maa esmak*
My name is...	اسمي...	*esmee...*
Nice to meet you.	تشرفنا.	*tasharafna*
Where are you from?	من أين أنت؟	*min ayn anta*
I'm from the US/UK	أنا من أمريكا/بريطانيا.	*ana min amreeka/breetanya*
What do you do?	ماذا تعمل؟	*maaza ta'aamal*
I work for...	أنا أعمل في...	*ana a'aamal fee...*
I'm a student.	أنا طالب♂/طالبة♀.	*ana taalib* [M]/*taaliba* [F]
I'm retired.	أنا متقاعد♂/متقاعدة♀.	*ana mutaqaa'id* [M]/*mutaqaa'ida* [F]
Goodbye.	مع السلامة.	*ma' al-salaama*
See you later.	إلى اللقاء.	*ilal-liqaa'*
I understand.	فهمت.	*fahimtu*
I don't understand.	لا أفهم.	*laa afham*
Who are you with?	مع من أنت؟	*ma' man anta*
I'm with my...	أنا مع...	*ana ma'...*
– husband/wife	زوجي/زوجتي	*zohjee/zohjatee*
– friend/friends	صديق/أصدقاء	*sadeeq/asdiqaa'*

Arrival and Departure

I'm on holiday [vacation]/business.	أنا في إجازة/في رحلة عمل. _ana fee ejaaza/fee riHlat 'aamal_
I'm going to...	أنا ذاهب♂/ذاهبة♀ إلى... _ana zaahib_ [M]/ _zaahiba_ [F] _ila..._
I'm staying at the... Hotel.	أنا نازل♂/نازلة♀ في فندق... _ana naazil_ [M]/ _naazila_ [F] _fee funduq..._

Money and Banking

Where's...?	أين...؟ _ayn..._
– the ATM	الصراف الآلي _al-saraaf al-'aalee_
– the bank	البنك _al-bank_
– the currency exchange office	مكتب تبديل العملات _maktab tabdeel al-'umlaat_
I'd like to change dollars/pounds into ...	أريد تبديل دولارات/جنيهات إسترلينية إلى... _ooreed tabdeel doolaaraat/ jinayhaat esterleeneeya ila..._

Transport

How do I get to town?	كيف أصل إلى المدينة؟ _kayf asil ilal-madeena_
Where's...?	أين...؟ _ayn..._
– the airport	المطار _al-mataar_
– the railway [train] station	محطة القطار _maHatat al-qitaar_
– the bus station	محطة الباص _maHatat al-baas_
– the underground [subway] station	محطة مترو الأنفاق _maHatat metro al-anfaaq_
How far is it?	كم هي بعيدة؟ _kam hiya ba'eeda_
Where do I buy a ticket?	أين أشتري تذكرة؟ _ayn ashtaree tazkara_
A single [one-way]/return [round-trip] ticket to...	تذكرة ذهاب/ذهاب و عودة إلى... _tazkara zehaab/zehaab wa-'ohda ila..._
How much?	بكم؟ _bi-kam_
Which...?	أي...؟ _ay..._
– gate	بوابة _bawaaba_
– line	خط _khat_
– platform	رصيف _raseef_
Where can I get a taxi?	أين آخذ تاكسي؟ _ayn 'akhud taksee_
Can I have a map?	ممكن خريطة؟ _mumkin khareeta_

Accommodation

I have a reservation.	عندي حجز. _'aandee Hajz_
My name is...	إسمي... _ismee..._
Do you have a room...?	عندك غرفة...؟ _'aandak ghurfa..._
– for one/for two	لواحد/لاثنين _li-waahid/li-itnayn_
– with a bathroom	مع حمّام _maa' Hamaam_
– with air conditioning	بتكييف هواء _bi-takyeef hawaa_
For...	لـ... _li..._
– tonight	الليلة _al-layla_
– two nights	ليلتين _laylatayn_
– one week	أسبوع _usboo'_

Is there anything cheaper?	hal yoojad ay shay هل يوجد أي شيء أرخص؟
Can I see the room?	mumkin ara al-ghurfa ممكن أرى الغرفة؟
When's check-out?	mata waqt tasleem al-ghurfa متى وقت تسليم الغرفة؟
Can I have my bill/a receipt?	mumkin al-Hisaab/eesaal ممكن الحساب/إيصال؟

Internet and Communications

Can I access the internet?	mumkin adkul 'alal-internet ممكن أدخل على الإنترنت؟
How much per (half) hour?	kam al-Hisaab li-muddat (nusf) saa'aa كم الحساب لمدة (نصف) ساعة؟
A phone card, please.	bitaaqa tilifooneeya min fadlak بطاقة تلفونية، من فضلك
Hello. This is...	al-salaam 'aalaykum ana... السلام عليكم. أنا...
Can I speak to...?	mumkin atakallam ma'... ممكن أتكلم مع...؟
Can you repeat that?	mumkin tu'eed ممكن تعيد؟
I'll call back later.	sa-attasil laaHiqan سأتصل لاحقاً.
Where's the post office?	ayn al-bareed أين البريد؟
I'd like to send this to...	ooreed an ursil haza ila... أريد أن أرسل هذا إلى...

Sightseeing

Where's the tourist information office?	maktab al-este'alamaat al-seeya - Heeya أين مكتب الاستعلامات السياحية؟
What are the main attractions?	maa hiya al-ma'aalim al-ra'eeseeya ما هي المعالم الرئيسية؟
Do you have tours in English?	'andakum johlaat seeyaaHeeya bil-engleezee عندكم جولات سياحية بالإنكليزي؟
Can I have a map/guide?	mumkin tu'ateenee khareeta/kitaab 'an al-makaan ممكن تعطيني خريطة/كتاب عن المكان؟
We'd like to see...	nureed an nara... نريد أن نرى...
Can we stop here...?	mumkin natawaqqaf huna... ممكن نتوقف هنا...؟
– to take photos	lil-tasweer للتصوير
– for the toilets [restrooms]	lil-zihaab ilal-toowaaleet للذهاب إلى التواليت

Shopping

Where's the market/shopping centre [mall]?	ayn al-sooq/al-markaz al-tijaaree أين السوق/المركز التجاري؟
I'm just looking.	ana atafaraj faqat أنا أتفرج فقط.
Can you help me?	mumkin tusaa'idnee ممكن تساعدني؟
How much?	kam si'rhu كم سعره؟
Where can I pay?	ayn adfa' أين أدفع؟
I'll pay in cash/by credit card.	sa-adfa' kaash/bi-bitaaqat al-e'atimaan سأدفع كاش/ببطاقة الائتمان.
A receipt, please.	eesaal min fadlak إيصال من فضلك

Business Travel

I'm here on business.	ana huna lil-'aamal أنا هنا للعمل.
Here's my business card.	haza kartee هذا كرتي.
Can I have your card?	mumkin aakhuz kartak ممكن آخذ كرتك؟
I have a meeting with...	'aandee ejtimaa' ma'... عندي اجتماع مع...
Where's the...?	ayn... أين...؟

– business centre	مركز الأعمال _markaz al-a'aamaal_
– convention hall	قاعة المؤتمرات _qaa'at al-mu'atamaraat_
– meeting room	قاعة الاجتماعات _qaa'at al-ejtimaa'aat_

Travel with Children

Can you recommend something for children?	ممكن تنصحني بشيء للأطفال؟ _mumkin tansaHnee bi-shay lil-atfaal_
Is there a discount for kids?	هل هناك خصم للأطفال؟ _hal hunaak khasm lil-atfaal_
Can you recommend a babysitter?	ممكن تنصحني بمربية أطفال؟ _mumkin tansaHnee bi-murabeeyat al-atfaal_
Do you have a child's seat/highchair?	عندكم كرسي خاص للأطفال/كرسي عال؟ _'aandakum kursee khaas lil-atfaal/kursee 'aalin_
Where can I change the baby?	أين أستطيع تغيير حفاض الطفل؟ _ayn astatee'a taghyeer Hifaad al-tifl_
Are children allowed?	مسموح دخول الأطفال؟ _masmooH dukhool al-atfaal_
Is it safe for children?	هل هو آمن للأطفال؟ _hal huwa aamin lil-atfaal_

Disabled Travellers

Is there...?	هل هناك...؟ _hal hunaak..._
– access for the disabled	مدخل مناسب للمعاقين _madkhal munaasib lil-mu'aaqeen_
– a wheelchair ramp	منحدر لكرسي المقعدين _munHadir li-kursee al-muq'aadeen_
– a disabled-accessible toilet	تواليت خاص للمقعدين _toowaaleet khaas lil-muq'aadeen_
I need...	أحتاج... _aHtaaj..._
– assistance	مساعدة _musaa'ada_
– a lift [an elevator]	مصعد _mis'ad_
– a ground-floor room	غرفة في الطابق الأرضي _ghurfa feel taabiq al-ardee_

Emergencies

Help!	النجدة! _al-najda_
Go away!	إمشي! _emshee_
Stop, thief!	امسك حرامي! _emsik Haraamee_
Get a doctor!	اتصل بدكتور! _ettasil bil-doktoor_
Fire!	حريق! _Hareeq_
I'm lost.	أنا تهت. _ana tuht_
Can you help me?	ممكن تساعدني؟ _mumkin tusaa'idnee_
Call the police!	اتصل بالشرطة! _ettasil bil-shurta_
There was an accident/attack.	وقع حادث/اعتداء. _waqa'aa Haadis/e'atidaa'_
My child is missing.	طفلي مفقود. _tiflee mafqood_
I need...	أحتاج إلى... _aHtaaj ila..._
– an interpreter	مترجم _mutarjim_
– to contact my lawyer	الاتصال بمحاميي الخاص _al-ettisaal bi-muHaamee al-khaas_
– to make a phone call	إجراء اتصال هاتفي _ejraa' ettisaal haatifee_

Health

I'm ill [sick].	أنا مريض♂/مريضة♀. ana ma<u>r</u>eed [M]/ ma<u>r</u>eeda [F]
I need an English-speaking doctor.	أحتاج طبيب يتكلم إنكليزي. a<u>H</u>taaj <u>t</u>abeeb yataka<u>ll</u>am engleezee
It hurts here.	يوجد ألم هنا. yujad 'alam huna
I have a stomach ache.	معدتي تؤلمني. <u>mi</u>'adatee tu'alimnee
Where's the chemist [pharmacy]?	أين الصيدلية؟ ayn al-<u>s</u>aydaleeya
What time does it open/close?	متى تفتح/تغلق؟ <u>m</u>ata ta<u>f</u>ta<u>H</u>/ta<u>gh</u>liq
How much do I take?	كم جرعة؟ kam jur'aa
Can you make up [fill] this prescription?	ممكن تكتب لي وصفة طبية؟ <u>m</u>umkin tak<u>t</u>ub lee <u>w</u>a<u>s</u>fa <u>t</u>ibeeya
I'm allergic to...	أنا أتحسس من... <u>a</u>na ata<u>H</u>asas min...

Eating Out

A table for..., please.	طاولة لـ...من فضلك. <u>t</u>aawila li-...min <u>f</u>adlak
Where's the toilet [restroom]?	أين التواليت؟ ayn al-toowaleet
A menu, please.	قائمة الطعام من فضلك. qaa'imat al-ta'aam min <u>f</u>adlak
I'd like...	أريد.... oo<u>r</u>eed...
The bill [check], please.	الحساب من فضلك. al-<u>H</u>isaab min <u>f</u>adlak
Is service included?	هل أجرة الخدمة محسوبة؟ hal ujrat al-<u>kh</u>idma ma<u>H</u>sooba
Can I pay by credit card/have a receipt?	ممكن استخدم بطاقة الائتمان/تعطيني إيصال؟ <u>m</u>umkin asta<u>kh</u>dim bi<u>t</u>aaqat al-e'atimaan/tu'teenee eesaal
Thank you!	شكراً! <u>sh</u>ukran
The wine list/drinks menu, please.	قائمة النبيذ/قائمة المشروبات، من فضلك. qaa'imat al-nabeez/al-ma<u>sh</u>roo<u>baat</u> min <u>f</u>adlak
I'd like a bottle/glass of red/white wine.	أريد زجاجة/كأس نبيذ أحمر/أبيض. oo<u>r</u>eed zujaajat/<u>k</u>a'as nabeez a<u>H</u>mar/abyad
I'd like a local beer.	أريد بيرة محلية. oo<u>r</u>eed beera ma<u>H</u>aleeya
A coffee/tea, please.	قهوة/شاي، من فضلك. <u>q</u>ahwa/shay min <u>f</u>adlak
Is the water safe to drink?	هل المياه صالحة للشرب؟ hal al-miyaah saali<u>H</u>a lil-shurb

Menu Reader

almond	لوز looz		halibut	هلبوت hali<u>boot</u>
apple	تفاح tufaa<u>H</u>		ice cream	آيس كريم aayis kreem
apricot	مشمش <u>mish</u>mish		lamb	لحم غنم la<u>H</u>m <u>gh</u>anum
banana	موز mooz		lemon	ليمون laymoon
beans	بقول bu<u>qool</u>		lentils	عدس <u>a</u>ads
beef	لحم بقري la<u>H</u>m ba<u>q</u>aree		mango	منجا <u>m</u>anga
beer	بيرة beera		meat	لحم la<u>H</u>m
blueberry	عنبية 'aana<u>bee</u>ya		melon	شمام shamaam
brown (fava) beans	فول fool		milk	حليب <u>H</u>aleeb
butter	زبدة <u>z</u>ibda		mineral water	مياه معدنية miyaah ma'ada<u>nee</u>ya
cake	كعكة ka'aka		mint tea	شاي بنعناع shaay bi-<u>na'</u>na'
cataloupe	شمام sham<u>maam</u>		mullet	سلطان ابراهيم sul<u>taan</u> ebra<u>heem</u>
cardamon	حب الهال <u>H</u>abb al-haal		mutton	لحم الضأن la<u>H</u>m al-za'n

carrot	جزر _jazar_	nougat	نوغة _noogha_
cheese	جبنة _jibna_	nuts	مكسرات _mukassaraat_
chicken	لحم دجاج _laHm dujaaj_	olive	زيتون _zaytoon_
chickpea	حمص _Hummus_	orange juice	عصير برتقال _'aaseer burtuqaal_
chilli	شطة _shatta_	peach	دراق/خوخ _daraaq/khookh_
chips [French fries]	بطاطس مقلية _bataatis maqleeya_	pigeon	حمام _Hamaam_
chocolate	شوكولاتة _shookoolaata_	pineapple	أناناس _ananaas_
cinnamon	قرفة _qirfa_	pistachio	فستق _fustuq_
coffee	قهوة _qahwa_	potato	بطاطس _bataatis_
couscous	كسكس _kuskus_	prune	خوخ مجفف _khookh mujaffaf_
cream cheese	جبنة للدهن _jibna lil-dahn_	quail	سُماني _sumaanee_
cumin	كمون _kammoon_	raisin	زبيب _zabeeb_
dates	بلح _balaa'_	saffron	زعفران _za'afraan_
dried dates	عجوة _'aajwa_	seafood	مأكولات بحرية _ma'akoolaat baHreeya_
egg	بيضة _bayda_	semolina	سميد _sameed_
falafel	فلافل _falaafil_	shish kebab	كباب _kabaab_
fig	تين _teen_	prawn [shrimp]	قريدس _quraydis_
fish	سمك _samak_	steak	ستيك _steek_
fruit	فواكه _fawaakih_	stuffed vine leaves	ورق عنب _waraq 'aanab_
goat	ماعز _maa'iz_	sugar	سكر _sukkar_
grapes	عنب _'aanab_	tea	شاي _shaay_
guava	جوافة _gwaava_	trout	تروتة _troota_
hake	قد _qadd_	yoghurt	لبن _labn_

Phrase Book

Index

Accommodation Index

303

Index

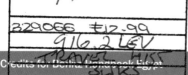

Credits for Berlitz Handbook Egypt

Written by: Ryan Levitt
Walking Tours by: Frances Linzee Gordon
Series Editor: Alexander Knights
Commissioning Editor: Siân Lezard
Cartography Editor: Zoë Goodwin
Map Production: Stephen Ramsay
Production: Linton Donaldson, Rebeka Ellam
Picture Manager: Steven Lawrence
Art Editors: Richard Cooke and Ian Spick
Photography: All Pictures APA Glyn Genin except:
Courtesy 4seasons 96 ;AKG London 110; Courtesy Al Capone 215; Alamy 3TL, 6BR, 8L/R, 12, 14, 18, 45, 56, 57, 79, 85, 86, 87, 93, 210, 216, 230, 231/T, 244, 246, 264; APA Chris Bradley 3ML, 6BL, 32, 33, 38, 39, 42, 59, 65T, 70, 71, 72, 75, 76, 77, 80, 81, 83, 84, 88, 91, 94, 95, 192, 199/T, 201, 203, 204, 205, 206, 207/T, 209, 219, 220, 222, 223, 224, 225, 226, 227, 228, 259, 266/267, 277; BBM Explorers 229; John C 190; Bonnie Ann Cain 149; Steve Copley 211; Corbis 15, 97, 119, 121, 144, 151, 189, 197, 212, 274, 280; Courtesy Eden Rock Hotel 213; ENTA/Bertrand Gardel 140, 14, 283; ENTA/ Arnaud Chicure 31, 36, 196, 221; ENTA/Bertrand Reiger 8T, 44, 48, 140, 162, 168, 169, 173, 175, 261, ; Mary Evans 50, 268; Isabel Gallay 245; Fotolia 239T; Getty Images 108, 117, 279; Karen Green 174; Joseph Hill 125; Istockphoto 6TL/TR, 7B, 9BL/BR, 20/21, 34, 37, 40, 41, 43, 111, 124, 142, 169T, 186, 218, 239, 270, 284, 285; Matt Jieffer 251; Clemens Koppensteiner 150Look 1; Martin lapotka 236; Daniel Meyer 73; Courtesy Movenpick El Gouna 233 ; Courtesy Nile Hilton 90; Courtesy Oberoi 5TR, 114; Bob Partridge 113T; Pictures Colour Library 60/61, 265; SJ Pinkney 287; Photolibrary 87T, 115; Lars Ploughman; Courtesy Redseawonders. com; APA Sarah Louise Ramsay 69, 122, 123Courtesy Starwood Hotels 2R, 4TR, 9TL, 30, 232, 234, 281, 284; Dustin P Smith 157; Superstock 6M,/TL; Courtesy Taba Regency Hyatt 214; Topfoto 271, 272, 273; Michael Tyler 226; Adam Wadler126; Sebastian White 89
Cover: LOOK picture agency (front); iStockphoto (back left, right), fotolia (middle)
Printed by: CTPS-China

Contacting Us
At Berlitz we strive to keep our guides as accurate and up to date as possible, but if you find anything that has changed, or if you have any suggestions on ways to improve this guide, then we would be delighted to hear from you. Write to Berlitz Publishing, PO Box 7910, London SE1 1WE, UK or email: berlitz@apaguide.co.uk

Worldwide: APA Publications GmbH & Co. Verlag KG (Singapore branch), 7030 Ang Mo Kio Ave 5, 08-65 Northstar @ AMK, Singapore 569880; tel: (65) 570 1051; email: apasin@singnet.com.sg
UK and Ireland: GeoCenter International Ltd, Meridian House, Churchill Way West, Basingstoke, Hampshire, RG21 6YR; tel: (44) 01256-817 987; email: sales@geocenter.co.uk
United States: Ingram Publisher Services, 1 Ingram Boulevard, PO Box 3006, La Vergne, TN 37086-1986; email: customer.service@ ingrampublisherservices.com
Australia: Universal Publishers, PO Box 307, St Leonards, NSW 1590; email: sales@ universalpublishers.com.au
New Zealand: Hema Maps New Zealand Ltd (HNZ), Unit 2, 10 Cryers Road, East Tamaki, Auckland 2013; tel: (64) 9-273 6459; email: sales.hema@clear.net.nz

www.berlitzpublishing.com